THE AESTHETICS OF PORNOGRAPHY

THE
AESTHETICS
OF
PORNOGRAPHY

Peter Michelson

HERDER AND HERDER

1971
HERDER AND HERDER NEW YORK
232 Madison Avenue, New York 10016

Library of Congress Catalog Card Number: 70–146299
© 1971 by Herder and Herder, Inc.
Manufactured in the United States

Contents

716261

TO DONNA
AND
WHEN THE TIME IS RIGHT
FOR KRISTEN AND HILARY

Preface

THE STARTING POINT of this book was a simultaneous interest in pornography and in aesthetics. At some point, a few years back, I noticed with more than casual interest that serious modern literature more and more made use of pornography to say what it had to say. Being encouraged by friends, colleagues, and a few editors of literary journals to pursue that observation, I did, and the result is this study—a descriptive attempt to examine why and how some modern aesthetic concepts accommodate the pornographic in literature. Aesthetics refer to theories of beauty in the arts; the aesthetics of pornography refer to those theories of "beauty" that incorporate the pornographic and its companion the obscene. This book, then, is more a study of literary aesthetics than it is a study in literary criticism. By that I mean that I have felt free to discuss writers and their works in a very selective way, using them to illustrate my own perceptions of literary and aesthetic practices. For example, though D. H. Lawrence abhored the idea of "pornography," I have not hesitated to discuss him in the context of my critical vocabulary rather than his own. Also, because aesthetics necessarily involve such things as ethics, morality, history, religion, and anthropology, I have drawn on and speculated about them as much as I have been able and have thought it useful. Inasmuch as this book proposes neither a representative survey nor a critical bibliography of pornographic literature, the body of writers and writings discussed is not at all supposed to be comprehensive. In choosing what or who to write about my only criterion has been what I thought of particular or illustrative interest in connection with the development of the aesthetics of pornography as I understand them.

Though I have avoided footnotes, my scholarly and intellectual debts, too eclectic to particularize here, will be clear one way or another from the text. I can, however, acknowledge my gratitude to friends and colleagues who have helped and encouraged me in the writing of this book. About six years ago, when I first conceived the idea of such a study, I was encouraged and abetted in proceeding with it by John Mcmanmon, Beverly Gross, Eugene Wildman, and Charles Newman. Since then, in the course of the book's intermittent progress, their support and advice have been invaluable. For so generously giving me their time and critical energy in reading portions of the manuscript I am grateful to Robert Turley, James Walton, Richard Giannone, Richard Bizot, and John Gerber. Beyond saying, they know how much I am indebted to them. For extraordinary assistance in research I thank John Wehrheim. For sustaining me through some trying times in the doing of the book, my gratitude to Thomas Lorch and John Matthias. Finally, for a graciousness that transcends debt and for assisting me through the most difficult times and tasks of this book, my deep thanks to Helene and Ernest Robischon.

Portions of this book have appeared, in different form, in *The New Republic, Tri-Quarterly, Continuum,* and *The Antioch Review.* I wish to thank the editors for permission to reprint them here in revised form. Finally, I wish also to thank the Olympic Press and Simon and Schuster for permission to quote extensively from *Barbara* and *The Adventurers.*

THE AESTHETICS OF PORNOGRAPHY

1.

An Apology for Pornography

TRICKSTER, the archetypal fool of Winnebago Indian mythology, was possessed of a phallus so large that he had to carry it over his shoulder. He did not, according to the legend, know either what it was or how it was to be used. But its very bulk reassured him against those who ridiculed his subjection to the huge burden and claimed he could not rid himself of it. For to carry it required, after all, a substantial and unique strength. This mockery, however, eventually took its toll, and Trickster wearied of the weight and mystery; he determined therefore to remove them. Whereupon he discovered, of course, that the joke was on him. Great as it was, his strength could not equably bear the burden, nor his wit devise a release from it.

This is a sobering myth. Rather than celebrating power and potency, like most phallic legends, it documents man's sexual anxiety and ignorance. But it is honest, more honest than men customarily are about their sexuality. There are, for instance, primitive Australian tribes whose traditional teaching does not recognize that copulation causes pregnancy. And the traditions are honored; pregnancy is explained by the woman having slept under a certain tree or having been graced by the light of the moon. In their hearts—and presumably their loins—they may know what's what, but they must nevertheless speak with a forked tongue.

Nor is this paralyzing duality peculiar to primitive cultures. The stable civilized culture is even more afraid of its own

1

beastly libido (this neurosis is the subject of Wayland Young's *Eros Denied*). Whether rational (as in Plato's *Republic*) or hysterical (as in the Salem witch trials) such a fear attacks the culture's particular libido image. In modern times sex and political revolution have been the fearful images most consistent in raising their ugly heads. Politics does not concern us here, but sexuality does. And pornography, the literature of sexuality, has been every bit as victimized by hysteria as ever were Sacco and Vanzetti. Pornography, it is supposed, constitutes both a social and psychic threat. Society will be terrorized by the rampant lewdness induced by pornographic books—our wives and daughters raped, law and order dissolved. And our sons (somebody, after all, has to do the raping) will either be driven to mad carnality or will become idiots driveling in the wake of luxurious onanism. *We*—that is, the Patriarchal we—of course remain impervious.

The legal starting point is the social threat. And here the machinations of the courts at all levels to find evidence of social value in "pornographic" books have resulted in monumental irrelevance to the one reasonable question. While there are responsible decisions, such as Judge Woolsey's judgment in favor of *Ulysses,* their irony is that, however good they are in particular, they are based on the wrong-headed obscenity laws. Judge Woolsey was critically right to find that *Ulysses* is a complex work the end of which is not obscenity. But he was both critically and legally wrong to feel compelled to explain away the pornography and obscenity that are in the novel in order to grant its freedom. The real issue is articulated by Judge Frank's dissenting opinion about the Roth case in 1956. He defined the issue as whether or not pornography, quite distinctly from its social or artistic merit, constitutes a "clear and present danger" to society. He argues quite rightly that there is no evidence that it does and that such research as has been done is either inconclusive or negates the idea that crimes or neuroses are caused by pornography. Until such time as there is evidence of this, Judge Frank's is the only reasonable decision a court can reach. There is nevertheless the irresponsible kind of deci-

2

sion reached through the Supreme Court's 1966 caprice in the Ginzberg case. In that decision, so incisively criticized by Justice Douglas' dissenting opinion, the character of the book is determined by the kind of advertising with which it is merchandized! An observation on censorship in *Rights and Writers* suggests the sort of Patriarchal hysteria which seems to prompt such decisions: "We know of no case where any juror or judge has admitted that *he* found material erotically stimulating or a stimulus to irregular conduct; on the contrary, the expression of concern is always that someone else or some other class of people will be corrupted."

The psychic threat is more ambiguous and for that reason more ominous. As usual in the event of emergency, it's women and children first; pornography is supposed to do incalculable harm to children. And as long as we are employing the logical and scientific technique of supposition, we suppose that women, whose minds are childish, are also damaged. *We* continue impervious. Impervious also to the hysteria motivating our moral earnestness, impervious to the ignorance of data that makes our zeal dangerous. This is the perfidious irony of submitting pornography to legal censorship. It makes us pass irrational laws, thus violating the nature of law itself; and this irrationality makes us prosecute where normally we would not. We don't prosecute books or television for misrepresenting marriage, or politics, or religion, or war. But we do prosecute where we think sex has been misrepresented. Plato, for all the dangers of his moral metaphysics, would have at least prosecuted all supposed stupidities equally. It would be neither more nor less criminal in his republic to represent man as pure sexuality than it would be to represent marriage as pure idyl or God as pure saccharine.

Such data as we have (for example, the Kinsey reports, the Glueck studies for the Harvard Law School, and the recently published report of the Presidential Commission on Obscenity and Pornography) indicate that pornography has little or no damaging effect on "normal" women or children. In point of fact, however, there probably is a psychic threat, but a threat

3

no greater than that posed by any popular fantasy literature. Emma Bovary shows that a mind deluded by Romance will make a bad job of reality. That is the danger of Romance or fantasy whenever and in whatever way it dominates the mind. And pornography is a kind of Romance. But it is no more socially or psychically pernicious than the Romance of passion that dominates the lives of Emma Bovary or Heathcliff or the mundane Romance of *Please Don't Eat the Daisies.* The representation of life as all passion or all idyll or all sexuality is a delusion. But it is not one that will determine the behavior of any but an already pathological personality. A *preoccupation* with pornography or any other kind of Romance may be an index of mental imbalance or even potential criminality, but it is certainly not a cause. To prosecute it as such, then, is no service to society but rather a manifestation of moral hysteria.

To understand the contemporary working of pornography we must conceive the term in its widest context. Originally it signified writings about prostitutes. But as we have come to recognize that the fantasy archetype represented in the prostitute is not at all unique to her, and as amateur promiscuity has increasingly supplied erotic fantasy material, pornography has revealed a new and larger being, *homo sexualis.* This has two images, the erect phallus and the carnal woman. The phallic symbol has become not only a psychological and literary commonplace, but also a cultural joke, and we are long since accustomed to finding one in everything from a new Buick to the Empire State Building. But the female image of *homo sexualis*—the essential pornographic image—is never funny, even in parody. Al Capp's cartoon women, for example, parody this image, enormously breasted and buttocked. But even the parody rides the edge of lust, and these images are much more desirable than ridiculous. For the pornographic world is peopled with men of limitless potency and women of limitless libido. O, the protagonist in *Story of O,* is a good contemporary example. No concerns in the narrative are allowed to obscure the translation of her total existence into terms of sexuality. Sex becomes the metaphor for being. In sophisticated pornography *homo*

4

sexualis metaphors the erotic dimension of imagination and is the basis of erotic fantasy. The fantasy in this case is archetypal, and is not dissipated even by ejaculation. In other words, in this expanded sense of the term, pornography creates an image of human sexuality which not only inspires erotic gratification but also suggests the anthropological dimensions of sexual libido.

This view of pornography, then, regards it in its broadest and best sense as the literature of sexuality. And it has therefore the same degree of dignity and complexity potential to it that the libido itself demands as an aspect of human nature. In what is perhaps the best analytical study of pornography, *Pornography and the Law,* Eberhard and Phyllis Kronhausen observe that "Both erotic realism and pornography, each in their own way, fulfill certain functions and answer basic needs in the human psyche which have been recognized by many societies and periods; for instance, in ancient Greece and Rome, in the Near East, as well as in China, Japan, and India, where erotic art and literature have always been integral parts of the total culture." In whatever art form, pornography documents both man's neurotic and his archetypal concern with sexuality. The neurotic (not to be confused with the pathological) engagement with pornography is the private confrontation of the individual psyche with its sexual needs. The larger cultural engagement with pornography is the public confrontation with archetypal—and usually subliminal—sexual impulses. Pornography then, for better or worse, is the imaginative record of man's sexual will. Let us look briefly at some of the psychological and artistic implications of this fact.

Steven Marcus (*The Other Victorians*) suggests that there is an inverse correspondence between a rising concentration on the dominating and sadistic image of masculine sexuality in pornography and the diminishing actuality of these qualities in real life. He finds evidence for this in the extravagant sense of phallic power so characteristic of pornography, where, as he puts it, "the penis becomes the man: it does the thrusting and not the man; it is its own agent." And in the world of pornog-

5

raphy, where sexuality is the prime mover, the penis takes on a kind of omnipotence. When viewed in an archetypal context this characteristic becomes an elaborate and central device of pornographic rhetoric. Theodore Reik, in *Love and Lust,* provides an important basis for interpreting this device:

Every analyst who has treated many women will have observed that most of them are often . . . assaulted by the conscious and often preconscious fear that their lover or husband will desert them, will not stay with them, but forsake them at a certain time. A fear . . . that is very rare with men. . . .

I daresay that there is a pattern for this contrast of the two sexes in the psychology of the sexual act. The male who has shown such an immediacy, urgency and intensity of sexual desire has very soon after the emission the wish to leave the body of the women. The woman who has hesitatingly and much more slowly yielded to his and her own desires feels the wish that the man's genitals should stay within her. She now experiences a heightened affection for him and something akin to gratitude. . . .

There is no doubt in our mind that in her wish to feel his body inside her long after ejaculation, she identifies his genitals with him, with his person, as if it were not only part of him, but he, himself. Does she identify his genitals only with him or is there a yet undiscovered dynamic factor operating?

There is here the psychic basis for the symbology of phallic power and pleasure so significant in sexuality from ancient worship to modern pornographic rhetoric. The image of the penis becomes a synechdocal statement. How far the figure extends is difficult to say. Is it, in addition to a celebration of power and pleasure, a figure also for the social or cultural role of the penis, that is, the reproduction of the race and state? Is it an ironic figure subconsciously trying to exorcise a masculine fear of impotence? Does, in other words, the popular and literary persistence of this figure document in some as yet untranslatable way Reik's sense of the "undiscovered dynamic factor" in the psychology of sex? In any event, it must be clear that this pornographic convention testifies to the psychic and archetypal human impulses which are themselves the origin of pornography. Marcus tends to regard this extravagant phallic metaphor as another sign of pornography's juvenility. But its psychological dimensions signify something well beyond the rhetorical crudeness of its masculine vanity. It symbolizes real human intercourse—fear and desire, fire and ice.

In her book *Psychic Energy* M. Esther Harding, a colleague and student of Jung, analyzes what might be called the sexual ages of man. She defines a progressive correspondence between emotional complexity and sexuality. The more advanced stages have a more complex emotional involvement in sexual relations. The earliest stages are phallic, in which man is synecdochally conceived as penis. There are also intermediate stages, where sexuality is stylized and idealized. The graphic representations of the early stages are of course the graffiti of the ages —phallic imagery and symbology. The intermediate stages are represented in the expansion of man's image from penis alone to the whole body—e.g. in stylized nude statuary. The advanced stages, dealing in emotional as well as physical sexuality, are more difficult of representation. The dynamics of psychic sexuality are beyond the static restrictions of painting and sculpture, but perhaps the film can overcome this. Yukio Mishima's recent film *Rites of Love and Death* or the fire scenes in Kokianos' *Elektra* may be examples. But the point is that we do experience these archetypal sexual ages, perhaps all of them simultaneously, and in both a personal and cultural context. And it is a natural impulse to express them. Pornography, in the sense that I am defining it, is the primal manner of this expression.

Representing an archetypal sexuality as it does, pornography may be expected to reflect the archetype's own historical development. That is, as our knowledge of sexuality increases and is assimilated into the culture, as psychological studies (we are still explicating Freud, Jung, *et al.*), sociological studies (such as the Kinsey reports), and physiological studies (such as Masters' and Johnson's *Human Sexual Response*) give us greater understanding and wiser interpretation of human sexuality, so will pornography, the literature of that sexuality, exhibit a greater artistic sophistication.

7

A comparison of the contemporary *Story of O* with the eighteenth-century *Memoirs of a Woman of Pleasure* (*Fanny Hill*) will authenticate this evolutionary progress. *Fanny Hill's* mode is one-dimensional description. It describes a prostitute's life, with the end of exploiting the obvious orgasmic stimuli in the subject. Fantasy is of course central to this end, and to induce it a kind of realism is affected through description of an occupation where rampant sexuality is made believable so that the reader can identify (fantasize) with it. Thus the action adopts the epistolary narrative device, the trappings of a specific sociological setting (eighteenth-century London), and is resolved with a gratuitous moral apostrophe on virtue and honor. In these respects it parodies the techniques of the eighteenth-century novel. Like everything else in the age of reason a description of sexuality required the sanction of moral rhetoric. Fanny's first letter puts it thus:

Truth! stark, naked truth, is the word; and I will not so much as take the pains to bestow the strip of a gauze wrapper on it, but paint situations such as they actually rose to me in nature, careless of violating those laws of decency that were never made for such unreserved intimacies as ours; and you have too much sense, too much knowledge of the ORIGINALS themselves, to sniff prudishly and out of character at the PICTURES of them. The greatest men, those of the first and most leading taste, will not scruple adorning their private closets with nudities, though, in compliance with vulgar prejudices, they may not think them decent decorations of the staircase, or salon.

This is a good and true argument. But in context it is rather a rhetorical gambit persuading the reader to believe in the descriptions and not feel guilt, which would of course ruin their effect. From this point the novel turns a standard eighteenth-century plot into a paradise of erotic fantasy. Fanny, a poor, provincial innocent, goes to London where she is deflowered and debauched by urban decadance and aristocratic profligacy. The bulk of the action is description of the standard variety of sexual experiences. In a nice touch, the story is resolved when Fanny is reunited with her first despoiler and true love; they marry and live ever after in virtue, honor, and penitence.

The key here is that the story is essentially description of sexual acts to the end of inducing some kind of orgasmic fantasy. Although the standard situations of the early English novel are employed—Fanny's world is shot through with the vicissitudes of poverty and innocence in the clutches of City and Aristocracy—the story is altogether focused on fantastic sexuality. There is a suggestion of moral causality, but it is so slight and so overshadowed by sex that it signifies nothing. There is no attempt to *explore* any of the implicit moral or psychic problems.

The essence of *Fanny Hill* is simplicity, simplicity of theme and simplicity of description. *Story of O,* on the other hand, adopts the complexity of abstraction and metaphor so characteristic of the modern novel. *Fanny Hill* is the description of a prostitute's life; *Story of O* is a metaphor of love as libido. If that figure contains all the paraphernalia of pornography—whips, chains, tortures, sadism, masochism, masculine power, feminine submission, sexual anonymity (at one point O is blindfolded and brought into a room where *"A* hand seized one of her breasts, *a* mouth fastened on the tip of the other"—sex without superego), and so on—it also contains the complex apparatus of the psyche. O submits herself to a brotherhood of sexuality which exploits and punishes her body, exorcises her will, dominates her total being, and finally is the cause of her self-destruction. She gives herself again to her surrogate lover, proving and taking refuge in her capacity to love; he abandons her also and she kills herself, but only after securing her master's permission.

The story provides, thus, two erotic points of view. From the masculine perspective it describes a complete liberation of the sexual libido. Men possess and enjoy O anonymously, without consequence or emotional responsibility. Her need for love brings her to them, which is a nice male power fantasy. And once they are through with her she is simply discarded; they have in fact the power of life and death, another nice male power fantasy. But from the female viewpoint the story arouses intense anxiety, a sure antidote to pornographic fantasy. O's captivity may be ended whenever she wishes, but to wish it is to forfeit the love she so desperately needs. Thus she is confronted constantly by the fear of loss, that archetypal anxiety observed by Theodore Reik. And of course she does lose that love, twice. And the consequence is suicide. Here is another classic female anxiety, that love for a man will subsume self-identity, and the loss of the love will leave her without reason to be. The novel, then, employs a multi-dimensional and complex descriptive and metaphorical methodology, exploring simultaneously the antitheses of sexual fantasy and anxiety.

What is important here is that O becomes the ur-woman in quest of love. She is thus exposed to its complete domination and consequent agony. Is she, then, an allegorical figure, perhaps the first *Everywoman?* Certainly everything about her is feminine stereotype—her love, her submissiveness, her sexuality, her annhilation of self, her anxieties, everything. At one point in *Peyton Place* (also written by a woman), a young girl says to her paramour, "Come on Honey. Love me a little . . . Come on Honey . . . Hard . . . Do it hard, Honey. Bite me a little. Hurt me a little." This is O's position; except she says, "Hurt me a *lot*." She is the archetypal woman in an archetypal situation. She has been described by every psychoanalyst who has written on the subject. On the one hand, she is the answer to every man's secret dream. On the other hand, she is an object awful in her implications. It is the former quality that makes her story pornographic. And it is the latter quality that takes her story beyond simplistic exploitation of sexual fantasy and lets it metaphorically explore a fundamental human condition.

The dramatically different technqiues of these two works parallel, of course, narrative forms characteristic of their respective times. But more than that they document the evolving psychic and artistic complexity of pornographic literature. Admittedly, these examples have higher artistic claims than most pornography. But I am interested here in its nature and artistic potential, and must consider therefore its highest stages of development. Because it has always been a sub-cultural phenomenon it has never been formally assimilated into the standard

10

literature. It can therefore be regarded, like musical comedy or opera, as a separate genre, with its own conventions and characteristics. But at the same time we must recognize that it is without a clear definition of its artistic ends. And to further complicate matters it must be regarded as a genre that will be—is being—absorbed into the standard literature. On the one hand, hard core or commercial pornography is static. Its ends are served by the simplest of descriptive techniques and rhetorical gambits. But, on the other hand, there is another and higher form of pornography which might be called *literary*. Rather than being only an exploitation of orgasm stimuli, it is rather an exploration of human sexuality. This is real pornography (not what the Kronhausen's call erotic realism); and it does exploit its subject. But it does more than exploit. We are, as Freud observed, *all* of us more or less neurotic. One aspect of human neurosis is the rhythm of expectation and frustration which marks our sexual lives. Pornography on its lowest level exploits this rhythm by providing easy fantasy gratifications. But on its highest level it *explores* this rhythm, its moral and psychic implications, and to the degree that it does this it is poetic in the highest sense. This kind, of course, is the pornography being absorbed into what we call Literature, and it is represented by such works as *O*. The fact of pornography's evolution out of its own genre and into the larger literature means that pornography must also be considered as a rhetorical device for that literature. Faulkner, for example, although no mere pornographer, is certainly one of the most pornographic of modern writers. He often uses pornographic scenes and situations (the cockpit copulation in *Pylon,* the romance of Mink Snopes in *The Hamlet,* etc.) to articulate his total scheme. It is perhaps in this latter rhetorical role that pornography will assume its best form and have its greatest significance.

What I have been arguing is that pornography, like any literature, is a way of knowing. The irony of its subject, sex, is the irony of another social pariah, the whore. We either deny its existence or privately acknowledge our private intimacies with it; and we are correspondingly either astonished or embarrassed

11

to meet it on the street. Critically, if we don't ignore pornography altogether, we condescend to it like reformed sugar-daddies. Legally we invoke "contemporary community standards" against it as if they were not a fantasy morality derived from vestigial Puritanism rather than human experience. And thus we insure our ignorance of what it can tell us about—the interaction of moral imagination and sexual being. Meanwhile science, having escaped community standards and academic condescension in the guise of a white coat, goes on documenting a reality we deny our imagination.

Further, we forget that contemporary pornography is a natural product of the contemporary moral and aesthetic imagination. Our sense of the beautiful has become too psychologically complex to permit its reduction to either moral idealism or artistic formalism. For Plato the True was necessarily the Beautiful. For us the true is much more likely to be the ugly or grotesque. A whole tradition argues this. In *A Streetcar Named Desire* Stanley Kowalski calls on his "colored lights," but it is finally the bright white light of revelation that brings the play's moment of truth and beauty—Blanche, Stanley, and Mitch all exposed, ugly, and helpless. And in Edward Albee's *Who's Afraid of Virginia Woolf?* Martha and George expend their full energies to show their young guests the true, the blushful Hippocrene—their monumental ugliness. Our literature adopts an aesthetic that aims to reveal the ugly as the true, and it often uses the sexual libido, which our culture has turned into a species of the ugly, as part of its rhetoric.

For the eighteenth and nineteenth centuries ugliness was artistically tolerable only when used as a dialectical agent (e.g. satire) to enforce the idea of a beautiful and harmonious Nature. It was an aesthetic which conceived of Nature, and therefore Truth and Beauty, as an archetypal norm that dismissed all aberrations as irrelevant. Contemporary aesthetic practice uses this process but reverses the values. Like Satan, it says, "Evil, be thou my good," and plays the role of devil's advocate, using the ugly to penetrate a cosmos no longer thought to be either benevolent or harmonious. It is at best indifferent, at

12

worst malign. The ugly, then, becomes an ironic figure of revelation, exposing an implacable universe unrelieved by moral or spiritual design. Sartre's concepts of *slime* and *nausea* are eloquent statements of an aesthetic of the ugly. Pornography, the kind represented by the *Story of O,* is a manifestation of the ugly. It does not romanticize sexuality; sex, unlike John's other wife, is not beautiful. It is simply there, at the center of man's life. And its meaning is that it *is there,* dominating love, aspiration, happiness, all human experience. Its extravagance is often fearful because it so ruthlessly reflects our own libido.

Perhaps, as Freud suggests, our sexual impulse cannot be gratified without our becoming cultural outlaws. Perhaps sexuality requires being worked out through cultural taboos. If so, this argues a fearful human necessity. A fact of life that may be true, but hardly what we can think of as beautiful. Such prospects as these make us defer from intimidating truth by equating it with beauty. The true for us must be a thing in itself; it may or may not be an analogue of something still better—the beautiful. We take LSD trips in an effort to find (or escape from) the true and maybe the beautiful. The danger is that our vision (perhaps of ourselves) will be destructive and make us flip altogether. But our ignorance is desperate enough so that we take the risk. Although the dangers are much smaller, pornography is part of this contemporaneous urgency to pursue the true. It too explores the unknown and therefore fearful in us. Our glimpses into that world refute our private and public lies. We can keep going—into the psyche as into space—and risk the dislocations that new knowledge brings, or we can collapse at the naked sight of ourselves. Not to explore the impulse to pornography is a form of denying human sexuality. We are, willy-nilly, brought to the overriding question of the modern imagination: how much deceit can we afford?

13

2.

Pornography as Poetic Genre:
Three Myths

I.

IN its elementary form genre refers to the manner in which literary action is presented to an audience. Thus, dramatic action, on a stage before us, happens in space and time, and, if there is dialogue, it happens audially. Lyric action happens audially—that is, either actually or imaginatively heard. Narrative action happens imagistically, an evocation of incidents analogous to a life, the sequential pattern of which describes narrative and plot, and so on. These are traditional distinctions that remain useful so long as we remember that they are perfectly violable and may be mixed at will, subject only to the restrictions imposed by a given artistic talent. The common ground for all such genres, the one inviolable thing, is the imagination of the audience, which, as even Aristotle pointed out, receives and interprets action on the same principles regardless of the accidental differences in representation.

The more complex idea of genre refers to the mythic sensibility invoked in an audience by poetic action. It is useful to regard myth in its philological context, where it refers to the telling of stories, traditionally stories of gods and heroes. In mythic tradition the storyteller has been in one way or another an exotic cultural figure. His experience, the basis for his stories, provides him not only with materials of entertainment

but also with the mantle of a special knowledge. He is a traveller, bringing to "villagers" ("audience," in this notion of genre,
is analogous to society) the thrill of his adventures, and by
virtue of those adventures he is a seer. As a visionary he
teaches us of a world beyond our own and, by analogy, we
often learn from him about our own world. The storyteller
gives our world a setting, a basis for interpretation and understanding. In so doing he provides us a vehicle for our own
mythic sensibility—who we are, where, and what potential the
cosmos holds. In this sense the traditional storyteller is paradigmatic of the poet.

The mythic sensibility of a culture takes various forms—
religious myths, nationalistic myths, heroic myths, and is
powerful enough that it can even define a sense of reality. For
the impulse to make myths is the impulse to construct a univocal and comprehensive explanation of things on the basis of
a special knowledge. The storyteller tells stories, and after a
while his stories tend to form a pattern, or perhaps in-
terpreters of myths find a pattern within the otherwise discon-
nected stories of a number of storytellers. However it happens,
when a pattern begins to emerge it is necessarily reductive,
intimidating new stories into its mold or excluding dissonant
ones from cultural significance. This rendering of dissonance to
coherence is the mythologizing process. It provides a conve-
nient way to see the world. And, as one sees the world so the
world inclines to be.

The natural impulse is to simplify, sift the important from the
unimportant, construct a mythic sense of things that is complete and satisfies the human need to feel in control of environment. It is through our mythic sensibility, then, that we
construct religion, morality, ethics—those things that define a
culture. And the process of definition is always exclusive, including what pleases us, excluding what does not. Thus Plato,
for example, in formulating his mythic sensibility in *The Republic,* gave priority to philosophers and excluded poets altogether. Thomas Jefferson and his colleagues, likewise, gave
priority to the equality of men in their pursuit of life, liberty,

15

and happiness, and denied the valid authority of despotism in their formulation of mythic sensibility via the Declaration of Independence.

But, as Plato feared and Jefferson and later the framers of the Constitution did not, cultures evolve and their interpretation of priorities change accordingly. Plato, hoping to stabilize mythic sensibility in a coherent state rooted in permanent forms of order, banished that imaginative dimension of mythic sensibility, poetry, that has always been not only celebrant but also the vehicle of exploring, ridiculing, and challenging mythic formulations. While he could tolerate those martial poets who celebrated *his* mythic vision, he could not tolerate those whose mythic sense was not locked into dialectic. Plato knew the power of the storyteller, and was himself a good one. He feared still better ones, like Homer and Euripides, who followed rather than channeled their imaginations.

By insisting that storytelling be dialectically functional Plato reduced poetry to rhetoric. As such it was not regarded as a mode of knowledge, only an instrument of persuasion or demonstration. He sought, of course, to neutralize the power of poetry, notwithstanding the fact that he was himself much more significantly a poet than a philosopher. Luckily Aristotle, no poet at all but a much more useful philosopher, was around to articulate the counter-argument that not only was poetry a mode of knowledge but that it was one of the highest modes, the nature of which was in a process of evolution, precluding therefore the reasonableness of any sweeping interdictions against it. The history of aesthetics and poetics has been essentially a commentary on the debate between these two positions. Because Plato's idealistic synthesis of all things has the appeal of cosmic unity and is consequently more socially portable, his view has dominated western aesthetics. Aristotle, partly because his total philosophy was not until relatively recently understood and partly because his method of differentiation is not so neat and partly because the *Poetics* does not adequately develop the idea of poetic evolution, has been wrongly regarded and sometime despised as a poetic formalist. Ironically Dante, neo-

16

Platonic as he was philosophically, provided the pragmatic wedge in western poetics for an Aristotelian notion of evolution. When Dante not only argued for the poetic propriety of native languages but demonstrated their possibilities in his poetry it was only a matter of centuries before sociology caught up with poetics to provide Aristotle's view the substance it needed. Once poetry was released from the static citadels of church and academy, once it was put back into the languages people used, it was only a matter of time until someone like Dryden turned up to argue the superiority of the "moderns" over the "ancients" on the basis of vitality. After that, it was a relatively short and easy critical jump to Schiller, Wordsworth, and then Arnold. Whatever anxieties Arnold may have had about popular literature and culture, which he shored up with such doctrines as "high seriousness," he knew the essential truth—that poetry *was* a mode of knowledge, that it had its own evolutionary rhythms of criticism and creativity, and that it would prevail perhaps even over religion as a cultural force.

If, then, poetry is a mode of knowledge disobliged to the univocal presuppositions of an idealistic dialectic, deriving its authority rather from the existential imagination, it is not only qualified to express mythic sensibility but it may help that sensibility to change, to assimilate the seemingly undammable stream of new truths being revealed to it. In this theory of "disinterested" poetics, a legacy of naturalism, poetry is not only disobliged to dialectic, it is as well disobliged to beauty, as we shall see in the following chapter. So it may as properly explore the ugly or obscene as the beautiful. Whereupon, enter pornography as a poetic genre.

As a genre, pornography has a political implication that perhaps more than any other factor has locked it into a sub-cultural role and thereby obscured its generic artistic character. In his solid history of English censorship (*A Long Time Burning*) Donald Thomas astutely observes that "there is an anarchic quality in obscene writing (as there is in satire), an urge to undermine what is intellectually or morally the accepted standard of the age." If Arnold was right about cultural rhythms

17

of criticism and creativity, as I think he was, then we may see something more positive in the anarchic impulse of obscenity. More and more, as our cultural values are obscenely perverted (by an atrocious war, capital punishment, poverty, chauvinism, racism), our arts use the obscene and the pornographic to let us see, in William Burroughs' metaphor, the "naked lunch" on the end of "that long newspaper spoon." Richard Wright's *Native Son,* Burroughs' *Naked Lunch,* Jack Smith's *Flaming Creatures,* Bruce Connor's *Cosmic Ray,* LeRoi Jones' plays and poems, Ronald Tavel's *Gorilla Queen,* Allen Ginsberg's poetic and prophetic role as culture hero—all of these and many more announce a reformation of mythic sensibility that requires a poetics of obscenity. The pornographic genre, precisely because of its moral anarchy, has provided a touchstone for a modern imagination disgusted with the blind and mechanical (or electronic) optimism of rich and powerful societies. If, as Kurt Vonnegut suggests, we must infect ourselves with humanity; and if, as Burroughs says, we have to get past *shame* (fig leaf as archetypal censor) to know our humanity, then our best artistic virus may be nakedness, and right now nakedness, perforce, means obscenity. The anarchy implicit in the pornographic genre is not simply an urge to undermine accepted standards, it is the urge to refute them, to demonstrate that they are humanly destructive. That anarchy is itself no antidote only means that the anarchic stage of criticism is preparing the way for creative responses to the placid murderousness of modern culture. There is indeed an anarchic quality in pornography. The anarchy necessary to remind us of what the makers, crew, and passengers of the *Titanic* forgot, that there is no such thing as an unsinkable ship, and the rhetoric that croons otherwise lures our sleepy navigators into the path of some ineluctable iceberg.

The erotic imagination, because it has until very recently been culturally repressed, is itself a species of the obscene— that which is kept out of sight. The very act of bringing it onstage, then, is aggressive and, at least implicitly, political. But its starting point is much darker and more private. Dark and

18

private enough that, although pornography has existed as long as literature, it could not be defined, or perhaps ever recognized, as a genre until Freud, Jung, and subsequent depth psychology articulated the murky connections between sexual neurosis and human behavior and imagination. Beyond that, it perhaps needed also the more "objective" support of such studies as the Kinsey reports and the Masters and Johnson investigations to document the "normality" of sex activity and erotic fantasy. Whatever ignorance remains, and there is much, we are certain at least that sexuality and the erotic imagination are significant facts of life. Though their precise significance remains hypothetical and speculative we are nevertheless sufficiently informed now to deal with them analytically. To discuss pornography as a genre, then, is simply to acknowledge that there is a substantial body of literature and other arts that are either wholly or in part pornographic, and that by inquiring into it we may discover something about both poetic evolution and erotic imagination.

Pornography, as a genre, is the literature of eros—the formulation of love's mythology. In classical cultures that mythic formulation was by and large coherent, incorporated into religion and the mainstream of cultural life. In "modern" cultures that mythology has lost coherence, become obscene. Phallic worship (or even curiosity) has become something to be repressed and consequently a source of shame. Relegated to the underground, erotic mythology—and pornography, its fictive literature—has been dissociated from our larger cultural mythos. This alienation has not only helped confirm pornography's anarchical role but has cut off society from an important source of mythic self-knowledge. Recently, as I have been arguing, pornography has become a more complex thing and its various forms are being assimilated into the mainstream of cultural life. Being everywhere—billboards, magazines, novels, poems, television, museums, and so on—we cannot ignore it. We are obliged to accept it as a fact of our cultural life, and let it tell us so much as it can.

But, though pornography is a mode of knowledge, it is no

more able to give us a complete knowledge of self or culture than any other poetic (or for that matter philosophic) mode of knowing. Its subject, sexuality, is as fragmentary a statement of human experience as any other. It is, however, nonetheless true for being fragmentary. The idealistic syndrome has deceived us into thinking that there are univocal answers available for the resolution of existential problems. Christ or Buddha may help us transcend our problems, help, that is, to put them in a cosmic perspective, but the problems remain. Neither as societies nor as persons do we escape confronting our desires and revulsions. Pornography is neither more nor less damnable than any other partial mythology, religious revivalism for example. Exploitive revivalism is every bit as personally and socially dangerous as exploitive pornography. Exploitation, whatever its immediate agency, is exploitation. And ignorance, whatever of, is ignorance. It breeds exploitation. It breeds vulnerability. It breeds manipulation. It diminishes human potential. Knowledge, as the myths of Faust or Eden argued, may have its dangers, but they are balanced and calculated—with the reasonable expectation that knowledge itself will help us deal with its own dangers. Ignorance has no options. The moral judgment, therefore, to be made of the pornographic genre must be based on the extent to which any given example of it gives us knowledge, however partial, of the truth of human being, whether or not we find that truth agreeable or even, apparently, useful.

The difficulty in dealing with pornography is that it customarily excites simultaneously our desire and revulsion (often at the simple fact of desire). Further, it has a wide range of artistic and philosophic ambitions, making it difficult to assimilate. Some, for example that of de Sade, seeks to articulate human degradation; some, for example that of Cassanova, seeks to articulate human graciousness. Some, for example *The Story of O,* is psychically complex and exploratory; some, for example *Barbara,* is simple and vapid. Such polarities and contradictions make gleaning knowledge from the genre an arduous job. So, inasmuch as I am regarding all pornography as

20

poetry, it will help to keep its mytho-poeic basis in mind as we examine its generic characteristics.

II.

As a genre, pornography is a mode of representing the obscene. Though obscenity, as an aesthetic concept, is not limited to sexuality—the explicit subject of pornography—pornography has become a popular analogue of the obscene. Thus, in the popular and frequently in the legal mind, while all obscenity may not be pornographic all pornography is obscene. And insofar as pornography's rise in popularity owes considerable to the rise of a "pop" aesthetics the popular association of pornography and obscenity is a reasonable one. "Soft-core" pornography, such as that in *Playboy* or the novels of Harold Robbins or Jacqueline Susann may attempt to dissociate itself from the obscene, but to a large segment of social taste even it is obscene. Consequently it seems more useful to provide a comprehensive basis for interpreting obscenity than to deny a deeply imbedded cultural association. The object of this study therefore is to demonstrate that obscenity is not simply a cultural aberration but that it is a complex expression of human imagination, humanistically vital enough to have its own poetics. If one is to have any commerce whatsoever with this interpretation of obscenity, then he must necessarily be attuned to the moral relativism characteristic of the modern mind. For it is this relativism that has permitted a separation of the good, the true, and the beautiful and made it possible to see that there is no necessary or constant equation between them. Rejecting that holy trinity of association also makes it possible to see that there may be positive connections between, for example, the good and the obscene.

There is a sense, however, in which we need to distinguish between the popular notion of pornography and the notion of it presented here. The quality by which pornography is usually identified is its inducement of auto-eroticism. Auto-eroticism is an important part of pornography, especially at its simplest levels, but it is not itself a defining characteristic. For one thing, auto-eroticism is highly variable from personality to personality. A shoe fetishist and a "normal" homosexual will not likely respond to the same stimuli. And it is quite possible for a "straight" heterosexual to respond to both fetishist and homosexual stimuli, even though he, at least consciously, regards them as "perverted" and himself as "normal." More significantly, pornography as a mythic genre is too complex to be capsuled into a masturbation syndrome, though it is obvious enough that pornographic material has a greater potential of inducing masturbation than, say, gnomic verse. The point is that pornography, in the sense that it is being discussed here, is a *poetic* genre, and like any such genre concerns itself with a full range of psychic and social dynamics, *including* the explicit sexuality by which we may recognize if not define it. For legal or rhetorical purposes one may be tempted to give a comprehensively synthetic definition of pornography. But that is no more truly possible for *pornography* than it is for *poetry,* which has never been comprehensively defined. In this study I attempt to indicate what pornography is by describing how it relates to cultural sentiments, poetics, and aesthetics. At this point I shall attempt further to define it by describing some of its workings, some of its kinds, and some of its mythic implications.

Perhaps the main business of poetry is to bring body and soul together, fuse the animal with the spiritual, and in so doing it provides a mythic basis for interpreting human experience. Poetry energizes itself and its audience by reference to and stimulus of instincts, and it elevates itself and its audience to mythic sensibility, to the poetic sense of the story of man, by connecting instincts with human spirit. Any art, then, that avoids either the animal or spiritual natures of man is by that much a lesser art. What "instincts" are exactly we must leave to philosophers and psychologists. But, as with discussions of poetry, we may proceed sans definition on the reasonable assurance that even so we more or less know what we are talking about. We may not be so confidant about agreeing on the nature of human spirit. I am using the concept in a naturalistic

22

rather than transcendental sense. That does not preclude our impulse to transcend or surmount despair, it simply means that the avenues to such transcendence are expanded from the traditionally apocalyptic ones to include the full range of human consciousness still being explored. That knowledge of human consciousness is never exhausted is the principal epistemological argument for poetry. And in arguing that pornography is a mode of this exploration I argue that, in greater or lesser degree, it is either spiritual or has the potential of telling us something of the human spirit. Such a notion of spirituality is probably not a traditionally acceptable one. For it requires accepting the depraved, the perverted, the neurotic, the psychotic —in short, the obscene—as agencies of spiritual knowledge. There are precedents for this notion in Christian tradition— Augustine, John of the Cross, Abelard—but they have not been a part of its mainstream. They do, however, suggest that this notion of the human spirit has a distinct if suppressed role in the history of even Christian humanism.

At its simple level (whether "hard-core" or "soft-core"), pornography is not itself spiritual. That is, insofar as an artistic product reveals its "intention," simple pornography does not intend to provide spiritual instruction. Whatever its intention, however, simple "hard-core" pornography does articulate the sexual aspect of what might be called the mythos of animality. The characteristic concerns of "hard-core" pornography, from its celebration of "normal" sexuality to its confusions of pleasure and pain in sado-masochism, document man's intrigue with his sexual animality. Until relatively recently—with Freud and Krafft-Ebing and others—graphic and literary pornography provided the only documentation of it. In this sense, as Steven Marcus's study of Victorian pornography shows, the mere fact of pornography's existence tells us something, something of both private and social personality. That there is an audience, and contemporaneously an increasing one, says that men are intrigued in a variety of ways, from the scholarly to the auto-erotic, with sexual animality.

The persistence of simple pornography as a coherent genre

and the expansion of its audience argue that there is a cultural mythos of animality. "Soft-core," the right wing of simple pornography, titillates its audience with animality, but seeks to socialize that mythos by sublimating its physically egocentric energies to a materialistic culture's analogue of spirit, the mythos of sentimentality. One must remember at this point that, while "hard-core" pornography has had a long—if underground—history, "soft-core" pornography is relatively recent, and its mythos consequently is tied more closely to the materialism of modern culture than is that of "hard-core." While "hard-core" looks back to the cave man for its model, "soft-core" looks ahead to technocratic and executive man. As I will discuss later, "soft-core" is probably best examined in the context of transformational psychology, because it provides a locus for the transformation of explicitly sexual energy from genital activity to "productive" energy of a more socially acceptable nature—commodity. And commodity has come to have a peculiar moral sentiment in modern technological culture. "Soft-core" pornography has emerged from underground by its ability to make sexual energy contribute to the Gross National Product. And, in the mythos of sentimentality, a man who keeps the economy churning is a man of implicit good will, that is to say, a modern equivalent to the man of feeling.

Finally, in the mythic structure of the pornographic genre, there is that artistic or complex pornography that has been around since at least Solomon and is of course the richest pornographic source of spiritual knowledge. It presents the mythos of love. It differs from "soft-core" in that it is culturally disinterested, not concerned to serve cultural sentimentalities. It differs from "hard-core" in that it is poetically complex, committed to exploring the full consciousness of love rather than restricting itself to animality, however much it may use the imagery of explicit genitalia and genital activity characteristic of "hard-core" pornography. Although it is complex, and may include many other concerns than sexuality, this mode of the genre is pornographic by virtue of making sexuality a major metaphor in the construction of its mythos of love. It need not, though it usually will, include explicit sexual imagery. Thus

24

Mary Renault's novel *The Charioteer* is an example of this mode because, although it does not use genital imagery, it does make homosexuality a major metaphor of the anguish of love and the human obstacles to recognizing and achieving it. D. H. Lawrence's *Lady Chatterly's Lover* is also an example (very likely over his own semantic objections). Though the action of Lawrence's novel is not even predominantly genital, it does image much genital activity to the end of exploring the antitheses of potency/impotency and man/nature to develop Lawrence's dialectical mythos of love. Whereas the mythoi of simple pornography tend to stereotype, flattening into conventions that will not disturb their audience, the mythos of complex pornography varies, sometimes diametrically, according to the imagination of a given poet. The erotic sensibilities of Jean Genet and D. H. Lawrence, for example, could not be more antagonistic, yet both of them can use the same themes, for example homosexuality and moral inversion, and the same explicit genital imagery, and both explore the possibilities and failures of modern love. The imaginative approaches to the theme of love, to the making of a mythos for it, are manifold, and poets in this artistic mode of the pornographic genre *are* poets. Their use of pornography, therefore, follows the dictates of imagination. And, as with any poetry of integrity, complex pornography is not obliged to confirm cultural norms of what love is. If, for example, Allen Ginsberg finds love to be homosexual, then his obligation as a poet is to pursue that and make as honest a story of it as possible. Not to do so because it threatens or contradicts the cultural norm is to fail not only himself but to fail his cultural role as poet. The responsibility of society, if it accepts poetry as a mode of knowledge, is to remain open to what poets of all genres, including the pornographic, have to say. Otherwise all mirrors will soon reflect the same imbecilic smile.

III.

To see how these mytic levels of the genre work we may begin with the simplest (and "dirtiest"). In *Pornography and the Law* Eberhard and Phyllis Kronhausen have so thoroughly analyzed the structure of "hard-core" pornography that their "formula" has become a model for commercial exploiters of the form. They have, in effect, articulated pornography's *conventions,* and in so doing have helped make it recognizable as a genre. They define its fictive principle thus: "A book which is designed to act upon the reader as an erotic psychological stimulant ('aphrodisiac') must constantly keep before the reader's mind a succession of erotic scenes. . . . The characteristic feature in the structure of 'obscene' books is the *buildup of erotic excitement* in the course of the text." Verbal and imagistic conventions of "hard-core" pornography exist to implement this movement of action. The imagistic conventions that the Kronhausens identify are seduction, defloration, incest, the permissive-seductive parent figure, profaning the sacred, supersexed males, nymphomaniac females, negroes and asiatics as sex symbols, homosexuality and flagellation. An impressive list of possibilities for animal delight and instruction.

In "hard-core" form these actions comprise the symbolic basis for making a mythos of animality. The form in fact depends on their predictability—that is, that they are predictably the basis of narrative and that they can be erotically expected to mind their business and not introduce extraneous non-sexual matters. Conventional "hard-core" narrative describes stereotypical actions performed by stereotypical actors. It is the predictability of pornographic action that permits the buildup of erotic excitement—one knows where the action is going and it remains only to "see" it. In this, perhaps Humean, sense "seeing" is believing (that is, an aphrodisiac) because sexual activity is imaged with an exclusiveness and purity that real-life experience of it does not have. "Hard-core" pornography focuses almost exclusively on the physicality of sex, animal desire and animal pleasure. Consciousness is seldom or never evoked. Normal anxieties, for example, that a couple might expectably have in their first sexual experience are, if included at all, token overtures to verisimilitude. They do not interfere with spectacular sexual performances. There is little or no "mind" represented in "hard-core" pornography, and certainly

26

none of its consequence—such as impotence or frigidity. Whatever diminishes sexual performance is excluded from the "hard-
core" pornographic world view. The imagistic conventions of
"hard-core" are not imagistic at all. They are superimpositions
of a pornographic thesis on images of nature, to the end of
fictively reconstructing nature according to the mythos of animality. In that mythos, libido rules the universe. All the conventions of the genre testify to that, but especially the
permissive-seductive parent figure, where libido is not only
given opportunity but becomes an implicit moral imperative—
one *should* indulge the libido, through the ethic of sexual frolic.
In such a convention parental authority, at once the most inti-
mate and cosmic kind, enforces the sexual ethic and thus fictively provides a place for the mythos of animality under the
canopy of heaven.

One must remember that in this mythos *all* manifestations
of animality from affection to violence are approved. One must
also remember that the morality of this, as of any, mythos is
fictive—thus figurative, thus incomplete. All mythoi, for poetic
and rhetorical purposes, represent their view of things as if it
were absolute. That selectivity makes art possible, and as any
teacher knows it makes knowledge possible. It is the audience's
responsibility to place the special pleading of myth in the context of its total experience. This is at once the freedom and re-
striction of poetic imagination. Being disobliged to the literal,
it is free; knowing that its creations are bubbles, the audience is
free, and the poet bound to his art. Unlike the philosopher or
scientist, the poet trades in proximate and suggestive truths,
the value of which does not depend on the intimidation following from exactness. Gravity is an exact truth, intimidating one's
behavior accordingly. Animality is an inexact, even contradictory, truth, the knowledge of which may influence behavior but
cannot intimidate it. Because society, for example, knows human animality, the policing of prostitution is correspondingly
inexact. Neither prostitutes nor their customers are intimidated
by the law or its enforcement, but they are influenced to be
discrete about their behavior. It is only in small communities

27

where discretion is impossible that such laws are in fact effective. The long history of pornography testifies to the archetypal truth of its animal myth. The irregular passing of laws against it and related activities, and the still more irregular policing of them, testifies that though men may want the myth out of sight they don't want it destroyed. Pornography, in its "hard-core" form, invigorates man's animal character, reminds him of it, suggests behavioral possibilities for it, approves. Morally, it not only certifies that man has this nature, it serves to remind him of the curiously intriguing game of fast and loose that he plays with his mythic sensibility.

The characteristic narrative of "hard-core" pornography consists in a series of sex scenes more or less inventively described. "Classics" of the form (*The Autobiography of a Flea, The Lascivious Hypocrite,* and so on) are for that reason usually rather short. The action, in E. M. Forster's terms, is all *story* and no *plot.* Plot requires a sense of causality, both immediate and cosmic. But in this form all causality is the same—the mythos of animality. Everything sharing the same cause, there is no need to represent anything other than its effects, carnal pleasure in various modes. Thus, "hard-core" pornography's fictive recommendation rests in the inventiveness of its descriptions rather than the energy of its imagination. Its imaginative energy is in the mythos of which it represents a particular variation. This is one reason why publishers of "hard-core" pornography tend to revive classics as often as they commission new works. One such publisher, Maurice Girodias of Olympia Press, complains that one of the problems of contemporary pornographers is that they get too "literary," consequently diminishing pornographic focus as they introduce psychic or moral complexities into the narrative. The principle of "hard-core" form is to tap into the mythos of animality and derive its energy and appeal therefrom. Its audience directs its imaginative energies, and the function of this pornographic mode is to provide the vehicle for surfacing the animal dimension of its audience's mythic sensibility. Thus animality is not only acknowledged but in large part its subliminal power over the psyche is exorcised. Recognizing animality subjects us less to it. Thus "hard-core" pornographic action is locked into its symbolic function. When we read it we know, roughly, what we want from it. We want its erotic stimulus to remind us of the animal nature we spend our civilized energies suppressing. And we want approval for it. And we want the pleasure implicit in approval. Thus, at its best, "hard-core" pornography provides a psychic joy that transcends the bounds of its imagistic physicality, the joy of acknowledging our own lust, and of being figuratively assured that it is not necessarily destructive of our humanity. This is why John Cleland's *Memoirs of a Woman of Pleasure* is and will remain one of western literature's great books. It is a great work of art because it is a brilliant example of its genre, and it surpasses most other examples of its genre in its civilized celebration of sexual pleasure. It reminds us, apart from its trappings of eighteenth-century ecology, that sex, as sex, is a source of joy and, frequently enough, amazement. A professional lady of pleasure, the pornographic heroine Fanny Hill, manifests human animality and yet retains a compassion, generosity, and humanity that fictively argue the compatibility of man's animal and spiritual natures. But, because *Fanny Hill* has a literacy and grace that make it nearly artistic or complex pornography, I want to use another less marginal example to illustrate the workings of "hard-core" pornographic form. "Frank Newman's" *Barbara* (Traveller's Companion Series, 1968) is an unequivocal instance of "hardcore" pornography. Where *Fanny Hill* reflects the stylistic gentility of its aristocratic eighteenth-century origins, *Barbara* reflects the most antagonistic flaunting of the pornographic imagination before social conventions that is so contemporaneous. Like most examples of its kind, it does not have a plot, though it frequently toys parodically with moral associations, and its story line is simply a convenience on which to hang a series of sexual descriptions. Each chapter is a variation on some form of "hard-core" convention, though by virtue of its up-to-date context (the action takes place at Provincetown, and it incorporates all the "hip" characters possible), it as-

29

sumes a particularly aggressive posture toward social standards. Here is the first chapter:

Max lying on the warm sand. The June wind cold on his back and he pressed his body against the smooth and yielding texture of the sun-warmed dune. Down in the hollow below two college kids were fucking dog-fashion, the boy long-haired and blond, with a wispy blond beard and mustache, the girl with much shorter, dark hair, both very tanned although it was only June, both slim, tall, supple. The white skin usually covered by their bathing suits so white that, from this distance of ten yards, had they not been fucking, would have seemed like bathing suits. His eyes just above the level of the dune, behind a screen of beach plum—pale blue eyes, pale sandy beard, hair—Max watched impassively as they fucked furiously, throwing the sand around, the boy on his knees behind the crouched girl, bending his body like a bow while he fucked to bite her neck and her back, reaching around her body and grabbing at her tits; squealing, both of them squealing, she twisting her arse in jerky, rapid rhythm, he pounding faster and faster until he screamed, threw back his arms and fell on his back—lay there like dead. The girl quite still in the same position, on knees and elbows, eyes tightly shut, slowly let her legs and arms slide straight till she lay flat on her belly, face in the sand. Max watched, still except for the slow movement of his hips, rubbing his cock against the incredibly warm softness of the sand—watched for minutes, slowly got up and carefully, slowly walked down the dune, took off the faded cut-down blue jeans—all he was wearing—and dropped them on the pile of the kids' bathing suits and suntan lotion. He walked over till he stood behind the prone girl, her arse slightly elevated from the wind-blown sand. He watched her, eyes closed, slow shallow breathing. Stood astride her, his feet level with her knees, then carefully and quietly lowered himself to his knees so that his cock slid into her cunt from behind. She stayed quite still, her eyes still shut. Max began to fuck her with long slow strokes, rocking back and forth on his knees, until she began twisting her arse in time to his slow, regular strokes, his cock going almost all the way out on each stroke, slowly, longly, each cycle growing slower and slower on the outstroke and faster and faster on the instroke. At the peak of the instroke Max felt her vagina begin to contract in the onset of orgasm; slower, painfully

30

slowly he drew back, elongating the delicious preliminary shudders of orgasm, while her hips twisted frantically, out of phase with the muscular jerks that twitched her back and her legs mmmmmmmmmmmmmmmm. . . .

When she came, Max squatted quite still, his cock still deep inside her, his balls squashed into the crack of her elevated and now softly relaxed arse. She lay quietly, her arms straight before her, her face flat in the sand, every muscle entirely slack; then she turned her head, sandy lips, started to open her eyes slowly . . . they grew wide with, actually rolled with, terror; she exhaled all at once, stunned, before she could catch her breath. Max grabbed her around the hips and forced them to bend, simultaneously sinking back from his knees to his heels; he held her tight against him so that she was sitting on his lap impaled on his steel-hard cock, the tip jammed against the vulva entrance. He began a pounding, rocking, jerking of the hips, switched one hand so that it covered her mouth and chin and jammed them shut, and his other arm locked around her waist, held her to him hard. In minutes she began to come again; Max kept up the pounding as she came and the orgasm turned into a serial orgasm, not passing its peak and subsiding, but turning into a strobe flash of continual shudders and explosions of sensation up her spine and through her limbs, shooting current through the marrows of her bones, repeatedly, until, through sheer exhaustion, the intensity of the climaxes began to decrease; Max slowed and softened his stroke, sat still, and let her shudders die away. Again they were still, the girl this time with wide-open eyes, staring at nothing, much white showing below the dark, completely opaque irises. Max still clasping the girl to him with an arm around her waist, with his cock still deep in her, now walked on his heels so that they were alongside and at a right angle to the boy who was lying on his back, arm thrown over his eyes to shield them from the sun; the girl was quite slack, mouth open, tongue lagging out. With caressing but firm motions of his other hand Max arranged her legs and arms so that she was kneeling, supporting her own weight, her head hanging loosely, directly over the boy's cock, which lay slack and dull with dried juices and come among the blond hairs. Max withdrew his cock until only the head remained in her cunt and began to make very slight motions with the head, going almost entirely out of her outer lips, the tip just penetrating the inner lips on each instroke; at the same time he pushed her head down toward the boy's prick With the strokes her

31

hanging tongue began to wake up and lick the boy's cock, now at the base, now along the side; as it stirred and grew, she became absorbed in her licking and took it into her mouth, softly with slack, so exhausted was she, lips sucking harder and harder, taking more and more into her mouth. Max, still with only the tip of his cock in her, was decreasing his motions, making each outstroke slightly longer than each instroke, imperceptibly leaving her to the excitement of sucking her lover's cock in long, soft, deep gobbles now; the boy still until, as Max withdrew entirely, unnoticed by the girl, the boy tensed his hips and connected thigh-muscles, moving no other part of his body. At this motion, the girl began to gobble frantically, plunging her nose into his pubic bush, twisting her head as she gobbled up and down. The boy, with a sudden, single spasm of his hips, came and the girl just sucked, stopped moving her head, but shuddered in her legs and sucked the juices deep down. Max had moved around until he was on the side of the boy, lying on his side, parallel to him. As the boy came, Max suddenly grabbed him by the nape of the neck and the thigh, roughly turned him over on his belly, jumped on top of him, holding his face and shoulders down into the sand with his hand on his shoulders, the boy's legs immobilized between his. He shoved his hard-on, somewhat, but not enough, lubricated by the juices of the girl's cunt, directly into the boy's arsehole. The boy screamed—the peculiar hissing high-pitched scream of those who are suffering the pain of first buggery—and fought to get loose, but Max's knobby legs held the boy's face and shoulders flat down in the sand. Max buggered away with hard strokes that burned and tore the boy's arsehole. The girl still stunned, still in the akimbo position she had been thrown into when Max turned the boy over. Max kept up his stroking until he felt the struggles of the boy's hips assume a rhythmic character; then, taking his hands off the struggling boy's shoulders, he put one on the back of his neck to hold him down and slipped the other underneath until it grasped the boy's cock, which was hard again, like a rock. When the boy felt Max's hand on his throbbing cock, he suddenly lay still. So did Max. Max withdrew, and using the boy's prick, firmly grasped, like a handle, turned the boy over onto his back. Then Max sunk his head down and placed his bearded lips on the boy's belly. The boy shuddered at the touch of a man's lips. Max moved his lips and his tongue across the boy's belly down to his cock. The boy shuddered again as Max took his cock in his mouth and began slowly, without much head motion, to gobble. The girl lay still, but her eyes had lost their glaze and were following Max's actions. Max with his eyes ordered her to get up and come over; she, understanding and not knowing how she understood, came. Max giving place to her, she straddled the boy and sank down onto his cock. She sat there, quite still, his cock deep inside her, waiting for Max, who had come around and was now lying, belly down in the sand between the boy's legs. Spreading the girl's cheeks with his hands, Max licked all around her arsehole, starting at the top of the crack; he licked down over the hole to the space between arsehole and cunt, the back edge of the cunt; now he was licking the back edge of the cunt and the base of the boy's cock and his balls all at once. His tongue moved back up to the hole and began to work its way in and his licking assumed a rhythmical character, his tongue darting in and out of her tight arsehole, and both the girl and boy began to stir in their hips. Max stopped his licking and watched for a moment as the couple's beating, twisting movement grew visible; then, rising to his knees, he slipped his cock slowly into the girl's tight arsehole gleaming with spit, where he felt the slow movement of the boy's cock against his cock through the thin stretched walls of colon and womb, so tightly stretched that he could feel the ridge of the boy's circumcision against the base of his cock. Max stayed still, establishing no conscious movement of his own, but let his hips be sucked into the rhythm of the rocking couple; when his hips were moving in the same slow counterpoint, he began to introduce variations and grace notes, to lead the young couple, as a great dancer leads a good dancer, to bring out of them rhythms and thrusts they had never known they knew, a three-part movement, now fast, now slow, each part growing into and amplifying each part in time and space. The young couple was fully awake, filled with concentration and wonder that they were able to fuck like this, were doing, swinging, building structures that danced like the summer cumulus over the ocean, each more intensely aware of his individuality than ever before, while lost in work of art, a bird's flight that took them entirely beyond any sense of the bodies that they felt so clearly—the sweat, the slide of skin against skin that was there. Contradictions implicit. They fucked for an hour. Playing with the new power, bringing out sensations beyond sensation. Finally all of them, knowing each other, knowing what they wanted, agreeing to slow, played a coda and stopped all motion, absolutely still for two or three minutes, the three of them

33

still. They all, slowly, by a willed act of nonwill, as the mountain peak tilts and falls, they each together, into depths beyond depth, came—not moving. Quite easily, relaxed, with a touch of languor, but with more of freshness, their limbs glowing with sweat like dew, they separated themselves and sat on the sand in easy positions, like friends talking, though they didn't talk but merely looked at one another in quiet. Then, rising up, they walked over the dune, down to the beach, holding hands, girl in the center; they went down to the beach, Max carrying the pile of clothes, which he dropped above the high tide mark. They plunged into the water and swam for a while. Still no word spoken. All in the easy manner of affectionate old friends, they sat down on the beach to dry themselves in the sun, and put on their clothes. They boy got out a pack of Camels. Gave one to each, took one himself. Lit them with a Zippo lighter.

"I'm Max."

Leaning over and kissing him softly on the shoulder. "My name is Leslie."

"Tom."

"Well, Tom and Leslie, how long are you going to be here?"

The girl answered, looking first at Tom. "We . . . we're going to stay for the whole summer. We're working at a motel in town."

Max smiled. "Well, if you want to, why don't you quit your jobs and move in with me. I have a shack out here on the dunes about three dunes up the beach. I don't believe you have to work. Think it over. Don't decide for a couple of days. Right?" They both nod— "Don't even talk about it for a couple of days. It's the fourth shack up from Sail Road. With a green roof. Come out any time. It's never locked."

"OK, Max," Tom says, and with a conscious effort, as Max was getting up: "Won't you kiss me before you go?"

Max leaned over and rubbed his cheek against the boy's. Leslie sitting alongside, reached out at the same time and put her hand on Max's shoulder.

"Bye, Tom, Leslie," and kisses each of them lightly on the lips. Leslie's lips trembled more than Tom's.

Barbara illustrates the "hard-core" form so well because, unlike many others, it is maximally inventive within the framework of its conventions. It does not transcend those conventions as *Fanny Hill* does, unless one regards its peculiarly satirical ending as getting somehow beyond those limits. But its sexual descriptions are clearly good within the limits of the form. The ingenuity of this passage "Max, still with only the tip of his cock in her, was decreasing his motions, making each outstroke slightly longer than each instroke, imperceptably leaving her to the excitement of sucking" borders on inspiration, from perhaps a diabolical rather than divine muse. But of course it isn't quite, even diabolically, inspired. Its inventions simply bring the reader into the framework of a libidinous world, where his interests and excitements may pursue their own paths. Max does organize his pornographic cell of sexual novitiates, and their fun and games work systematically through the whole host of pornographic conventions—from Max's defloration of a more than willing twelve-year-old through homosexuality, lesbianism, incest, and group sex to conclude with a prodigious outrage to one of the greatest of all cultural taboos—incest between father and son, mother and daughter. After which we are given a bucolic family portrait—"They stood quite content on the peak of the last dune before the tidal beach. Arm in arm, Barbara and Franz between their mother and father." This is the mood with which the book closes, and its parodic absurdity reminds us of the distance between archetypal awareness and ethical instruction. Having belabored nearly every possible sexual act, position, and relationship, *Barbara* ends with the suggestion that when confronting our sexual fantasies we do well to keep our own ridiculousness in mind. And not the least of the joke is that the demands of our animality are such that we read to the end, to find ourselves and our fantasies, both the pornographic ones and the sentimental ones, ridiculed.

But, unlike such a pornographic novel as *Candy*, satire is not the real business of *Barbara*. The apostrophe of *Barbara's* ending is merely the author reminding us that, after all, pornography is just another game, like metaphysics. But such fun is not the usual animal tone of either this novel cr the form generally. *Barbara* evidences another dimension of the animality myth, violence. Violence, as Gershon Legman's *Love and Death* argues so persuasively, is a cultural sublimation of

35

sexual impulses, and is a vital part of the pornographer's arsenal. In *Barbara* it has a particularly modern nuance; the fusion of violence and pleasure provides an appropriately modern sense of subtlety. It is a kind of "hard-core" analogue of Burrough's far more complex treatment of Dr. Benway, who parodies the subtle fascistic sado-masochistic genius of technocracy.

In *Barbara* violence is kinetic, giving what might otherwise have been rather flat pornographic conventions a suspense and tension apropriate to the nature of the "civilized" mythos of animality, where this peek-a-boo game of intrigue constittutes a basic rhythm. As with sex, we at once want it and fear it. So sex and violence complement one another nicely. In addition to which they are both very much a part of the act of sex, especially insofar as the violence is kinetic or controlled. Such violence is an analogue of sexual power, and is therefore a central part of the fictive representation of the mythos of animality.

If violence may be defined to include the violation of another's will, then Max rides the thin ridge of it, molding Tom's and Leslie's wills by literally manipulating their pleasure, thus fictively surfacing that archetypal relationship between pleasure and pain, will and submission, so crucial to the pornographic genre. One submits to his animality under the aegis of pleasure, even if it must be forced upon him. The omnipotence of pleasure is precisely his excuse: Faust says of the Helen that Satan has conjured to keep Faust from backsliding to salvation, "Her lips sucks forth my soul." This sado-masochistic pleasure is central to the pornographic ethos because it is so deep in our archetypal sense of self, however disturbing and therefore repressed.

Further, pleasure is given a kind of "purity"; that is, like beauty, it is in pornography its own excuse for being. In his "rape" of Leslie, Max demonstrates a depersonalized sexual pleasure both as a lesson to Leslie and analogously to the reader. Leslie experiences it unequivocally in mistaking Max, a stranger, for Tom, her lover. Aside from the parodic theme of

36

the mysterious stranger, the point is that Leslie's pleasure is not tainted in this scene by affection for her sexual partner. Max does much the same with Tom, expanding the lesson in "pure" pleasure by making him enjoy buggery and homosexuality. In both lessons there is enough force used to make the reader wonder where things are going, but the anticipation of violence (in "hard-core," unlike complex, pornography one does not fear violence—it is an aphrodisiac) is elevated into the novel's pornographic version of the flower-power admonition to "love" one another. The final sublimation of violence comes in Max's creation of the *ménage à trois,* where Tom and Leslie learn that sex is not only pure pleasure (their first pornographic "zen" lesson), but also *art* and *knowledge* (their second): "each more intensely aware of his individuality than ever before, while lost in a work of art." Only after these lessons have been learned by the neophytes does the master introduce himself, transforming bodies as instruments of pure pleasure into personalities. And then the chapter drifts with post-orgasmic bliss into a modern pornographic theme—don't get uptight, there's enough to go around. So much for the tragedy and violence of the eternal triangle. Here, then, is a "good" example of pornography—that is, one that uses the mythic conventions, gives them the dynamics of a tantalizing manipulation of violence, which is finally sublimated to the pornographically omnipresent and necessary theme that sex is good for you.

The verbal conventions of simple or "hard-core" pornography—what the Kronhausens call " 'dirty' words in 'dirty' books"—are in fact the most complex and evasive aspect of that mode of the genre. Their brief but basic statement suggests the many implications in the use of dirty words:

The use of taboo words in "obscene" books is closely related to the frequent mixture of the sacred and the profane which we discussed in the preceding section. Its chief attraction lies in the open defiance of the "superego," or conscience, the flagrant violation of the social conventions of polite discourse, the flaunting of one's independence, the throwing off of social responsibility, and the assertion of the instinctual primitive side of life against all the restraining and inhibiting forces of the environment.

Verbal pornographic conventions are used to remind the audience of what it is getting away with, and in that way heighten its pleasu   Dirty words are at once an aphrodisiac and a repudiation of social restrictions. Their thrill, therefore, is both psychic and political. The dynamics of this relationship are difficult to get at and would require an examination of language as a mode in the "transformation" of psychic energy. This is not the place for that, but we can suggest how that psychological context helps us see that pornography is not merely a subcultural sign of depravity but is in fact a relatively common way for individual personalities to relate to their environment and exorcise some of its power over them.

One function of language is its use as a social index of a man's knowledge of and ease with social propriety. Comedy and satire are by and large peopled with mismatched vulgarity and "aristocracy," and the usual giveaway is language. Witness Eliza Doolittle in both the musical and dramatic versions of Shaw's *Pygmalion*. Dirty words, and the jokes and stories made from them, are a kind of transformation that permit one to "get even with" a social or cultural repression that he does not wish or dare to oppose directly. The preference of "lower-class" speech for dirty words probably derives from the preference of the Angles and Saxons (and the indigenous "lower classes" subsequently in their tradition) for their own words (e.g. *fuck*) over Roman imports (e.g. *copulate*). One might ask, as hip Saxons must have, inasmuch as the act is as natural to a Saxon as to a Roman, why not use an indigenous Saxon word? But inkhorn pretensions and Christian sublimation prevailed, and now no socially ambitious man whose native tongue is English will *shit* if he can *defecate,* and he will do neither if he can "go to the bathroom." If he is not much polished he will use the "men's room"; if a middle or working-class wit and bon vivant he will use the "little boy's room"; and if he is socially hopeless he will "go to the toilet." If one feels either oppressed or boxed

38

in by these linguistic niceties, he might very naturally—as a walk on the street or even a visit to a country-club locker room will show—advise such an intimidating system to "eat shit" or "get fucked." When he does, if he has not been too deceived by his education, he will be ripe for subscription to both an obscene aesthetic and a pornographic poetics. Actually the culture is a good deal more prepared for a smutty poetics than it knows, considering that most of us are better equipped by it to enjoy a dirty joke than a Keats ode.

One function, then, of smutty language is to resist social encroachment on individuality. Another use is its assistance to maintain a psychic balance. The two areas are of course closely related; if one can exorcise a sense of social oppression through language—his own or what he reads or hears—that will surely help him maintain some kind of psychic balance. That is, it will help him channel his psychic energy into socially acceptable modes of conduct, for instance swearing rather than bloodying somebody's nose. There is near universal approbation for letting dissidents—from children to political radicals —"blow off steam." This device, administrators of colleges and governments have discovered much to their advantage, helps maintain order.

Dirty words too, then, are an aspect of the myth of animality. Animality implies naked power; in the case of dirty words it means the covert power to dare defy social conventions. There is also the more psychically complex role of language as aphrodisiac. If we may think of language so as to include phonemic noises, that is, voice sounds such as moans that do not signify anything outside a specific behavioral context, then there is no question but that language does act as a sexual stimulant. Sexual partners are certainly guided, one way or another, by vocal responses. Positive vocal responses such as moaning or heavy breathing induce heightened sexual excitement and activity. Language is both a guide and an encouragement in sexual conduct. Two "soft-core" examples show how pornographers imitate this fact of sexual life. In one, cited earlier from Grace Metalious's *Peyton Place,* a girl at a peak of sex-

39

ual excitement says to her partner, "Hurt me . . . Hurt me a little," thus guiding and encouraging his activities. The other, from Harold Robbins' *The Adventurers,* is more specific. Here the passionate lady says to her partner, who has just called her a "dirty cunt," "That's right honey . . . eat me, hurt me, talk dirty to me, and fuck me. That's all I want," giving advice and consent for cunnilingus, sadism, vulgarity, and other delights of the animal nature.

Sex is a single-minded activity—the seeking of (frequently but not always at one with the giving of) pleasure. It is its own form of communication, and consequently does not usually involve conversation, which is a different form of communication. It is also at once an intense physical and psychic thing. Thus language, in its service, is intense to the point of primitiveness, a primitiveness that taps the mythos of animality. Dirty words, in sexual intercourse, like any aphrodisiac, are a form of liberation—liberating the libido verbally as manipulation of the body liberates it physically. Erotic language approves the actions of the body, approval is encouragement, and sexual encouragement is the point of all aphrodisiacs. It may be that the intensity of such language marks a given person's need of an aphrodisiac, in which case it is perhaps slightly neurotic. Those who are completely satisfied sexually by language alone, like those who are satisfied by voyeurism or flagellation, are certainly abnormal, possibly psychotic—that is, in some psychic way dissociated from their total being. But it may also be, and this is no contradiction, that an intense use of dirty words is a lyrical celebration, primitiveness being at the very heart of lyricism, of the release of animality. There is very likely something of both causes behind the use of erotic language or dirty words. That they are used in life makes it predictable that they will be used in pornography. They are used there like any other "hard-core" pornographic convention—to help articulate the mythos of animality.

The mythos of animality, being what it is, is threatening at once to personality and society. Consequently it is frightening. "Soft-core" pornography evades threat and fear both by sublimating the primitive energies that are their source into socially approved activities. In modern culture the most socially approved activities turn on economic productivity and its corollary, willingness to "defend" the capitalistic faith with rhetoric and/or arms. The corollary is in some ways most potent because it provides the emotional wherewithal to sentimentalize economic materialism. Patriotism, as a proper repository of virtuous emotionalism, has a long and distinguished history. As usual, the Greeks gave us the paradigm. Socrates, otherwise not much enchanted with emotional modes of behavior, was a strong patriot. Strong enough that, rather than refute even misdirected state authority, he chose to be executed by it. But Socrates had a more persuasive rationale than most modern chauvinists. His philosophical notion of justice, which he supposed to be on trial rather than himself, required a harmonious relationship of parts—both of a personality and a state. Therefore, for him to let fear for his life direct him to overtly act against the state would disprove the efficacy of his philosophy, and so prove the prosecution's case against him. By submitting to even a wrong judgment, he felt himself to be serving the cause of justice. He wanted to be an example, perhaps a martyr, to that cause. And he was. In fact, his choice was made for him by the rigor of his dialectic. He was unable to deal with the antithetical idea, not compatible with his dialectic, that the example of ignorant and self-serving men prosecuting a false cause successfully was every bit and probably more damaging as a precedent of social justice than the behavioral failure of his metaphysics. But such, apparently, is the solipsism of philosophers.

The moral example of Socrates' death is, not that he died for what he believed, nor even that what he believed was right, and certainly not that he died for his country, but that he knew whereof he believed and knew precisely why he was dying and what his options were. Socrates knew the issue, for him: ideal justice as the basis of the state. Modern chauvinism is much less philosophically exact in its pursuit of Socrates' example. For one thing, the chauvinists are doing the prosecuting; that is, they are *in* and not, like Socrates, gadflies *out* of power. They are more nearly the sophists who pressed Socrates' execution. Like those sophists they are not concerned with ideal justice, merely with preserving order, regardless of its justice. Draft boards, for example, are not concerned with the justice of a social order that conscripts men, often against their will, to prosecute an undeclared, "defensive" war 3000 miles from its shores. For the American social order, justice and power have become synonymous, and thus power is sentimentalized—that is, it takes on the emotional justification of justice by association. Assuming that value, power has the psychic appeal of all men for justice, even though a substantive justice and rationality are idled, in limbo. Thus, any war that the social order undertakes becomes a "holy" war, and he who participates in it is sanctified. He is not merely a soldier of his country, but a defender of the faith. The faith, in this case, means the capitalistic ethic. And, as Kurt Vonnegut says, so it goes. A by-and-large self-serving hypothesis about who should control capital wealth becomes the arbiter of moral justice. And he who doesn't like it can go back where he came from—except we have rockets that can get to him even there, if he continues being a wise guy.

From the time of the "Church Militant" violence has been sentimentalized as not only a morally proper but an ethically heroic model. In the sublimation of the means of economic production to moral virtue, the violence used in its "defense" becomes the sign of moral sensibility. He who does not (somehow perversely) see that expanding defense perimeters secure the social order, and that capital investment is necessary to that security, is not a man of good social sentiments.

Unlike either complex or "hard-core," "soft-core" pornography fortifies such social sentimentalities. It is not anarchical; it celebrates social order. In fact its pornographic character is only approved insofar as it associates itself with elevating cultural sentiments. The two staples of social elevation are, again, wealth and power. And "soft-core" pornography, from Samuel Richardson to Jacqueline Susann and Harold Robbins, focuses extravagantly on both. But naked wealth and power border on the obscene, so they need to be made presentable to "civilized" society. They need, in other words, to be dissociated from the mythos of animality (scarey) and connected to the mythos of sentimentality (gratifying). Consequently, "soft-core" pornography uses "realistic" settings and actions, including explicit, if carefully controlled, sexuality. The control usually comes in providing a sentimental context for such titillating nakedness as it might show.

Most characteristically the context for sexual excitement created in "soft-core" pornography is some analogue of wealth and power. The heroes, then, of "soft-core" are the rich and the powerful, and the narrative structure of these novels, much more complex than that of "hard-core" pornography, builds on the timeless romanticizing of these qualities. To achieve one or the other or, ideally, both justifies everything, including animality, that may be necessary to get there. Fictively, this means that society will readily approve a little obscenity if it is dressed elegantly and ultimately uses its animality for the good, true, and beautiful. Thus "soft-core" pornography flirts with animality, but does not descend into the naturalistic depths of its mythos. It rather connects animality with proper sentiments, and thereby sublimates it into the more socially acceptable mythos of sentimentality. In it, animal energies are occasionally revealed (usually in short pornographic scenes paced more or less regularly through the story), but are transformed into such productive contexts as making a fortune, becoming a successful politician, fighting for freedom (freedom somehow never has a rational basis, it is always connected with the glorious gore of sentimentalized violence; that this violence derives from the mythos of animality is not so much forgotten as hurriedly covered up by giving it a "civilizing" objective), and so on. For the mythos of sentimentality is based on the assumption that men are "civilized" creatures with "civilized" feelings.

The danger of that mythic ideal is that it easily becomes confused with the logic that, because men are civilized creatures, whatever they feel and do are consequently also civilized—

43

that confusion is what permits, for example, genocide in such civilized countries as Germany and the United States. And fictive treatments of the mythos of sentimentality tend, because their trappings are "realistic" and more broadly based socially than fictive treatments of animality, to assume a guise of ethical possibility. No normal person expects to live in a "hard-core" world of total sexuality; but he knows very well that he lives in one where wealth and power are premiums, and might rather easily be induced to think that such types as Mike Hammer or James Bond do define a possible ethic. This ethical susceptibility is what makes the generalized sentimentality of the "soft-core" pornographic view so appealing. As a member of an audience it is gratifying to believe that the feedback of cultural sentimentalities articulates an ethic one can justifiably emulate. One popular fiction writer, Ayn Rand, who is occasionally a "soft-core" pornographer, has in fact argued in *The Romantic Manifesto* that Mike Hammer and James Bond are *the* heroic moral models for modern culture!

"Soft-core" pornography, then, happens most effectively in the context of popular romantic literature. Fictionally, conventions are analogous to those journalistic ones of *Playboy* and *Cosmopolitan*. The necessary thing is to place sexuality in context with a generally romantic rendering of life. The "realism" of violence and sexuality provide a "tough" realistic basis so that the reader (usually, bookstores report, middle-class women between 35 and 45) is titillated by this proximity to "life as it really is," which is to say, life as his boredom would like to imagine it. Wealth, or such analogues of it as detectives, politicians, movie stars, and other images of glamorous public life, provides an exotic assistance to the reader's fantasy elevation of animality to an admirable rather than fearful plane. In this sense, popular fiction follows the *Playboy* rule of thumb in its use of sex—giving it its place in a "well-rounded" bourgeois fantasy life.

Because it adroitly encompasses so many cultural sentimentalities and is also unequivocally pornographic, Harold Robbins' *The Adventurers* serves as a good example of the

44

"soft-core" form of pornography. Its title suggests its theme, adventure; and the political, economic, jet-set, and sexual adventures of the novel are a brilliant springboard into the effect of "realistic" romantic fantasy that such a novel requires. Robbins' use of adventure makes it a vehicle of sublimation. Its story fuses many sentimental myths. He skillfully handles the Horatio Alger myth in the fortune of his hero, Diogenes Alejandro Xenos, Dax for short ("Diogenes after the fabled seeker of truth; Alejandro after the conqueror of the world . . ."). Dax, from Corteguay—yet another decadent Latin American republic in turmoil, rises from humble beginnings to become the heir-apparent to *el Presidente's* military dictatorship. His grooming for this position sends him to Harvard and then on to become part of the international jet set, where he conquers women, money, influence, and all the rest of it. But Robbins knows the mythology well enough not simply to make a poor boy rich, sexy, and powerful. A hero needs the right sentiments. And, as Dax wearies of the venal life, he gets them. Having experienced all that wealth and power can provide, he is converted to the social gospel, and decides to return to Corteguay and topple the dictator, setting up a true republic in its place. But this, of course, involves the betrayal of *el Presidente,* who has been like a father to him, however evil otherwise. (To justify Dax and let us know just how evil and decadent *el Presidente* is, we are treated to a Turkish delight; when Dax breaks in to tell his surrogate "father" he is through he finds *el Presidente* in [perverse] *flagrante* with Amparo, who as it happens is not only *el Presidente's* daughter but also Dax's wife: "They were naked on the bed, Amparo's legs wide, *el Presidente* on his knees between them, a huge black dildo strapped around his waist. In his hand a riding crop." Not, as they say, a pretty scene.) This kind of thing, that is, the father-son business, Robbins knows, is the stuff of pathos; and he gets the most from it. *The Adventurers* is not, therefore, a simple success story. It is a pathetic success story. Or perhaps, depending on one's taste, a bathetic one. It won't do to get away with treachery, even in the interests of justice. So, though Dax

45

successfully engineers a coup and refuses the offer (thrice) of the presidency in order to institute a government by, for, and of the people, he is killed at the very moment of his selfless triumph by a bandit who wrongly thinks Dax is still an agent of *el Presidente*. Tragic irony. Enough to make you cry. If that won't do it, the dying scene will, where the two companions touchingly play out their role to the end: "Fat Cat, I'm afraid . . . Fat Cat raised his head and into his eyes came a look I had never seen there before. It was all the looks of love in one expression. Of a friend, of a father, of a son. Then he pushed his hand out over mine and covered it. I gripped his fingers tightly. His voice was hoarse but soft. 'Hold my hand, child,' he said, 'and I will take you safely through the mountains.' " And if those sentimental myths don't get you, the postscript chapter will. Dax may be dead, but not his son, also named Dax. He is in the care of his mother (not the infamous Amparo) and a foster father less adventurous than Dax Sr. But Robbins knows his Faulkner, and Dax Jr. will be a chip off the old block: this scene ends the book, as Dax Jr.'s mother says of his father, dropping his Harvard ring down the incinerator, " 'Now he is gone . . . and there is nothing left of him but a dream we all had when we were young.' Jeremy started to speak but then he saw the tears standing in her emerald eyes. Instead he too got up, taking her into his arms and holding her closely to him. He felt the trembling in her and the salt of her tears against his lips. She was wrong. And he knew that she knew it. There was always the boy upstairs."

But if Robbins is a genius at compounding sentimental formulas, he is no less skillful at lacing them with pornographic conventions. He may not use them all, but then he has a lot of fish to fry, so to speak, and the ones he does use he uses inventively. The following scenes illustrate.

A little blood and rape:

With an angry curse he let her go, then his hand came up with a knife. It slashed quickly down the front of the dress. The coarse shift fell away like the husk from an ear of corn. A thin pencil-like streak, starting at her throat and running down between her breasts and across her brown Indian belly into the heavy matting of pubic hair, suddenly began to well crimson. She screamed and tried to get away, scrambling on her hands and knees, but he laughed aloud and pulled her back by her hair.

She tried to get away again. Quickly he reversed the knife in his hand and hooked the butt end viciously upward between her legs, and this time she screamed in pure agony.

She crumpled to the floor at his feet, writhing in pain. The sharp blade end of the knife reflected the crazy yellow lights from the candle as it stuck upright from between her legs. He put his heavily booted foot on her belly to hold her still and started to pull at the rope belt that held up his *pantalones*.

A little virginal humor:

I could feel their eyes following my hand as I unbuttoned my fly. I took out my cock and began to fondle it as I had seen Roberto do. After a moment I looked down. Nothing was happening.

"Maybe you're doing it too fast," Marta whispered. "Diego did it much slower."

I looked at her in bewilderment. I wondered if she could know more about it than I did.

She saw my hesitation. "Here," she said, reaching out her hand, "let me show you."

Her hand felt hot and damp. I began to feel its heat and a pressure began to build up in my abdomen. I looked at them both. They didn't raise their eyes; they were too busy watching. I could see Vera move her tongue over her dry lips, and for once she wasn't giggling.

I began to feel a spastic shudder in my loins. I looked down at myself. Pride came surging through me like the heat of the sun in the morning. My pecker was hard. It wasn't as big as I thought it would be, but it was hard.

"I told you I could do it. You better stop or I'll rape you."

"You wouldn't dare!" Marta whispered.

"No? You better let go and get out of here fast!"

They didn't move. I took a step toward them. Their eyes were still on my pecker. I could feel it throbbing. "You better leave!"

"Which one would you rape first?" Marta asked in a low voice.

"I don't care which one," I said. "You just better go, that's all."
The sisters looked at each other. "You're the oldest," Vera said.
I stared at them. I didn't know what to do. I hadn't expected this.
"Are you going?" I asked in my most threatening voice.
Marta looked at me. "All right. You can do it to me first."
"You won't like it. You better go."
Marta lifted up her skirt. "Are you going to or not?" she asked
impatiently.
I stared at the thin black fuzz between her legs. There was a
challengingly expectant look in her eyes.
"All right," I said. "But just remember. You wanted to."
I went at her the way I remembered Roberto had done with the
putas in the forest. We tumbled backward to the ground. I shoved
her legs apart and climbed between them, jerking my hips in a sudden spasmodic motion that seemed to come from deep within me. I
could feel myself going everywhere but where I wanted to go. Then
I felt her hand on my prick as she guided it to where she wanted it
to go. The hair was thin and prickly there, and felt like a thousand
tiny needles.
"Stop wriggling," she whispered angrily. "Push!"
But I couldn't. There was a wild exciting pain tearing through my
loins that wouldn't let me. No matter how hard I tried I couldn't get
past the very edge of her flesh. I heard her grunt with the effort of
trying to get me inside her.

A little peek at the quiet side of a soldier's life:

The first soldier rolled over on his side. "I fucked all of them," he
bragged. "As soon as I unloaded in one, I got up and joined another
line."
The second soldier shook his head. "No wonder you're so pooped."
"Which one did you screw?"
"The hysterical one. I don't see why she made such a fuss. She had
a cunt big enough to accommodate a stallion. I couldn't even feel
the sides."
"She wasn't very good," one of the others agreed.
The first soldier grinned broadly. "The blond was the best. You
could tell she was getting it regularly. She pressed down the moment
you put it in and—pop—you had it. If there hadn't been so many
behind me I'd have slipped it to her again. The next time she

48

wouldn't have got off so easy." He reached for his canteen. "I need a drink. All the liquid has been drained out of me."

A little candor about cunnilingus:

Her voice was soft and slurry. "Honey, nobody, but nobody, eats me the way you do."

Dax rolled over on his side and looked up at Sue Ann. Her eyes were almost closed and her mouth partly open. Her long blond hair spilled out over the pillow and her full breasts, with their oddly tiny pink nipples, rose gently with her deep breathing.

"I can't believe that."

Her eyes opened. They were blue and they looked at him with a fierce intensity. "I mean it, Dax. All the others—well, they act as if they didn't really like eating me, that they were just doing it as a favor."

He grinned, reaching for a cigarette. "Well, they're stupid then."

Her hand stopped his and guided it back. She sighed softly. Her eyes closed again. "And when you're inside me," she whispered, "man that's so much livin' it's almost like dyin'."

He laughed and rolled her on her side facing away from him, then, almost jackknifing her, pulled her back against him. He felt her shudder as he went inside her.

"Oh, God!" she cried. "Don't you ever stop?"

"Only when you've had enough."

"I never get enough!" she cried. A frenzied shiver rose through her. "I'm coming again!" She yelled wildly, trying to pull away from him.

His hands gripped her shoulders, holding her tightly. A moment later her frenzy passed but she kept shivering and squirming. "Don't stop! I want to come a thousand times."

"I won't stop."

Her head fell back against his shoulder and her face twisted around to look up at him. Her eyes were almost closed again and her voice was very low. "No wonder they don't want you to fuck niggers!"

He had been long enough in the States to know what she meant. It was all he could do not to hit her. "You dirty cunt!"

Her eyes closed tight and she pressed herself against him. "That's

49

right, honey," she whispered, "eat me, hurt me, talk dirty to me, and fuck me. That's all I want!"

A little underwater experiment:

Without a word she grabbed a mouthful of air and let herself sink into the water. He felt her slipping from his grip and turned after her, but already she was back at him under the water. He felt her hands grabbing for his trunks, pulling at them, and then one hand was inside holding him.

Her head came out of the water in front of him. "Surrender?"

He felt the heat rushing into his loins. He looked back over his shoulder. The flash of light glinted at the window. Hadley was still watching them. Well, to hell with him, he thought, they hadn't yet invented binoculars that could see into water. He turned to Sue Ann. "A Corteguayan never surrenders!"

"No?" She tightened her grip.

He laughed, tensing himself against her fingers. Then he put his hands under the water behind her and found the seam in the crotch of the silk bathing suit. With a quick motion he ripped the light fabric then, reversing the grip, thrust two fingers inside her.

He laughed at the sudden surprise on her face. She squirmed, trying to push him away, but he held her easily. Then his feet found the bottom and she couldn't move at all. "Best you get is a draw."

"Let go," she said, pushing at him. "The old man is watching!"

"Let him. He can't see what's happening under the water."

Suddenly she was soft against him. "Oh, God. Oh, God!" Frantically she climbed on him. "Put it in me," she cried wildly, "get it in there!"

He braced his legs and pushed himself into her. He felt the heat of her body close him off from the water. "Put your arms out straight and keep your upper body away from me," he said harshly. "That way it won't even look as if our bodies are touching."

She leaned back in the water, her arms straight out, her legs around his hips, almost as if she were floating. "Oh God," she moaned, already in a paroxysm of delight. Suddenly her blue eyes were on his face. "I can't hold it, Dax! I can't!"

"You'll hold it," he replied grimly, his fingers tightened unmercifully into the flesh of her buttocks. She started to scream. Violently he thrust her head under the water. She came sputtering up and coughing, then went limp in his arms as she climaxed.

50

A moment later, she looked up at him smiling. "I needed that," she gasped, "it's been so long." She glanced over his shoulder at the house. "You better let me go, he's still watching."

Dax shook his head, not letting go of her buttocks.

She looked at him in surprise. "You're still hard," she exclaimed, a note of wonder coming into her voice. She threw her head back in a half scream as he thrust himself into her again. "Oh God," she cried. "Oh God! God!"

A little theory of sports cars and sporting ladies:

He grinned. It worked every time. No matter how sophisticated they were, no matter how snide about things American. All you had to do was get them beside you on that front seat. Whatever it was— the speed, the sense of power, the masculine smell of new leather— it never missed.

He looked at her again. There was a place just off the road around the next turn, and there was no doubt about her being ready. She fell on him almost before he had time to cut the motor, her fingers frantically tearing at the nonexistent buttons. He pulled down his zipper, and she gasped as his youth and life sprang free. Then her hot moist mouth covered him.

And thus *The Adventurers* gives us an enticing view of life as it might be, neatly balancing sex, money, and violence to provide a socially redeeming world view.

Complex or artistic pornography differs from "hard-core" or simple pornography in not being exclusively committed to the mythos of animality and its explicit sexual imagery. And, while "soft-core" pornography offers ethical encouragement to the sentiments of the status quo, complex pornography, like most artistic modes, explores the moral recognition that necessarily precedes and informs true ethical instruction. In the sense, then, that art is moral rather than ethical, artistic pornography is moral. It may use both "soft" and "hard-core" conventions, but is distinguished from both by the degree to which it meets the criteria of all serious art—how honestly and thoroughly it pursues its imaginative vision. Formally, because it is a rather recent form, it is not so sophisticated as other art forms. Though when complex pornography appears in more sophisticated modes, as in

Molly Bloom's pornographic soliloquy at the end of James Joyce's *Ulysses,* it exhibits a corresponding formal sophistication. The conventions of complex pornography are, then, indistinguishable from those of whatever form it may take. And it has the same freedom available to it that any artistic mode has. It is generically distinguishable by its treatment of the mythos of love. Complex pornography is unique in synthesizing the mythos of animality with that of love—while animality is a naturalistic premise, it is expanded to fuse with the more complex psychic consciousness of love. Such books, therefore, as D. H. Lawrence's *The Rainbow,* in which the theme of sexuality is used to help explore the mythos of love but not through explicit genitalia imagery, are perhaps more erotic than pornographic. *The Rainbow* focuses on the consciousness of love rather than the act of love (which, though present, is treated on an archetypal level of consciousness rather than in the pornographically descriptive manner of *Lady Chatterly's Lover*), and therefore represents a modified pornographic mode of the myth.

The mythos of love itself tends to have two basic philosophical approaches, the idealistic and the naturalistic. Shelley's *Prometheus Unbound* and "Epipsychidion" are examples of an idealistic or erotic approach, though it has pretty much atrophied so far as serious modern literature goes. Pornographic treatments are usually naturalistic, partly because depth and behavioral psychology have provided naturalistic documentation of sexuality, and more significantly, because naturalism dominates the modern imagination. More precisely, complex pornography may be said to preoccupy itself, appropriately for the age of anxiety, with a *neurotic* interpretation of the mythos of love, though we must remember Freud's sound premise that neurosis is a normal phenomenon. As we have become increasingly aware of the range and influence of neurosis on behavior, we have come more and more to see love and love relationships as neurotically structured. Whether or not psychologists will agree to this generalization, there has developed a substantial body of literary and artistic works that turn on this theme.

That some of them, such as Vladimir Nabokov's *Lolita,* have not only been bestsellers but transformed into popular movies argues that both the artistic and popular imaginations are highly conscious of the dynamic and dangerous association between neurosis and love. In fact, the narrative structure of Nabokov's novel hands the problem directly to society. When Humbert Humbert addresses his defense to the "ladies and gentlemen of the jury," he addresses the whole of modern culture. Humbert does not deny his guilt; he is guilty of crimes against both man and nature—the murder of his rival in "love" and the systematic violation of his juvenile "beloved," of both her body and, finally, her soul. Humbert's defense consists in defining the *terms* of his guilt, in explaining how the confusions of modern culture, an almost hopelessly mix-mastered paste of "decadent" old and "progressive" new world demonologies, made his crimes inevitable. He wants, as he says, to save not his head but his soul. His murder of Quilty, his rival and fellow despoiler of Lolita, is a symbolic purge of the new world. Humbert's own execution, as inevitable as his crimes, is the symbolic purge of the old world. And yet, as things of the soul are wont to be, it is only a symbolic purge. We, the ladies and gentlemen of the jury, are left with the neurotic modern culture that produced the neurotic characters that people the neurotic plot of Nabokov's brilliant telling of his neurotic version of the mythos of (failed) modern love.

What makes the mythos of love so fascinating for the modern mind is that, having lost confidence in its divine or idealistic nature, we do not know what it is. We do know, as the history of tragedy testifies, that it is often destructive. But we also know, from both mythic and personal history, that it makes the world go round. Our fascination comes from this dichotomous and ineluctable nature, like a cobra weaving and hypnotizing, luring us to some glorious demise. So long as we know little more than our confusion, so long will the mythic literature of love, including pornography, be a valuable and inescapable mode of groping for some knowledge of what love is.

One of the best, and most celebrated, examples of complex

53

pornography is *Story of O*. It uses all the devices of "hard-core" pornography, but manages to transcend those conventions with its profoundly depressing exploration of the neurosis of modern love. In opening up the anxieties of love, in probing its archetypal fears and desires, *Story of O* is not only a true statement of human experience, it is anarchical at a deep and distressing personal level. For it is, in effect, a cultural suicide note, articulating the failure of love in an allegory depicting an obsessive masculine need for the security of possession and an obsessive feminine need for the security of love. Ironically, masculinity can only prove itself by destroying what it most desires (and is most contemptuous of), woman—and thus its very need carries the seed of its own insecurity. And woman, needing as much to give herself over to that neurotic masculine irony, is at once gratified and destroyed by it. O's story records the disintegration of human personality as it clumsily thrashes and writhes in a death struggle with the incomprehensible antagonism of body and soul seeking a harmonious synthesis in love. But the idea of love that promised such a harmony was a dialectical chimera, and in the rough and tumble of psychic reality it often as not fails to deliver. As Plato knew, the only hope for the ideal of love lies in suppression and control of animality, harnassing it to the service of sweet reason. However, he also knew that that was pretty unlikely without the complete restructuring of society that he recommends in *The Republic*. But since no utopian social structure has proved amenable to human idiosyncracy we are, twenty-five hundred years later, still left with the wars of body and soul, and the carnage it makes of tranquility. This, after all, is what the allegory of O is about.

O being the protagonist, her story is a largely feminine projection of the mythos of love, but it has masculine implications. For, although the story represents the characteristic pornographic sense of gender—masculine domination and feminine submissiveness—these stereotypes take on bisexual ambiguities. O is completely feminine in relation to men, but she also plays a dominant lesbian role in relation to women. In fact, until she falls in love with René, her lover and master, she prefers lesbian sexuality, partly because of the simple pleasure she derives from caressing women and partly because of the more complex pleasure she gets from dominating them, and finally because of the highly ambiguous reassurance she gets from finding in her attraction toward women an analogy of men's attraction toward her. It is interesting that, again from this peculiarly feminine mythos of love, while O's story includes a fair amount of lesbian activity, it has no homosexuality whatsoever. The yin and yang principle, westernized to signify sexual ambivalence and perhaps neurosis rather than the personal harmony it suggests to the eastern mind, operates only in women. But it is *always* overshadowed by their willing subservience to men. In E. M. Forseter's critical terms, then, men in O's story are always *flat* (that is, predictable) characters, while women are *round*—capable of psychic changes and complexity within the framework of narrative action. Men are used to represent one mythic quality, power. But it is a strangely complex power, symbolized by sexual domination, yet signified more ominously by its manipulation of feminine will, the ability to make that will consent to its own obliteration. O, having been imprisoned in a kind of obedience school for mistresses of a secret sexual society (not dissimilar in its murky international omnipotence to those political conspiracies Ian Fleming conjures), reflects thus on her bondage:

And yet nothing had been such a comfort to her as the silence, unless it was the chains. The chains and the silence, which should have bound her deep within herself, which should have smothered her, strangled her, on the contrary freed her from herself. What would have become of her if she had been granted the right to speak and the freedom of her hands, if she had been free to make a choice, when her lover prostituted her before his own eyes? True, she did speak as she was being tortured, but can moans and cries be classed as words? Besides, they often stilled her by gagging. Beneath the gazes, beneath the hands, beneath the sexes that defiled her, the whips that rent her, she lost herself in a delirious absence from herself which restored her to love and, perhaps, brought her to the edge of death. She was anyone, anyone at all, anyone of the other girls, opened and forced like her, girls whom she saw being opened and forced, for she did see it, even when she was not obliged to have a hand in it.

The invocation of love and death, in conjunction, is crucial. For love, in this anxious mythic exploration of it, demands a corresponding death. O, the archetypal woman, must destroy her sense of self to secure love. She must consent to whatever men desire of her, even if it means forfeiting the consciousness by which any human being certifies his existence. Thus the mythic statement is that there is only one consciousness possible in love, that of masculine authority. All power to masculine will—which means the anarchical destruction of a feminine reality. There is, in this mythic vision, psychically only one sex, one reality, one essence. The feminine differential is an accident, suitable, like slaves in the Athenian democracy, only for service. Even O's lesbianism, in which she assumes a masculine role, argues for the myth of a masculine metaphysics.

Woman's need for love forces her into a masculine cosmos, where morality is defined by masculine power and desire. O is ordered by her lover to seduce Jacqueline, a haughtily confident and thoroughly feminine woman ("Since Jacqueline was sure of herself, she had nothing to redeem; she had no need to be reassured, all she needed was a mirror") who consents to O's lesbian ministrations because they give a "safe" animal pleasure, into the secret sexual society that metaphors the universe of love. O recognizes that to do so is to betray both Jacqueline's essentially feminine nature and the trust that Jacqueline has in her. To manifest betrayal is to don absolutely the masculine ethic, and O has still enough resistance to have this awareness. But her need for love, which means the approval of her lover, and her own "masculine" desire for the possession of Jacqueline (the proof of which in *Story of O,* it will be recalled, is a kind of primitive version of conspicuous consumption—that is, the ability to give to someone else certifies one's complete "ownership") force her to be

obsessed with the burning desire to have Jacqueline at any price, even if attaining her goal meant handing her over to Sir Stephen. After all, she rationalized to herself, Jacqueline's beauty is quite sufficient protection for her, and besides, why should I get involved in it anyway? And what if she were to be reduced to what I have been reduced to, is that really so terrible? —scarcely admitting, and yet overwhelmed to imagine, how sweet it would be to see Jacqueline naked and defenseless beside her, and like her.

With this betrayal O moves unequivocally into the masculine world view. Her act parallels her own lover's betrayal of herself into the secret society, into the demonic hypothesis that love demands complete surrender of being. So with this act O becomes the moral equal of her lovers, men. And she further enforces that morality by betraying Jacqueline, who with her mockery and self-containment threatens the masculine solipsism that has become for O love's salvation:

O was happy that René had had her whipped and had prostituted her, because her impassioned submission would furnish her lover with the proof that she belonged to him, but also because the pain and shame of the lash, and the outrage inflicted upon her by those who compelled her to pleasure when they took her, and at the same time delighted in their own without paying the slightest heed to hers, seemed to her the very redemption of her sins.

And what if, in spite of that, Sir Stephen was right? What if she actually enjoyed her debasement? In that case, the baser she was, the more merciful was René to consent to make O the instrument of his pleasure.

It is, then, imperative to the mythic view represented by O that she betray Jacqueline, that she does signifies the deep need in her. But she is in fact unsuccessful, for Jacqueline's animality is far greater than her need for love, and so she is impervious to the satanic guiles and temptations of the secret society. Not being in love, she has no need for O's diabolical selflessness. In

57

the dialectic of love's mythos Jacqueline presents the only other option to the slavery of love, not being in love. But, though Jacqueline does not love, she is loved by someone outside the secret society. So her dialectical option is real, so far as the reader is concerned. It tells us that O's condition is not the result of a simplistic cosmic determinism, it is rather the result of her particular (perhaps neurotic) need for love. O's condition is a result of *choice*, however little, given her psychic needs, she is in control of that choice. O's decision, and the novel repeatedly emphasizes that she is free not to love, to choose love and its bondage may be the most terrifying dimension of the mythic sensibility she represents.

For one of the great human aches is the desire to be free from oneself, to have the gratifications one associates with the self without the obligation of making the choices by which moral character and personality are defined. This is the sense in which *Story of O* is a suicide note, the ultimate anarchy, proclaiming the human will to self-destructiveness as a way to that constant state of felicity that has been promised in all our mythology, a state, if it exists at all, no more constant than Juliet's moon. Keats, "half in love with easeful death," knew that temptation, the temptation that somehow nature will make it possible "To cease upon the midnight with no pain." But he also knew he was talking in his sleep. For Aristotle hit the mark long ago when he told us that the object of human actions is happiness, and our choice of actions is what brings us happiness or the reverse, and no single choice (Christianity to the contrary) lands us in heaven. Life, Joyce said in a profound addendum to the *Nicomachean Ethics,* is every day, day after day. But O's mythic being testifies to the archetypal human fear of that great labor, the steady seeking after happiness. Like most of us, O does not want always to be in transit. She wants to be *there.* And our mythology also tells us that love is where it's at. O's story articulates at least one version of the price for a one-way ticket:

In the space of a week she learned fear, but certainty; anguish, but happiness. René threw himself at her like a pirate at his prisoner,

58

and she reveled in her captivity, feeling on her wrists, her ankles, feeling on all her members and in the secret depths of her heart and body, bonds less visible than the finest strands of hair, more powerful than the cables the Lilliputians used to tie up Gulliver, bonds her lover loosened or tightened with a glance. She was no longer free? Yes! thank God, she was no longer free. But she was light, a nymph on clouds, a fish in water, lost in happiness. Lost because these fine strands of hair, these cables which René held, without exceptions, in his hand, were the only network through which the current of life any longer flowed into her.

However fictively exaggerated, O's story spreads before us the dark terrors and the near nihilistic rewards waiting in the labyrinth of love. Hers is the mythic story of the love-pilgrim's progress to a celestial city the existence of which we are no longer sure of. And thus the progress is understandably fearful, its severe demand promising so ambivalent a reward. Being mythic, fictive, her story sets our options before us with a clarity and force, however disturbing, that no other mode of knowledge can attain.

One might, then, discuss this novel in many terms other than its sexual theme, that is, without needing to be preoccupied with the explicit sexual scenes, because it deals with life as any poetic work does—on a level of significance beyond its literal imagery. Its sexuality at all levels is a natural part of the novel's narrative rhythm, and, once accustomed to its subject, one is not particularly conscious of pornographic spectacle. One is in fact a good deal more aware of its psychic ominousness, of its particular rendition of the mythos of love. If one brings himself to accept the possibility of a pornographic art, he may critically consider this novel as he would any other. And there are, of course, as many possible interpretations of the mythos of love as there are artists to interpret it. Nor are they necessarily a product of philosophical naturalism. No artistic dimension of complex pornography is obliged to anything other than its art. Unlike either "hard" or "soft-core" pornography, complex pornography is structured according to its own demands rather than those of its audience. The conventions of

59

"hard" and "soft-core" pornography are geared to what their audiences expect, and as audience expectations broaden so will the use of the conventions. They are, therefore, popular rather than serious arts. Complex pornography, following its author's imagination rather than that of its audience, is a serious art form, or rather a synthesis of serious forms. I have discussed only fiction here, but journalism, graphic arts, theater, poetry, and films are all increasingly using pornography as a mode of artistic statement. Inasmuch as the pornographic genre is determined by its treatment of subject rather than its formal structure, any art form which treats its subject pornographically— that is, by tapping the mythos of animality and either exploiting it alone or extending it to other mythic figures—may either centrally or peripherally be regarded as a manifestation of the pornographic genre. It is quite likely that an exclusively pornographic art will diminish as pornography continues to move out of its sub-cultural role and becomes therefore less potent as a weapon of attack on cultural standards. Its most effective future probably lies in its synthetic potential, in its utility to other forms. In this sense, pornography is perhaps more accurately a rhetorical rather than poetic genre. But, inasmuch as the history of rhetoric and poetics are inextricably entwined, that distinction is not particularly useful. Neither is it of much use to belabor the question of whether pornography is a pure or synthetic genre. For, again like poetry, whether or not we can construct flawless definitions, we can certainly know when we are in the presence of it. If nothing else will, a quivering of the loins should tell us.

3.

Decadence and the
Poetics of Obscenity

I.

NAT King Cole used to sing a calypso song about a homesick Trinidadian comparing the decadent, civilized States with healthy, natural Trinidad. Gringo women, he lamented, were submerged beneath their arty use of padding, cosmetics, and clothes. But with the Trinidad girl, "what you see is what she got." This topical calypso format presents the archetypal problem for all lyrical impulse—the antithesis of art and nature. From Plato to pop this tension permeates the history of art and art theory. Aubrey Beardsley's recent vogue articulates a particularly contemporaneous version of this dilemma.

His artistic elegance—both graphically and literarily—satisfies our desperation for the beautiful, while his blatant pornography adds another raspberry to the popular assault on moral transcendentalism. The dilemma is that poetically we want the beautiful without its constant companion, the ideal good. But the tradition of our aesthetics makes them inseparable. The "decadent" art with which Beardsley was much involved made the first direct hit against the monolith of aesthetic idealism. Beardsley, in keeping with the central principle of decadence, demonstrated that artistic beauty was not obliged to traditional morality in any way for its being. His two most extreme state-

61

ments of this are of course the *Lysistrata* illustrations and his unfinished pornographic novel, *The Story of Venus and Tannhauser*. Beardsley was one of the first to present pornographic satire in a lyrical guise and make both satire and lyricism convincing. His story of Venus and Tannhauser is at once a rebuttal of the transcendental melodrama of Wagner's libretto, on the one hand, and a parody of pornographic "romance," on the other. Simultaneously it is also a lyrical tour de force celebrating its own purely artistic beauty. Whereas Wagner's libretto is patterned on the morality play—Tannhauser's despair, for example, is at last resolved in Christian faith and spiritual beauty—Beardsley's treatment denies the artistic potency of moral conflict by simply dismissing it, and thereby he exorcises morality and celebrates style. Wagner's Tannhauser, for instance, is introduced in profound angst—"No more, no more. . . ./how long this nightmare?"; when Venus cloys, his conscience boggles. Not so with Beardsley's dandy, who is introduced thus:

The Chevalier Tannhauser, having lighted off his horse, stood doubtfully for a moment beneath the ombre gateway of the Venusberg, troubled with an exquisite fear lest a day's travel should have too cruelly undone the laboured niceness of his dress. His hand, slim and gracious as La Marquise du Deffand's in the drawing by Carmontelle, played nervously about the gold hair that fell upon his shoulders like a finely curled peruke, and from point to point of a precise toilet, the fingers wandered, quelling the little mutinies of cravat and ruffle.

The decadent Tannhauser, unlike Wagner's moralistic counterpart, relishes losing himself in the Hill of Venus, and is neatly poised in the face of his ambiguous perdition: "Goodbye, Madonna," he says casually, and then sighs to heaven for "the assurance of a looking glass before I make my debut!" As Socrates says, first things first. In similar manner, Beardsley satirizes pornography and romance (antithetical variations on the same theme): "It is, I know, the custom of all romancers to paint heroes who can give a lady proof of their valliance at least twenty times a night. Now Tannhauser had no such Gargantuan facility, and was rather relieved when, an hour later, Priapusa and Doricourt and some others burst drunkenly into the room and claimed Venus for themselves." Beardsley proves the decadent thesis by creating a pornographic narrative at once denying the necessary connection between either pornography and vulgarity, or immorality and ugliness. Characteristically he casts hard-core pornographic images into elegance and wit; for instance,

I wish I could be allowed to tell you what occurred round table 15, just at this moment. It would amuse you very much, and would give you a capital idea of the habits of Venus' retinue. Indeed, for deplorable reasons, by far the greater part of what was said and done at this supper must remain unrecorded and even unsuggested.

Venus allowed most of the dishes to pass untasted, she was so engaged with the beauty of Tannhauser. She laid her head many times on his robe, kissing him passionately; and his skin, at once firm and yielding, seemed to those exquisite little teeth of hers, the most incomparable pasture. Her upper lip curled and trembled with excitement, showing the gums. Tannhauser, on his side, was no less devoted. He adored her all over and all the things she had on, and buried his face in the folds and flounces of her linen, and ravished away a score of frills in his excess. He found her exasperating, and crushed her in his arms, and slaked his parched lips at her mouth. He caressed her eyelids softly with his finger tips, and pushed aside the curls from her forehead, and did a thousand gracious things, tuning her body as a violinist tunes his instrument before he plays upon it.

Priapusa snorted like an old war horse at the sniff of powder, and tickled Tannhauser and Venus by turns, and slipped her tongue down their throats, and refused to be quiet at all until she had had a mouthful of the Chevalier. Claude, seizing his chance, dived under the table and came up the other side just under the queen's couch, and before she could say "One!" he was taking his coffee "aux deux colonnes," Clair was furious at his friend's success, and sulked for the rest of the evening.

The appeal of Beardsley's brilliant rhetoric to the literati in an age of fading aristocracy was ironically similar to his appeal for ourselves. To his time Beardsley represented the triumph of an aristocratic, classically oriented aesthetic taste over a modern puritanic, know-nothing moralism. To a contemporary (democratic, middle-class) mind he recalls a traditional aesthetic—line, symmetry, and representation highly stylized—without its vestigial moralism. Thus Beardsley is the kind of avant-garde gift the man who has everything can understand and feel comfortable with. His popularity is a pop culture analogue of the now famous "forward-looking return to the past." In short, *The Story of Venus and Tannhauser* is a tour de force carrying formal poetic tradition to extremity and at the same time ridiculing the moral idealism so long concomitant with that poetic tradition.

Of the four major treatments of the Venus and Tannhauser legend that I know in the nineteenth century, only Beardsley's has artistic potential for us today because his was the only treatment that was in touch with poetic evolution in a really vital way. Not simply because his is pornographic (although a good pornographer is no mean thing), but because he used pornography to make a statement about the nature of art. The others resorted to more acceptable traditions not so dynamic (or pregnant) as pornography. William Morris's "Hill of Venus" (from *The Earthly Paradise*), for instance, uses allegory; it is an allegory of psychic despair in which Tannhauser leaves the Hill of Venus, and gropes his way to Rome where he is refused absolution by the Pope except if his holy staff should bloom. In despair Tannhauser returns to his venal life. Meanwhile, back at the Vatican, the Pope's staff blooms. Although unknown to him, Tannhauser's salvation exists through the miracle of God's grace. Thus the poem argues allegorically the need for faith. It is a nice poem if you like clean poems, but both its vision and its structure throw us back on tradition, not forward to either a new vision or a new poetic. Wagner's opera libretto is similarly unrewarding. It uses the morality play as vehicle. Morris resolves despair theologically; Wagner resolves it morally, through Tannhauser's repentance. The ending is directly from morality format, with Venus (Knowledge, evil) and Elisabeth (good, Innocence) contending for his will. Naturally Elisabeth's Christian virtues win. Not even Swinburne, from whom we might expect some decay, could get out of the traditional "poetic" bag. His "Laus Veneris" is a good clean poem too. But it articulates a sort of inverted Pascal's Wager in the lyric stoicism with which Tannhauser recognizes that he is doomed, but not doomed until the last judgment (and there is always the hope that there is not any judgment to come, in which case he is home free). Swinburne cannot seem to figure out whether there is a God or not; so he resolves the whole thing by going back to a lyric version of Dryden's "All for Love," on the hunch that the millennium is a long way off.

The Story of Venus and Tannhauser did for English pornography what *Tristram Shandy* had done for the English novel, gave it dimensions of artistic possibility hitherto unexplored. And it perhaps lay dormant so many years for about the same reason that *Tristram Shandy* did—because no one quite knew what to make of it. Unlike Sterne, however, by the time Beardsley came back he was artistically obsolete, and however much one may enjoy him he has little now to teach artists. Like the decadents (and many liberals since), he gave up everything for classical beauty. Even in his time it was a desperate investment. On the truth exchange, the politics and religion markets had already collapsed; science was ominously rising, and artists tried to head off a bull market by pulling everything out of politics and religion and investing in beauty. It was, despite its brief and glorious success (Beardsley, Beerbohm, Rossetti, Swinburne, Wilde, Symons, Pater, and Yeats in England; Rimbaud, Verlaine, Mallarmé, Gautier, Baudelaire, etc., in France), a strategic failure. The rendezvous between the art of monolithic beauty and the art of analytic exploration was already begun with Claude Bernard and Emile Zola. After that the future lies ahead.

Beardsley's pornographic novel is important because it shows how completely the decadents were persuaded that, as Oscar Wilde put it in "The Decay of Lying," "Things are because we see them, and what we see, and how we see it, depends on the Arts that have influenced us." The decadents could produce Beardsley's effete *tour de force* because it affirmed for them what Zola denied, that art brings reality to man rather than bringing man to reality. But in fact they could not really accept it—it is not altogether accidental I think that Beardsley never finished it—because it was the nihilistically logical conclusion of their poetics. For in saying that nothing mattered but artistic beauty they had sooner or later to confront the implication that beauty did not matter either. One sees Arthur Symons wrestling with this when he says of Zola (1919) that "He sees the beast in all its transformations, but he sees only the beast. He has never looked at life impartially, he has never seen it as it is. His realism is a distorted idealism . . ." Symons really means that Zola's scientific-poetic formula challenges Symons' own symbolic-decadent formula. One must remember that Symons' idea of realism, of "telling it like it is," is Mallarmé's mystical "confidence in the eternal correspondences between the visible and the invisible universe." Symons did not understand that Mallarmé's mysticism, like any mysticism, is simply an idiosyncratic idealism, and that the very idiosyncrasy he so admired was an ominous fissure in his revered edifice of Beauty. For not only did Mallarmé write *prose*-poems, thereby refuting the necessity of artistic convention, but he also located beauty in the perceptions of his mind (in "the horror of the forest, or the silent thunder afloat in the leaves; not the intrinsic, dense wood of the trees"). Such beauty is not in a unified Nature; neither is it in artistic presentation of vision; it is in the vision itself. And the logical conclusion of Mallarmé's theory is that he not write *about* his visions at all, but that he simply *have* them. And, as Symons laments, this is pretty nearly what Mallarmé did. If beauty does not have its own form to control art, and if artistic convention is no authoritative vehicle for conveying the beautiful, then every man is his own artist and every vision has its own beauty. Symons' preference for Mallarmé over Zola is simply a matter of taste, not aesthetic necessity. Beardsley's pornography carried the grand decadence as far as it could go in creating a cosmos where morality was non-existent, sentiment was merely an ironic rhetorical device, and classical artifice was the nature of being. It is more than a little historically prophetic when Yeats laments that that place where "Fish, flesh, or fowl, commend all summer long whatever is begotten, born, and dies" is no country for old men or monuments of unaging intellect. In recent years art and literature have been much more concerned with those dying generations, their long, hot summer, than with the artifice of eternity.

II.

When Schiller noted that the difference between classicism and modernity was in the latter's loss of confidence in a coherent sense of nature, he identified also that component in romanticism which revolutionized western poetics. Once such philosophers as Kant and Hume relocated reality from external space and time to perceived space and time it opened poetic possibilities that recreated the imagination. In the poetic tradition evolved from Plato's moral idealism and Aristotle's theory of artistic imitation, art was supposed to imitate nature. Nature was supposed to have an order more or less coherent and comprehensible. Correspondingly, art too was supposed to be ordered, and its truth lay in the rightness with which it represented the correspondence. Thus Dr. Johnson, one of the great products of this tradition, judged that *Tristram Shandy* could not last because "nothing odd will do long." Sterne's psychically idiosyncratic novel anticipated the romantic modernity that Dr. Johnson could not be expected to appreciate. Decadence, as I am using it, is a development from romanticism. There was never, of course, a comprehensive romanticism; if Schiller, for example, doubted a coherent natural order, that was certainly not true of Wordsworth. But if one can talk about a generalized and synthetic impression then one can observe that, for all its revolutionary aesthetic potential, romanticism kept to a conventionally unified poetics as an expression of the coherent moral sense which still prevailed. And if we except a tendency to narrative and descriptive impressionism in such decadents as Gautier, Huysmans, Baudelaire, Swinburne, and Wilde, the

67

structural poetics of decadence too was conventional enough. Early decadence manifested itself in subject and imagery rather than form. By introducing the ugly, the grotesque, and the "immoral" as agencies of beauty and "harmony" the early decadence refuted moral idealism, but maintained the poetic unity so long associated with it. Thus decadence attempted to "liberate" art from morality, and even life. A later decadence—beginning perhaps about 1915 (Vorticism, Imagism, Dadaism, and others), subsiding in the new critical Thirties and Forties, and strong again in the Fifties and Sixties—took the next logical step; having long since accepted the refutation of moral idealism, this "movement" proceeded to repudiate artistic unity and wholeness as necessary poetic principles. In this larger sense, then, decadence refers to the contemporaneous rejection of complementary moral and artistic unity, the heritage of western poetics.

A premise of moral unity derives from a univocal metaphysics (for example, Platonic idealism), or such romantic analogues as Wordsworth's or Coleridge's moral transcendentalism. Decadence denies romantic morality (that is, the upward good for which Nature is figure) while extending the implications of romantic poetics. Romantic theory (as in Shelley's *Defense*) holds that art leads to truth. Oscar Wilde, in "The Decay of Lying," implicitly reverses that with marvelous chop logic: art is lying; art is truth; therefore lying is truth. Thus decadence confronts romantic poetics with a radical contradiction. The result is the absurd paradox fundamental to decadence, the paradox that cuts romanticism off from its vestigial idealism. Romantic poets, the popular front for romantic theory, had been unable to do this. They had instead wallowed in elaborate but unconvincing attempts to integrate deep-well psychology with Olympian morality. And in so doing, as Byron says, they "proved unintelligible." It is true that Keats, for example, recognized an incipient decadence. Negative capability was an unsystematic awareness that dialectical preoccupations like those of Wordsworth, Coleridge, and Shelley were an "irritable

reaching after" facts that were clouded by the very presuppositions through which they were to be reached. But Keats unfortunately (though true to decadent tendency) died young,
and doctrinaire decadence was left for a later generation in
England. When Wilde, echoing Gautier, said that art expresses
only itself he was articulating the decadent wish to find a world
of beauty that neither the natural nor moral worlds provided.
Thus the decadents wanted essentially a romantic beauty, but
they denied its source in nature. Man, they said, defines nature and not the converse. So art, not nature, is the source of
beauty. The later decadence simply makes the next logical assumption—that if there is no beauty in nature, neither is there
any in art. Thus, by our time, the basic generalities of poetic
tradition—that art reveals the good and the beautiful—are
largely disbelieved. Like the early decadents, we say that art
expresses itself, but that self no longer necessarily implies
beauty. Beauty, as an artistic concept, has largely become
rhetorical. It was meaningful only when it applied to creation
or formal analogues of creation. Since the author of nature has
ceased to exist it is no longer necessary to honor him by prais-
ing his works. And with his passing so too passed the analogy
between his works and ours. Although the early decadents tried
to grasp beauty a while longer without its metaphysical basis,
they had to do so by appealing to an aristocratic sensibility.
And that too was doomed. When democracy caught on it
swept away the last refuge of monolithic beauty.

The decadent connection between art and metaphysics is
that perception is controlled by the arts (for contemporary
decadence, *art* is expanded to mean something like Marshall
McLuhan's "media," hence, for example, pop art) which convey experience to us, and that we can therefore be informed
only by what these arts intend or are capable of conveying to
us. Thus we know only what we perceive; our perceptions are
controlled by the arts which represent "reality" to our senses;
reality therefore depends on the character of the art or medium
that represents it; and consequently rather than art imitating

Nature (the constant), nature (the relative) imitates or takes on the qualities of art, which has now become the arbiter of reality. Thus Wilde:

Consider the matter from a scientific or a metaphysical point of view . . . For what is Nature? Nature is no great mother who has borne us. She is our creation. It is in our brain that she quickens to life. Things are because we see them, and what we see, and how we see it, depends on the Arts that have influenced us. To look at a thing is very different from seeing a thing. One does not see anything until one sees its beauty. Then, and then only, does it come into existence.

If we substitute "irony" or "absurdity" for Wilde's "beauty" and expand Wilde's use of "Arts" to include popular culture and its "media" we have here a contemporaneous statement of decadent poetics. Nor is what McLuhan describes, excepting of course his electronic thesis, substantially different from what Wilde observed:

We have all seen in our own day in England how a certain curious and fascinating type of beauty, invented and emphasized by two imaginative painters, has so influenced Life that whenever one goes to a private view, or to an artistic salon, one sees here the mystic eyes of Rossetti's dream, the ivory throat, the strange square-cut jaw, the loosened shadowy hair that he so ardently loved, there the sweet maidenhood of *The Golden Stair,* the blossom-like mouth and weary loveliness of the *Laus Amoris,* the passion-pale face of Andromeda, the thin hands and lithe beauty of the Vivian in *Merlin's Dream.* And it has always been so. A great artist invents a type, and Life tries to copy it, to reproduce it in a popular form, like an enterprising publisher.

In short, to say that life imitates art is to say that artistic media influence our perception and knowledge of complex reality and to that extent control our lives.

The "documentary" or the news film illustrates contemporaneously what I mean. A recent telecast from Vietnam filmed the battle for Hill 888 (or some such number) in which the camera and reporter created a drama from the battle by featuring an interview with one of the young soldiers and using his descriptions to punctuate visual scenes from the battle and battlefield. It was a curious synthesis; the soldier was exhausted and confused about the significance of the victory. What he knew was that he was tired, that he had been afraid, that many friends had been killed, and that he did not want to have to go through it again. What he did not know was why (or perhaps *if*) Hill 888 was so important, or how it was part of a larger view of the war's conduct. He knew only what he had experienced. The reporter (or more likely editors back in the States) bridged the soldier's gaps in information and understanding by reconstructing a *drama* of attack and counterattack, while machine guns, artillery, and medics were playing out the spectacle of war on the screen. The supposition of film and narrative was that Hill 888, being, one guessed, somewhere between Hills 887 and 889 and having an elevation, had specific strategic importance. But that importance of course was not documented nor precisely determined; although it remained an assumption, it was structured to have the dramatic impact of certainty. The important thing here is that the maker of the film (reporter, editor, whoever) wanted some kind of coherence. The soldier's description without the film shots didn't have it. And the film without the soldier didn't have authenticity. So, in the interest far more of art than documentary, the two were brought together to give a view of the war that was neither that of soldier, nor reporter, nor camera. This synthetic artistic view is the one upon which the audience, those of us who have no other data for comparison, has to depend for its knowledge of the battle's reality. So it is that decadence prevails, and life imitates art. We "see" only what we *can* see through the medial apparatus by which we see.

The next evening's news announced that Hill 888 had been recaptured by the Vietcong. Now what was the reality of that battle? To us at home, its reality was formulated by art. But, at the time we perceived it, we were watching a "victory." Was it a victory then and later a defeat? Was it the same

71

battle? For the soldier it was perhaps a new battle, defined by the rhythm of resting and fighting or advancing and retreating or however he perceived the passage of time. And what if he is killed? From at least one perspective of reality there will be no more battles and no more war. And then our own sense of the battle's reality will have been largely determined by a perspective no longer existing. Where then *is* the reality of the battle? For us it must remain in the realm of art; it must in fact take the shape that the film maker and his art *permit it* to take. And so too for the reality of the war itself. We know its reality only through the artistic representations of it that we perceive. The war takes on the qualities and character of its artistic representation—that is, the war imitates art.

The limitations of perception are clear enough, then. But suppose the artist has some rhetorical purpose beyond even the restrictions of his art. Suppose that the film-maker wanted to show the battle so as to make it noble or make it foolish. Then the image of reality that he presented to us would be still more complex because reality would be not only artistically structured but it would be structured so as to persuade us to the artist's purpose. Now reality will have come to us filtered through the art with its limitations *and* the artist with his limitations and peculiar motives. In short, when we add the artist who controls the art to the art which controls our perception, then we must get a very decadent idea of the reality of the house that Jack built.

The theory that art, as medial purveyor and reflector, controls reality means also—and more significantly—that it controls moral reality. Moral categories, the traditional way of moral knowledge, are consequently absurd. That is, they exist because of faith rather than necessity. Categories have a way of becoming disengaged from experience by way of their own "artistic" (that is, dialectical) structure and taking on their own intimidating existence. Contemporary decadents attempt to fight this intimidation by articulating the gap between real moral authority and chimerical moral faith. They assume the stance of an existential Socrates demonstrating that the philis-

tines, like the sophists, are epistemologically dangerous because they believe shadowy categories to be reality. And thus
the dominant decadent motif is, in William S. Burroughs'
words, "Let them see what is on the end of that long newspaper spoon."

III.

The early decadence of which Beardsley is representative
conceived art as celebration. But, having lost moral faith, it
was able to celebrate only its own elegance. The later, or new,
decadence is analytic rather than celebratory, having been
for some time convinced that there is nothing under the sun
so true or beautiful as to inspire celebration. This contemporary sensibility rejects Art and Beauty because they have,
like transcendental morality, proved incapable of the latitude
necessary for dealing with a highly fragmented and incoherent
reality. Being persuaded that there is nothing to sing about, it
is not surprising that it satirizes those who persist in singing.
Nor, with the rejection of beauty as artistic center, is it surprising that its primary imagery draws from the ugly and obscene.
It is possible to employ the poetics of satirical obscenity more
than William S. Burroughs, but not much more. So I would
like to use his work as a paradigmatic instance of the later
decadence at work.

Excepting the latter's rejection of Beauty and unified form,
the artistic premises of the two Decadences are similar—the artistic image is the true reality and its function is to illuminate the
ironic falseness of programmatic preconceptions. For instance,
it is a culturally programmed generality that drug addition is
evil. Burroughs' *Naked Lunch* "demonstrates" by satiric dispo-
sition of images that it is human nature to be addicted, and
that drug addiction is in fact the most easily recognized addiction virus. The novel's structure is a dialectical tension of
obscene images designed to persuade us that addiction in all its
manifestations is man's normal state, and that ignorance of
this phenomenon makes us morally absurd.

We are morally absurd when our actions or ideals are dissociated from the moral values authorizing them. Morally abstracted ideals are sure-fire decadent avenues to absurdity. As Burroughs demonstrates, for example, our programmed association of addiction with abnormality depends on subsuming human nature into preconceived and simplified moral categories. Burroughs assaults this idol of the mind by counterasserting that the central issue of addiction is not moral vice at all, but rather the freedom of human will. Then he reconstructs our popular images of freedom through knowledge and order (for example, the scientist, the jurist, the police agencies, the political parties, the business corporations, and so on) and reveals them to be agencies of control addiction. They are all aspects of the Nova Mob. Thus not only are our cultural ideals cast in criminal context, but we are also shown that complex reality (that is, the true nature of addiction) is falsified by popular image makers, whose art demands and whose purposes are served by programmatic simplifications of reality. Thus the decadent thesis. And/ thus the title *Naked Lunch;* in reference to charges of pornography against his orgasm-death gimmick, Burroughs says,

These sections are intended to reveal capital punishment as the obscene, barbaric and disgusting anachronism that it is. As always the lunch is naked. If civilized countries want to return to Druid Hanging Rites in the Sacred Grove or to drink blood with the Aztecs and feed their Gods with blood of human sacrifice, let them see what they actually eat and drink. Let them see what is on the end of that long newspaper spoon.

In short, he conceived both the obscenity and the dialectic as devices to make it possible for men to perceive the reality of cause and effect in such basic cultural addiction syndromes as capital punishment.

Burroughs defines the novel's central metaphor thus:

Junk is the mold of monopoly and possession. The addict stands by while his junk legs carry him straight in on the junk beam to relapse. Junk is quantitative and accurately measurable. The more junk you use the less you have and the more you have the more you use. All the hallucinogen drugs are considered sacred by those who use them —there are Peyote Cults and Bannisteria Cults, Hashish Cults and Mushroom Cults—"the Sacred Mushrooms of Mexico enable a man to see God"—but no one ever suggested that junk is sacred. There are no opium cults. Opium is profane and quantitative like money. I have heard that there was once a beneficent non-habit-forming junk in India. It was called soma and is pictured as a beautiful blue tide. If soma ever existed the Pusher was there to bottle it and monopolize it and sell it and it turned into plain old time JUNK. Junk is the ideal product . . . the ultimate merchandise. No sales talk necessary. The client will crawl through a sewer and beg to buy. . . . The junk merchant does not sell his product to the consumer, he sells the consumer to his product. He does not improve and simplify his merchandise. He degrades and simplifies the client. He pays his staff in junk. Junk yields a basic formula of "evil" virus: *The Algebra of Need*. The face of "evil" is always the face of total need. A dope fiend is a man in total need of dope. Beyond a certain frequency need knows absolutely no limit or control. In the words of total need: "Wouldn't you?" Yes you would. You would lie, cheat, inform on your friends, steal, do anything to satisfy total need. Because you would be in a state of total sickness, total possession, and not in a position to act in any other way. Dope fiends are sick people who cannot act other than they do. A rabid dog cannot choose but bite. Assuming a self-righteous position is nothing to the purpose unless your purpose be to keep the junk virus in operation. And junk is a big industry. I recall talking to an American who worked for the Aftosa Commission in Mexico. Six hundred a month plus expense account:

"How long will the epidemic last?" I enquired.

"As long as we can keep it going. . . . And yes . . . maybe the aftosa will break out in South America," he said dreamily.

In a world whose chief business is JUNK, the object of man is to profiteer. And in a world where JUNK is the principal industry, its end is to make of man an addiction machine. The decadent absurdity of such a world is imaged in Bradley the Buyer, the narcotics undercover agent who destroys the institutions he was created to protect because their knowledge of reality has been so categorically deformed that they cannot comprehend or control the monster they have made; Bradley

75

goes berserk, schlupping up the District Supervisor, other agents, junkies, and finally the Narcotics Commissioner himself. Finally he is destroyed by flame thrower, "the court of inquiry ruling that such means were justified in that the Buyer had lost his human citizenship and was, in consequence, a creature without species and a menace to the narcotics industry on all levels."

The Algebra of Need, so central to this deformation, is a Decadent phenomenon too. On its literal level, in reference to drugs, it means being controlled by physiological need. On the larger metaphorical level need is more subtle, more artistic, and so more decadent. Dr. Benway, himself a control addict, is perhaps the consummate artist at turning man into the soft machine. Benway is a bureaucratic Frankenstein, the burgeois scientist whose arts of power over human nature and reality describe a massive cultural obscenity. Here is Benway at work:

"I deplore brutality," he said. "It's not efficient. On the other hand, prolonged mistreatment, short of physical violence, gives rise, when skillfully applied, to anxiety and a feeling of special guilt. A few rules or rather guiding principles are to be borne in mind. The subject must not realize that the mistreatment is a deliberate attack of an anti-human enemy on his personal identity. He must be made to feel that he deserves *any* treatment he receives because there is something (never specified) horribly wrong with him. The naked need of the control addicts must be decently covered by an arbitrary and intricate bureaucracy so that the subject cannot contact his enemy direct.

"I digress as usual. Pending more precise knowledge of brain electronics, drugs remain an essential tool of the interrogator in his assault on the subject's personal identity. The barbiturates are, of course, virtually useless. That is, anyone who can be broken down by such means would succumb to the puerile methods used in an American precinct. Scopolamine is often effective in dissolving resistance, but it impairs the memory: an agent might be prepared to reveal his secrets but quite unable to remember them, or cover story and secret life info might be inextricably garbled.

"Many subjects are vulnerable to sexual humiliation. Nakedness, stimulation with aphrodisiacs, constant supervision to embarrass subject and prevent relief of masturbation (erections during sleep automatically turn on an enormous vibrating electric buzzer that throws the subject out of bed into cold water, thus reducing the incidence of wet dreams to a minimum). Kicks to hypnotize a priest and tell him he is about to consummate a hypostatic union with the Lamb—then steer a randy old sheep up his ass. After that the Interrogator can gain complete hypnotic control—the subject will come at his whistle, shit on the floor if he but say Open Sesame. Needless to say, the sex humiliation angle is contraindicted for overt homosexuals. (I mean let's keep our eye on the ball here and remember the old party line . . . never know who's listening in.) I recall this one kid I condition to shit at sight of me. Then I wash his ass and screw him. It was real tasty. And he was lovely fellah too. And sometimes a subject will burst into boyish tears because he can't keep from ejaculate when you screw him. Well, as you can plainly see, the possibilities are endless like meandering paths in a great big beautiful garden. I was just scratching that lovely surface when I am purged by Party Poops. . . . Well, 'son cosas de la vida.' "

Finally, of course, the system produces its logical consequence, a man who becomes the perfectly efficient soft machine—and is then banished as an unnecessary adjunct of the anal aperture: here is part of the story of the "Man who taught his asshole to talk":

After a while the ass started talking on its own. He would go in without anything prepared and his ass would ad-lib and toss the gags back at him every time.

Then it developed sort of teeth-like little raspy incurving hooks and started eating. He thought this was cute at first and built an act around it, but the asshole would eat its way through his pants and start talking on the street, shouting out it wanted equal rights. It would get drunk, too, and have crying jags nobody loved it and it wanted to be kissed same as any other mouth. Finally it talked all the time day and night, you could hear him for blocks screaming at it to shut up, and beating it with his fist, and sticking candles up it, but nothing did any good and the asshole said to him: "It's you who

77

will shut up in the end. Not me. Because we don't need you around here any more. I can talk and eat *and* shit."

Human reality has now been subsumed so completely by function, that the functioning parts themselves commandeer Being and exile humanity.

Thus the arts of addiction, the Algebra of Need, define and control complex human reality. We are all the junkie naked in sunlight; we are all the pusher; exploiter and exploited. This is the tension that defines nature. Nature is not, as Wilde saw, our voluptuous mother. Nature is the obscene, the naked reality of our personal being in conflict with impersonal being. Impersonal being, imaged as the Nova Mob, makes it a crime to manifest personality. Benway's arts, the arts of our culture, are designed to redefine identity in "corporate" terms. Thus the crime of separate life:

The black wind sock of death undulates over the land, feeling, smelling for the crime of separate life, movers of the fear-frozen flesh shivering under a vast probability curve. . . .

Population blocks disappear in a checker game of genocide. . . . Any number can play. . . .

The Liberal Press and The Press Not So Liberal and The Press Reactionary scream approval: "Above all the myth of other-level experience must be eradicated. . . ." And speak darkly of certain harsh realities . . . cows with the aftosa . . . prophylaxis. . . .

Power groups of the world frantically cut lines of connection. . . .

The Planet drifts to random insect doom. . . .

Thermodynamics has won at a crawl. . . . Orgone balked at the post. . . . Christ bled. . . . Time ran out.

The center indeed cannot hold. But Yeats was not really persuaded; Burroughs is. The "red shift" is paradigm for both physical and spiritual cosmos. The comprehensive dialectic of Burroughs' whole canon of work articulates the cause of disintegration. In *Naked Lunch* the cultural industry merchandises addiction; Benway programs our interior isolation, dehumanizes us, defines our mechanistic reality for us. *The Soft Machine* explores the destructive human consequences of this reality—

". . . are these experiments really necessary?" *Nova Express*
provides an antidote to nova control:

I have said the basic techniques of nova are very simple consist in
creating and aggravating conflicts—"No riots like injustice directed
between enemies"—At any given time recorders fix nature of absolute need and dictate the use of total weapons—Like this: Collect
and record violent Anti-Semitic statements—Now play back to
Jews who are after Belsen—Record what they say and play it back
to the Anti-Semites—Clip clap—You got it?—Want more? Record
white supremacy statements—Play to Negroes—Play back answer
—Now The Women and The Men—No riots like injustice directed
between "enemies"—At any given time position of recorders fixes
nature of absolute need—And dictates the use of total weapons—
So leave the recorders running and get your heavy metal ass in a
space ship—Did it—Nothing here now but the recordings—Shut
the whole thing right off—Silence—When you answer the machine
you provide it with more recordings to be played back to your
"enemies" keep the whole nova machine running—The Chinese
character for "enemy" means to be similar to or to answer—Don't
answer the machine—Shut it off—

And *Nova Mob*, by articulating the criminal source and character of nova control, shows nature—the cosmos—in a state of
total moral emergency.

We have come a long way, here, from Wilde's or Beardsley's
aloof, artistocratic superiority to nature. And we have come
still farther from the naive romantic idealizing of nature. But,
though "art" and nature have lost coherence in their respective expansions, they still have design. Design is not univocal;
it means simply that events happen according to cause and
effect, or probability and necessity. The artist's business, that
which makes him poet rather than mere artificer, is to locate
causality in the events of nature. That is the center of poetic
imitation. For Burroughs, as for all contemporary sensibility,
cause cannot be referred to such categories as the good or the
beautiful. Knowledge of causal reality requires penetrating
to those points in time where cause is revealed. Even plot, the
long-time poetic agency of showing cause, is a falsification

79

—because it means the artist must superimpose a linear and chronological order on the chaos of his perceptions. The maker of plots is, at least to some degree, the maker of causes rather than the discoverer. Dr. Benway represents the dangerous potential of giving life a plot. Our arts work on the premise that knowing requires ordering; Burroughs, realizing that the mind has greater perceptual capacity than we have thought, counters this by showing that superimposed order makes life take the shape we give it, and in so doing it prevents our perception of cause in natural events. Knowledge so derived is a chimerical self-indulgence.

Nakedness is all. Nakedness means images, structured as little as possible—enough structure to show the artist's perception of causal connection, not so much as to give an order that may gratify the mind's ease but which must falsify our knowledge of nature. Thus, direct experience and perception is the aesthetic base of Burroughs' poetic:

> I awoke from The Sickness at the age of forty-five, calm and sane, and in reasonably good health except for a weakened liver and the look of borrowed flesh common to all who survive The Sickness. . . . Most survivors do not remember the delirium in detail. I apparently took detailed notes on sickness and delirium. I have no precise memory of writing the notes which have now been published under the title *Naked Lunch*.
>
> There is only one thing a writer can write about: *what is in front of his senses at the moment of writing.* . . . I am a recording instrument. . . . I do not presume to impose "story" "plot" "continuity." . . . Insofar as I succeed in *Direct* recording of certain areas of psychic process I may have limited function. . . . I am not an entertainer.

When he says that he is no entertainer he denies that component of poetic tradition which the earlier decadents grasped so desperately. When he declines the continuity gambit, he rejects the traditional means by which art was supposed to instruct. How, then, instruct? Through an irregular rhythm of intersecting images which articulate causes and are, in their obscene nakedness, themselves the effects. By forcing us to concentrate on the imagistic connections—connections traditionally made for us by plot—we are kept, as he says, from taking our own pulse. The artist projects his montage, provides editorial control through the ironic inversion of beauty and obscenity, and that serves as catalyst to the reader's imagination rather than the determinant of it. The rhythmic recurrence of coordinated intersecting images acts as objective correlative. Here is Burroughs' own description:

You can cut into *Naked Lunch* at any intersection point. . . . I have written many prefaces. They atrophy and amputate spontaneous like the little toe amputates in a West African disease confined to the Negro race and the passing blonde shows her brass ankle as a manicured toe bounces across the club terrace, retrieved and laid at her feet by her Afghan Hound. . . .

Naked Lunch is a blueprint, a How-To Book. . . . Black insect lusts open into vast, other planet landscapes. . . . Abstract concepts, bare as algebra, narrow down to a black turd or a pair of aging cajones. . . .

How-To extend levels of experience by opening the door at the end of a long hall. . . . Doors that only open in *Silence*. . . . *Naked Lunch* demands Silence from The Reader. Otherwise he is taking his own pulse. . . .

The Word is divided into units which be all in one piece and should be so taken, but the pieces can be had in any order being tied up back and forth, in and out fore and aft like an innaresting sex arrangement. This book spill off the page in all directions, kaleidoscope of vistas, medley of tunes and street noises, farts and riot yipes and the slamming steel shutters of commerce, screams of pain and pathos and screams plain pathic, copulating cats and outraged squawk of the displaced bull head, prophetic mutterings of brujo in nutmeg trances, snapping necks and screaming mandrakes, sigh of orgasm, heroin silent as dawn in the thirsty cells, Radio Cairo screaming like a berserk tobacco auction, and flutes of Ramadan fanning the sick junky like a gentle lush worker in the grey subway dawn feeling with delicate fingers for the green folding crackle. . . .

This is Revelation and Prophecy of what I can pick up without FM on my 1920 crystal set with antennae of jissom. . . . Gentle

81

reader, we see God through our assholes in the flash bulb of orgasm. . . . Through these orifices transmute your body. . . . The
way OUT is the way IN. . . .

And, given JUNK as existential metaphor, the images are necessarily obscene in character. For we are all junkie analogues,
we all share—we all *must* share—his shamelessness and obscenity:

Take a shot in front of D.L. Probing for a vein in my dirty bare
foot. . . . Junkies have no shame. . . . They are impervious to the
repugnance of others. It is doubtful if shame can exist in the absence
of sexual libido. . . . The junky's shame disappears with his non-
sexual sociability which is also dependent on libido. . . . The addict
regards his body impersonally as an instrument to absorb the medium in which he lives, evaluates his tissue with the cold hands of
a horse trader. "No use trying to hit here." Dead fish eyes flick over
a ravaged vein.

Without that obscene vision of nakedness we know nothing.
But contemporary decadence is complicated by the peculiar
nature of its spiritual vision. Burroughs' doctrine of separate
life, that is, personality liberated from nova control, is a spiritual doctrine. But it presents spirit in psychic terms, spirit without theological apparatus, radically humanistic spirit. And the
form of his fiction is much influenced, though indirectly through
Swift, by a homiletic tradition. Swift's own sermons, of course,
were far more humanistic than religious. And the tradition
that both Swift and Burroughs share is the medieval "Saccus
Stercorum" homily. Fundamental to this thinking is the image
of the world as compost heap, decadent and obscene in the eyes
of God. Burroughs even has his own text; his book of knowledge is his own profound experience of addiction and its
obscenity. His novel, like the homily, takes its authority from
this book. Specifically it takes the form of his article on drugs
in the *British Journal of Addiction*. Though naturalistic and inverted, it is still a "revealed book," and ultimately speaks to
the human spirit. It tells us of new demonic gods, the tech-
nocrats, and their new arts. It explains their ways to man.

Burroughs, like so many contemporary decadents, is behind all that decadence and obscenity a man of intellectual faith, faith in the rightness of human personality, faith in the possibility of human dignity, faith that man can know if he will look past the demons he has himself constructed. And he brings the Word, in all its fractured complexity of perception. And perhaps most importantly he tells us that the artist, not the dialectician, is king—that his truth and his alone shall make us see.

IV.

This latter-day decadence, then, and the humanistic relativism behind it, are the root source of an obscene aesthetics. In the modern recording of Truth, obscenity has become the flip side of Beauty. Thus decadence has provided the philosophic audacity necessary to deny the aesthetic synthesis of the good, the true, and the beautiful on which western poetics have been based. So far as the true goes, Burroughs puts the function of poetry succinctly—"Let them see . . ." Conrad said it before, but for him moral truth was still a gorgeous operatic melodrama, however forceful, profound, and experiential. Still, though he was afraid of its rhetoric, he had at times—as in *Lord Jim* or *Heart of Darkness*—a fundamental grasp of the artistic possibilities of obscenity. Many are now persuaded, as Swift was, that obscene rhetoric is a necessary probe in the search for true understanding. If this view of truth is exaggerated, it is the exaggeration of selection and focus that we expect in art. And, because it has been so long sat on, the obscene vision is quite naturally aggressive in its flowering. Nor, so far as comprehensiveness goes, is the vision of Burroughs, say, any more restrictive in its kind than those of Dante or Milton are in theirs. And Burroughs had at least the humility not to pretend to represent what he does not know, namely, a beatific vision. In this sense the poetics of obscenity pretend only to as much truth as its poets have experienced. It contends, not that existence is obscene, merely that obscenity has existence. Obscenity, then, no less than beauty helps articulate the truth.

In short, obscenity takes itself quite seriously as a mode of moral knowledge, notwithstanding its elaborate network of ironies. "Whatever I say may be false and fantastic," say de Sade, Beardsley, "Pauline Réage," Burroughs, "or it may be true and terrible. Or, more likely, it is both. And that's the truth." Henry Miller's autobiographical novels, for example, quite clearly fuse experience with erotic fantasy (just as his or anyone's experience is in part *directed by erotic fantasy*) and so he produces fantastic documentaries. The truth he is after lies in exactly such a synthesis. Its reality demands that much complexity. But he also knew he had opposition, and being more or less normal he had to adopt an offensive line- man's stance—main thrust forward to meet opposition and make yardage. Hence the aggressive posture of much obscen- ity, willy-nilly. For there is a necessary and inevitable clash when antithetical aesthetics meet. When, that is, one contends that the good is the beautiful and the other that the good is the existential. Augustine, Chaucer, Donne knew it; Dante and Milton did not: when experience and dialectic conflict, an irresistible force meets a difficultly moved object. To assert an obscene truth is necessarily to deny the universal authority of a beautiful truth. And to do that, in the face of our cultural tradition, means that you carry a chip on your shoulder.

That chip now is pornography, as it was blasphemy in the nineteenth century and free form in the early twentieth. Por- nography has become, in effect, the principal genre of obscene aesthetics. Obscenity counters beauty in its dialectics (bring- ing "onstage" what heretofor was "offstage"); and sexuality is the imagistic, figural, and verbal basis of its rhetoric. It al- ready has, as the Kronhausens and Steven Marcus have shown, its own conventions. The critical problem has been that, fear- ing the aesthetic implications of acknowledging that pornog- raphy was anything other than an artistic aberration, we have not been critically prepared to recognize its artistic integrity. We no longer have a choice; in spite of the intimidating mono- lith of critical idealism and its domination of the academy, there are simply too many unequivocally good writers and artists using obscenity and pornography as vehicles of poetic statement.

Henry James rightly insisted that the art of fiction required a *"donnée"* from its audience—that is, the audience must grant the fiction its subject, for questions of *art* are questions of execution, not subject. And if the audience will insist on "taking its own pulse" there can be no artistic engagement with the artist. This is perhaps most profoundly true of pornography, because the kind of thing it is often puts people off. Some will grant obscenity and balk at sexuality. Others will accept sexuality but disallow obscenity. But both of these *a priori* attitudes impose on the artist's integrity. The artist has no obligation to confirm our own expectations, we rather want him to tell us something special. And the special thing that pornographic art tells us about is sexuality. *If* we are to have commerce with an artistic pornography, then, we must grant it its subject. Tennessee Williams like many other artists, echoing Terence, finds nothing human to be obscene. The sense of this idea is also served by saying that obscenity, too, is human, and that so far as we deny it we deny our humanity. It is in this context that we can most profitably see pornography as an artistic genre. What I am arguing is that, while pornography has been around as long as any mode of art, it is only lately— perhaps since Judge Woolsey's *Ulysses* decision, where law joined new criticism to blend art and life in a healthy decadence —that we have had an aesthetic, social, and poetic climate that would permit us to recognize pornography's more than pathological role and development in man's imagination—and in his art, the deepest statement of imagination. While criticism has always recognized the "erotic" (Solomon, St. John of the Cross), the "bawdy" or "vulgar" (Chaucer, Rochester), the "gallant" (Casanova, Cleland), and the "depraved" (de Sade), it has always regarded them as unique. Attributable to human idiosyncracy, but not—for that very reason—an artistic phenomenon. There is, sighed the Augustans, simply no disputing tastes. But lately, as Molly Bloom's mellow yellow (smellonispheres) have become a pop music hit, and as

85

Joyce, Faulkner, Genet, Burroughs, Nabokov, and others like them have become "classics" of modern literature, and as the atrocities of war and racism pile into our consciousness to make us recognize that *that* complex, sublimated obscenity is a good deal more dangerous than the trivial obscenity of naked sex (however "perverse" or acrobatic its posture)— lately with all of this we have begun to see enough coherence in this blooming of pornography and obscenity to suspect that a genre is in fact forming itself.

I am also arguing that this genre's existence has been accommodated by the evolution of philosophical and artistic theory. A pornographic genre is the natural product of the "triumph" of existential over moral metaphysics, and the corresponding change from stylized forms to the "naturalistic" representation of reality. In other words the sexual "giant"—masculine or feminine—has always been a human archetype for sexual desire; its manner of representation (the chief vehicle of which is art and literature) has evolved in accord with the evolution of theories of (sexual) being. In the main line of western artistic tradition sex has been sublimated to the status of myth. Not that there have not been frequent breaches of that line, but they have always been regarded as "curiosities" and been artistically disregarded. The history of "Bowdlerism," for example, has been the attempt of culturally aware people to bring such revered documents as the Bible and Shakespeare into alignment with the manners and tastes of a particular society. Thus, following Bacchic myth, the *goat* has been the symbol of lechery in western art. Occasionally there are variations. Picasso, for example, whose pornographic works have only recently begun to share in the universal Picasso popularity, uses the *bull* as an obvious enough symbol. Even the vernacular, where *fuck* has ready enough currency, symbolizes a lecher by the term *stud*. From the street to the ivory tower we have been taught by tradition that sexuality is best referred to in stylized and mythic terms. However, in spite of our attraction to the economy of referring to "a stud" rather than "a chap whose only interest in women is sexual," since the

naturalistic discovery of consciousness we have become interested in a depth image of such a man, his motives, his style,
feelings, effects. To satisfy that curiousity we need to see
what he does in fact, more than we need to be reminded that
he is very like a beast. We are already persuaded that man is
a beast. What we want to explore is what that means to his humanity, since he is of beasts the kind we call man. In short,
though we have had pornography a long while, it is only relatively recently that philosophy and artistic theory and practise
permitted the formation and recognition of a truly artistic
genre of pornography. I have suggested that the artistic line of
that evolution may be seen in the development from the
Decadence of Beardsley and Wilde to its contemporary revi-
sion in such writers as Burroughs or "Pauline Réage." That
line of development suggests that pornography has taken on
the moral and artistic "high seriousness" necessary to make
it a properly artistic genre. As a genre, then, pornography is
that literature which in its complex form treats sexuality as a
mode of nature and in its simple form excites sexual interest
by treating sex as the whole of nature. Simple pornography is
what we have termed "hard-core" pornography. But that designation is for legal rather than aesthetic purposes. Aestheti-
cally, as such books as *Story of O* demonstrate, there is no
clear line of demarcation. This genre, like all others, is in
flux. At its most ambitious—in Burroughs, Genet, "Pauline
Réage," Henry Miller, de Sade—it attempts to fuse the sub-
cultural conventions of "hard-core" pornography with the
moral seriousness endemic to western artistic tradition. To
understand it properly, therefore, we need to see the full range
of its artistic uses.

4.

Pornography as Moral Rhetoric

DEDALUS'S famous aesthetic, in *A Portrait of the Artist as a Young Man,* argues for a pure aesthetic emotion in which the mind is arrested by its artistic perception and lifted momentarily beyond the "loathing" or "desire" caused by "improper arts"—pornographic and didactic. Beauty, he says, is the proper end of art, and the end of beauty is to induce an "ideal pity or an ideal terror" at last resolved by the "rhythm of beauty." He defines art thus: "to express, to press out again, from the gross earth or what it brings forth, from sound and shape and colour which are the prison gates of our soul, an image of the beauty we have come to understand—that is art." There is here the antithesis that has buggered artistic theory at least since the formulation of romanticism in the late eighteenth century. For it postulates a naturalistic art ("from the gross earth") as the agency of an ideal beauty. Joyce has attempted to fuse the two poles of moral awareness—the transcendental and the naturalistic—and in so doing articulates the classic dilemma between flesh and spirit. His solution is a naturalistic idealism —faith that the gross earth must finally give us an image of beauty.

This is, too, the pastoral faith that the earth abides forever. And in this respect Joyce articulates a paradigm of the western aesthetic tradition. It is based on the Platonic analogy between the good, the true, and the beautiful. On one hand, his premise is idealistic and so he must deny the beauty, truth, or good of desire and loathing. On the other hand, however, his artistic theory is sensual, rooted in the sound, shape, and color of the earth and what it brings forth. Surely desire and loathing are indigenous to that. The aesthetic dilemma, then, is whether our art presents to us a world preordinately beautiful—and therefore good and true—or whether it presents to us a world that predicates only its perceived existence, and is not necessarily either good or beautiful. But of course it does both, and we are left with the realization that there is no univocally satisfactory theory of art. For those who feel the truth of Plato's analogy art does one thing. For those who do not feel that truth it does quite another.

Pornography, antithetically to Plato's truth, proceeds from a sense of moral dissonance rather than moral harmony. There is a distinction necessary here. The formulaic commercial sex literature defines itself, and we designate it by the term hardcore pornography. The end of this literature, as we have seen, is simply the exploitation of our sexual fantasies. It is a literature without moral context. When, as in the case of *Fanny Hill,* it has some artistic pretensions it superficially adopts whatever poetics is current. We are not, therefore, much concerned with it here. But rather with artistic pornography, the end of which is rather the exploration than exploitation of the sexual imagination. Because human nature is presented in exclusively sexual terms—sexuality in it is the metaphor of being —"Pauline Réage's" *Story of O* may be the extreme statement of this genre. If its figure for man is limited, it is the limitation of selection and focus that we expect in art. It is the limitation necessary to all literature conceived figurally. It is a limitation in kind with Camus' *The Stranger.* Although both Joyce and Lawrence opposed "pornography," they opposed it in its limited semantic context. But in our expansion of the concept, pornography creates an image of human sexuality which not only inspires erotic gratification but also suggests the archetypal and moral dimensions of sexual ibido.

In Lawrence's case the pornographic image serves as the symbolic vitality central to his moral dialectic. His opposition to what he understood as pornography was based in his belief that such a pornography denied humane vitality. But we shall see that it *need* not. For Joyce pornography was crucial to his extended epiphanal image of the existential comedy, as for example in Molly Bloom's soliloquy. In such instances pornography provides the agency for positive moral statement. On the other hand, the pornographies of the Marquis de Sade, Jean Genet, or "Pauline Réage" do not much feel vitality as a persuasive presence in life. Their sexual imagery is oppressive and destructive. They see vulgarity, hostility, and anxiety. This vision of life is ugly and without either cosmic or social redemption, but it is exploratory and authentic. Authentic because it is experiential, and exploratory because it attempts to construct images of the subliminal erotic imagination. We have now a philosophy of the ugly that is clearly operative, a philosophy that has been a long while with us—in, for example, the Gothic—but has only recently become predominant. If we continue to identify the beautiful with the true, the truth now explores the human meaning of the grotesque and the ugly. Whether it articulates an affirmative or negative morality, then, pornography is an important figural vehicle of moral statement.

We shall return to pornography's figural character, but it will be helpful, first, to consider the moral basis of literature. If one must be asked how art *instructs,* it instructs quite simply by presenting the artist's vision of what life and nature are. If his vision is presented with sufficient vitality and truth to persuade us that it is authentic, then it will instruct us in the truth of the vision it presents. The vision itself is important only insofar as it permits of vitality, truth, and authenticity. This stanza,

> Trust no Future, howe'er pleasant!
> Let the dead Past bury its dead!
> Act, —act in the living Present!
> Heart within, and God o'erhead!

may have the highest truth, but it does not have vitality. It is dead in word, thought, and prosody. It cannot, therefore, have authenticity; its lack of life makes its truth commonplace and irrelevant. Conversely this poem from the Japanese:

90

Under the cloudy cliff, near the temple door,
Between dusky spring plants on the pond
A frog jumps in the water, plop!
Startled, the poet drops his brush.

Though insignificant in action this poem has the truth of nature, the vitality of figurative perception, and consequently the authority that persuades us of its moral being. It speaks profoundly of the delicate Japanese sense of man and nature. The form of a work will determine its moral magnitude. A lyric, like this, will not have the scope of an epic. But this difference is quite accidental. Essentially the lyric and the epic have the same moral center: the fall of man and the splash of a frog are only superficially different subjects; each has its kinetic truth, and each may inform our understanding of the potentialities of being. Having been so informed, we have before us necessarily the knowledge of choice, the basis of moral action. Moral instruction, then, means that one is made to understand the necessity to choose among viable alternatives, that choice has consequences, and that the consequences define one's moral character. One has moral knowledge, not when he "knows how" to act in all possible situations (an impossibility), but when he knows that his actions testify to his sense of what life is and what it should be. He is morally informed when that sensibility alone is of sufficient value to him to compel a running internal monologue of self-examination.

Morality is essentially the sense of good *and* evil as natural forces. The moral sense is correlative with the metaphysical sense. So that a sense of an ordered universe will induce its analogical morality. These are the synthetic poles of moral awareness, and either may have validity. The Judaic-Christian morality has derived its authority from its ideas of order. And human history sugests that man inclines toward a faith in some sort of cosmic order. Philosophically, however, order is not necessary, and our faith in it will depend on the kind of evidence we consider and the manner in which we consider it. The kinds of evidence available appear to be supersensory, extrasensory, or sensory. It is ironic that, while we have had no trouble accepting supersensory evidence—basically in religion—we have never taken extrasensory evidence very seriously. So in practice our sciences and arts have proceeded along the polar routes of religious or supersensory investigation, on the one hand, or naturalistic sensory investigation, on the other. And it is instructive to remember that the naturalist keeps to his own methodologies—indeed his value as a scientist is measured largely by his keeping that "faith"—while the theologian quite often enforces his theories with naturalistic data, methods, and interpretations.

At the transcendental pole of moral awareness, knowledge is dialectical, and subsumed therefore into axiomatic first principles. In Platonic dialectic the *idea* is the axiomatic first principle; in the Judaic-Christian dialectic it is God. In such systems knowledge is conceived as evidence for the truth of dialectically established first principles. Knowledge which does not so verify is ignored, considered chimerical, or dialectically reinterpreted. In the sense that it is within a dialectical parenthesis, then, knowledge is static in this system, and if any knowledge threatens the system it is considered vicious. Thus Christ and St. John of the Cross had to be dispatched because they brought a new threatening knowledge to the old dispensations. Conversely, in a naturalistic moral awareness knowledge is scientific and is obliged to no ultimate truth. Its restraints are methodological rather than axiomatic. In this thinking sensory experience is the measure of things, and thus the virtuous scientist is he who has the widest range of experiential knowledge. Insofar, then, as naturalistic knowledge is without arbitrary limits it is dynamic, and it is virtuous in proportion to the degree it realizes its undefined potential. In the one morality the good, true, and beautiful prescribe what knowledge is; in the other knowledge prescribes the good, true and beautiful. Morality, then, is a way of interpreting the happenings of the universe. And one's sense of cosmic order or its absence will profoundly influence, perhaps even determine, his sense of what is good and how and to what extent knowledge is a part of or means to the good.

The artist, like everyone else, has in a more or less sophisticated way his own moral sense. His moral vision will determine both the forms and themes of the art he produces. When we speak of the artist's *vision* or *imagination* we speak essentially of this moral perception of things. And when we speak of an artist's growth, we mean not only his technical mastery but also his increasing consciousness and artistic use of his moral awareness. Poets like Dante or Milton, for example, wrote in the context of specific moral dialectics, one highly Catholic, the other highly Protestant. The poetics of both the *Comedy* and *Paradise Lost* were conceived as testimonials to the truth and efficacy of their systematic moralities. There is of course also a naturalistic artistic tradition. It began—for example, in Zola—as an artistic analogue to scientific method and it was an important step away from the aesthetic imagination's intimidation by assumed first principles. Naturalism has had its own evolution and has formed its own metaphysics and morality. The most coherent latter-day statement of this is probably an eclectic non-dogmatic existentialism. God is final cause in a Christian metaphysics, but in an existential metaphysics no final cause is predicated. Such writers as Camus, Beckett, or Genet deal only in temporal causality and distinctly image human ignorance of ultimate cause. *Waiting for Godot* and *Malone Dies* are two radical examples of a literature built on existential morality. Where Dante schematized a morality to the end of gaining for man the beatific vision of God, Beckett's Malone is without the options necessary for moral choice, and his end is quite simply his end. The plot of *Malone Dies* is that Malone dies. Of powers beyond his own impotence he knows only that a pair of hands deposit a daily tray of vittles. Camus' summation of such a natural order is that the universe maintains a "benign indifference."

That Dante and Beckett have antithetical moralities is merely a doctrinal difference. Both have a moral sense of good and evil, however disparately understood, as operative forces in the universe. Dante's good is an ideal. Beckett's is existential. Dante's good may be more hopeful and inspiriting,

93

and we may prefer his morality therefore, but that is quite another matter. No man, and certainly no artist, is obliged to have a moral vision that pleases us. His vision may not even please him. But when we penetrate the implications of dissident moralities we often find a reality that gives us profound moral knowledge whether or not we subscribe to *its* particular metaphysics. It may be that, from a Christian point of view, a morality that refuses to transcend humanistic knowledge is highly limited. But, on the other hand, there will never be an Inquisition to enforce an existential truth. On the behavioral level Christians are not appreciably more humane than atheists or Hindus. And there is substantial historical evidence that Christianity's feeling of omnipotent authority has caused considerable human suffering, not only among disbelievers—the Jews and Arabs, for example—but among the faithful as well —witness St. John of the Cross, St. Joan, *et al.* And there is evidence, too, that shows men are seduced into supposing that being Christians—or Mohammedans—puts God on their side and makes their side right. That attitude is especially appealing when God's authority is buttressed by fire power. The point is this, that the supposition of truth—whether a Christian, Jewish, or Nazi truth—is as often as not translated into moral license for the self indulgence of human passions. And the passion for truth or authority very easily becomes vicious when it is given power. All human institutions are riddled with this danger.

I have dealt here with the antipodes of moral vision. There is a whole range between them. Much current theology is to a great extent attacking and revising notions of the inviolability of religious dialectic. Some naturalistic artists, like Lawrence, eschew science for their own dialectical systems. But all these are the consequence of genuine moral inquiry. The validity of moral inquiry and exploration—that is, the effort to reformulate moral knowledge—is a benefit of the naturalistic ascension. The lack of moral consensus that characterizes contemporary life and art indicates the viability of moral exploration, to say nothing of its need. In this process art is a means of seeing what we are, what we think we are, and what we want to be. For, if I may use Joseph Conrad's definition, art is an "attempt to render the highest kind of justice to the visible universe, by bringing to light the truth, manifold and one, underlying its every aspect. It is an attempt to find in its forms, in its colours, in light, in its shadows, in the aspects of matter and in the facts of life what of each is fundamental, what is enduring and essential—their one illuminating and convincing quality—the very truth of their existence. The artist, then, like the thinker or the scientist, seeks the truth and makes his appeal." Conrad's analogy between the artist, the thinker, and the scientist is important because it designates art as a mode of knowledge. Since western culture has been Christian, art has concentrated largely on rhetorical appeal; the artist's responsibility to delight and instruct largely meant that there was a truth available for him to instruct and his business was to make it appealing through invention. But we are now in the process of redefining ourselves, discovering what we are. Science has told us so much more than we previously suspected that the old definitions won't do. The business of art, now, is actually, rather than rhetorically, to *seek* the truth. Schiller understood this in his famous essay on sentimental poetry—romantic theory marks the start of modern literature—when he distinguished between the ancients and the moderns by virtue of their relation to nature. Ancient culture, he says, has a simple existential relation to nature in which the poet *is* nature. The modern, or sentimental, culture has a moral relation to nature wherein the poet seeks nature. Or, more succinctly, "The feeling we have for nature resembles that of a sick man for health." The ancients identified with nature and were confident of it and themselves and their proper relation. We are not confident in our knowledge either of nature or ourselves, and we are compelled therefore to seek where we have not previously been accustomed to finding. The artistic consequence, as Schiller stated it, is that "the power of the ancients consists in compressing objects into the finite, and the moderns excel in the art of the infinite." As we grope the shadows

95

of the infinite for its truth, one of the first principles of art will and must be that it is exploratory rather than persuasive.

Pornographic literature is one manner of artistic exploration—which is saying that pornography, as we have defined it above, is a mode of knowledge in the way that any literature may be said to be so. It deals in a dark knowledge, the implications of which have been for a long time denied or ignored by philosophy and have therefore been largely unavailable to our literature. But science has provided us with the information and procedures to verify our suspicions, and demonstrable natural truths—many of them sexual truths—have authenticated new directions for the imagination. So what we have thought of as simply perversion or titillation has been shown to have psychic, archetypal, moral, and therefore artistic significance.

The moral basis of pornographic literature, then, is that it is an imaginative avenue to greater knowledge of human being. Its point of view is of course naturalistic. But its methodology, like any literature, is the Word. The difference between its use of the Word and a transcendental use lies in the different reality that each attitude envisions. The basis in each, however, for verbalizing its reality is the same. I want now to explore a verbal strategy common to both religious and pornographic literature. It is what Erich Auerbach has defined as the figural interpretation of reality. Without going into the complex history of the concept we may say that figural interpretation is similar to allegory and symbolism in that it was a device for interpreting scripture that became as well a moral paradigm for literary structure. It is similar, too, in that it is a way to penetrate "deeper meanings" of both scripture and nature. It differs from allegory in having historicity where allegory has abstraction, so prophecy is central to it. It differs from the symbol in that the symbol is more directly related to nature, having some kind of magical power, whereas *figura* is not a talisman and relates rather to interpretation of history (for example, the Old Testament) than to nature directly. These are Auerbach's distinctions. But, as he acknowledges,

96

in rhetorical and exegetical practice the three methods of interpretation tended to be synthesized. The important point
here is that the figural method is a way of articulating an abstract reality (God, for example) by means of imagistic reference to an experiential reality (God as father, shepherd, or
lover). It is in this respect the immediate ancestor of what we
call figures of speech. But, unlike figurative language, it is not
simply a rhetorical way of speaking; it is a means of getting
at reality. Metaphor is comparison; *figura* is not similitude but
an imaging of reality. My thesis here is that pornographic
imagery is best understood in terms of its figural structure,
that it has that structure in common with religious literature,
and that both use it as a device of moral statement.

In mystical religious literature (the extreme mode of transcendental morality), for example, where the object is to communicate an ecstatic religious truth, it is common to employ
sexual figures. St. John of the Cross is an excellent example of
the use of figural sexual imagery through which to state the
power of the soul's union with God. In St. John of the Cross'
three major works—*The Ascent of Mount Carmel, The Dark
Night* and *The Spiritual Canticle*—he uses what we might call
the vocabulary of figural sexuality in order to convey the
ecstatic sense of divine love in terms of its figural analogue in
human life—sexual orgasm. Mount Carmel is his symbol for
the "union of a soul with God." To make its ascent one must
first pass through three stages of the Dark Night, which are the
mortification of the senses, the purgation of the spirit, and the
"passive purgation" of the soul, effected by God. Although
the end of this dark night is in fact the beatific vision, St. John
does not use, as Dante does, the basic image of light and revelation. He wants something more emotionally persuasive than
that, so he uses the "Song of Songs" as scriptural base rather
than "Genesis." Thus his basic image turns on *union with*
God rather than the *revelation of* God. This impels him, as a
user of the Word, to use a sympathetic instead of apocalyptic
imagery. The only natural source with sufficient sympathetic
force for his purpose is the imagery of courtship and sex.

97

Here is the figural theory as St. John himself describes it in *The Ascent of Mount Carmel.*

The soul, naturally speaking, possesses no means other than the senses (the windows of its prison) of perceiving what is communicated to it. . . . because the faculties of the soul cannot of themselves reflect and operate except upon form, figure, and image, which would be the rind and accident of the substance and spirit. . . . For the aim of this activity is the reception of substantial understanding and love through those forms. . . . In these apprehensions coming from above (imaginative or any other kind . . .) a person should only advert to the love of God they interiorly cause. He should pay no attention to the letter and rind (what they signify, represent, or make known). Thus he should pay heed not to the feeling of delight or sweetness, not the images, but to the feelings of love that are caused. Only for the sake of moving the spirit of love should the soul at times recall the images and apprehensions which produced love.

That such apprehensions may have a diabolical origin is the chance that a merely human being must take to perceive anything at all. Therefore the figural method is the only effective way of understanding the highest moral good—union with God. With this figural methodology in mind St. John wrote his "Stanzas" for the soul, which begin "One dark night,/Fired with love's urgent longings . . ." and conclude with this clear, though decorous, sexual imagery:

> Upon my flowering breast
> Which I kept wholly for Him alone,
> There He lay sleeping,
> And I caressing Him
> There in a breeze from the fanning cedars.

> When the breeze blew from the turret
> Parting His hair,
> He wounded my neck
> With His gentle hand,
> Suspending all my senses.

> I abandoned and forgot myself,
> Laying my face on my Beloved;

All things ceased; I went out from myself,
Leaving my cares
Forgotten among the lilies.

Also such images as this from the *The Spiritual Canticle:*

The bride has entered
The sweet garden of her desire,
And she rests in delight,
Laying her neck
On the gentle arms of her Beloved.

The point here is that even the religious mystic finds the imagery of sexuality necessary to transmit understanding of the reciprocal love of man and God, when that prodigious union is attained. He is dealing with a reality for which there is no other suitable analogue. He has gone beyond dialectic and theology to explore the realm from whose bourne no traveler returns—the felt power of God's presence, mystical knowledge.

St. John of the Cross does not, of course, write pornography. But he does use for his own purposes the kind of imagery and subject characteristic of writers who do write pornography. St. John, however, unlike the pornographer, disengages the ecstatic effects of orgasm from its material cause and conceives it only in terms of its final cause. The moral purpose of figuring God's love as sexual love is to transcend the merely human to a love still better and more ecstatic. And to keep focus on God rather than on the analogical "delight or sweetness" of the love images, he refrains from an indecorous description of "love's urgent longings." In his commentary on this phrase he observes that it is neither "appropriate" nor "possible" for him to make a "description . . . of these longings of love." Morally, however, we are, he says, instructed about spiritual love by analogy from physical love:

A love of pleasure, and attachment to it, usually fires the will toward the enjoyment of things that give pleasure. A more intense enkindling of another, better love (love of one's heavenly Bridegroom) is necessary for the vanquishing of the appetites and the denial of this pleasure. . . . For the sensory appeties are moved and attracted toward sensory objects with such cravings that if the spiritual part of the soul is not fired with other more urgent longings for spiritual things, the soul will neither be able to overcome the yoke of nature nor enter the night of sense.

This is not only a warning about the naturalistic world, it is also an analogical lesson in the great power of love and pleasure. The highest love and pleasure are therefore the proper concern of the religious man. But the access to their comprehension is necessarily physical love, because, as St. John says in reference to another of his verses, "the act of love is on the arm, since by the arm the beloved is held and caressed."

Thus St. John of the Cross uses the imagery of sexuality in his spiritual dialectic as a means of knowing the divine love of which it is the figure, or prophecy. *Love* is the key in distinguishing between his figural use of sex and the naturalistic figuration of sex in pornography. Religious figure prophesies that all the goods of earth—for example, love ecstacy—are such faint shadows of heaven that they are evil by comparison. And love of course is the central fact of Christian dialectic. Pornography is not necessarily concerned with love, although it may be (it is, for example, in the *Story of O*). Nor is it committed to a dialectical truth for which it acts as prophecy, although here again it may be (it is in *Lady Chatterly's Lover*). And, being naturalistic, pornography is inclined to use description and specificity in its treatment of sexuality, so its analytical concern is more immediately with the material cause of sexuality and its human effects. Its moral perspective will be determined, consequently, by the demands of its fictional function rather than by an external system.

To see pornography as a literary device for moral statement let us look at William Faulkner's morally pornographic use of three characters—Laverne Shumann (*Pylon*), Mink Snopes' wife (*The Hamlet*), and Lena Grove (*Light in August*). Faulkner's own moral vision is nicely synthesized in his famous Noble Prize acceptance speech. In that speech he consciously articulates the moral perspective from which he wrote and from which he thought all poetry must come:

I believe that man will not merely endure: he will prevail. He is immortal, not because he alone among creatures has an inexhaustible voice, but because he has a soul, a spirit capable of compassion and sacrifice and endurance. The poet's, the writer's, duty is to write about these things. It is his privilege to help man endure by lifting his heart, by reminding him of the courage and honor and hope and pride and compassion and pity and sacrifice which have been the glory of his past. The poet's voice need not merely be the record of man, it can be one of the props, the pillars to help him endure and prevail.

Laverne Shumann is one of Faulkner's highly idiosyncratic ur-women. She is a sensual woman who shares a hard, meagre, and dangerous life (they are a barnstorming team of stunt fliers) with two men and her son by one of them, she does not know which. She is a fecund (at the end of the novel she is pregnant again) but ambiguously feminine type. Like many Faulkner women, she is tough and hard superficially in order to survive and cover a basic sentimentality that is invariably fatal when indulged. Laverne's vulnerability comes from in fact loving one of her men. He is, of course, killed in a stunt, using a defective plane in an attempt to get extra money to cover the birth of the new child. He is the pilot, and so the team is left without means. Laverne must, therefore, give up her son to the parents of the dead "husband," and be cut off from him forever. Here her toughness serves her, and she is able to give him up, suppressing the destructive tendency to indulge sentimentality and keep the child. The child turns out to be the true son of his father in that, like his father, he is obviously a future pilot, and like his father he will give up easy and artificial prospects to embrace a natural life rhythm. And by the end, the drama of the stunt flying team has given moral knowledge to the sceptical newspaper reporter who brackets the novel's main action; and the "grandfather" who doubts his grandson is his grandson is given signs that at least spiritually he is. The novel, then, celebrates the life urge and the spiritual survival of man.

The plot quite candidly denies the existential authority of

conventional morality. Monogamy, motherhood, fidelity, thrift, cleanliness in thought, deed, and word—all of the standard moral sentimentalities are simply ignored. All the values antithetic to these triumph, in the sense that they provide the context within which life goes on. The stunt-flying team in its unorthodox, pitiful, and naturalistic way becomes the symbol of the courage, honor, hope, pride, compassion, pity, and sacrifice of which Faulkner speaks in his acceptance speech. The "glory" of man is that he finds a way to survive; he may pay, but he also prevails. At plot's end, the dead pilot's son stands defiantly with his toy plane in hand and his clothes ready to run away as his father before him. Laverne, a new baby in her womb, moves on with her remaining man to the life she chooses to live in the way she chooses to live it. And the sceptical, morally aloof newspaper reporter has been persuaded of a fundamental human dignity and the need to honor it. This vision of the dignity of life for life's sake is pornographically fortified.

The pornographic image comes on the eve of Shumann's death. He is going to make a probably suicidal flight in a defective plane to get a stake for the new child. This is his sentimental mistake, but also of course it is the virtue that defines him. But Laverne makes the fatal sentimentality clear as they lie in bed: she accuses him of knowing that the plane may kill him, and he responds,

"I guess I can land it, all right."
"You're lying," she said. "We got along before."
"Because we had to. This time we don't have to."
"But it's seven months yet."
"Yair. Just seven months. And one more meet, and the only ship we have with a shot engine and two wrenched longerons."
"You bastard," she said in a tense rigid whisper. "You rotten pilot, you bastard rotten pilot. . . ." Her hand shot out and snatched the cigarette from him; he felt his own fingers wrench and bend and then saw the red coal twinkle and arc across the dark and strike the invisible floor. . . . now the hard hand struck his cheek, clutching and scrabbling about his jaw and throat and shoulder until he caught it and held it, wrenching and jerking.

102

"You bastard rotten, you rotten—" she panted.

"All right," he said. "Steady, now. . . . All right, now . . . You want to take your pants off?"

"They're already off."

This scene sets up the pornographic image. It articulates Laverne's fury at death and existential defeat—"You bastard rotten pilot." Then the narrative returns to a previous scene in which she has exhibited this same vital fury. Faulkner presents it pornographically in order to underscore the symbolic defiance of mortality that Laverne's sexual passion celebrates. It is the occasion of her first parachute jump:

He sat in the back cockpit with the aeroplane in position holding the wing up under her weight, gesturing her on out toward the wingtip, almost angrily, when he saw her leave the strut and with that blind and completely irrational expression of protest and wild denial on her face, the hem of the skirt whipping out of the parachute harness about her loins, climb, not back into the front seat she had left but . . . scrambling and sprawling into the cockpit . . . astride his legs and facing him.

In the same instant of realizing (as with one hand she ripped her skirt hem free of the safetywire with which they had fastened it bloomerfashion between her legs) that she was clawing blindly and furiously not at the belt across his thighs but at the fly of his trousers, he realized that she had on no undergarment, pants. . . . So he tried to fight her off for a while, but he had to fly the aeroplane, keep it in position over the field, and besides . . . he soon had two opponents; he was outnumbered, he now bore in his own lap, between himself and her wild and frenzied body, the perennially undefeated, the victorious. It was some blind instinct out of the long swoon while he waited for his backbone's fluid marrow to congeal again that he remembered to roll the aeroplane toward the wing to which the parachute case was attached because the next that he remembered was the belt catching him across the legs as, looking out he saw the parachute floating between him and the ground, and looking down he saw the bereaved, the upthrust, the stalk: the annealed rapacious heartshaped crimson bud.

The pornographic fantasy involved here is clear enough, but at this point Laverne's sexuality takes on also a figural dimen-

103

sion. Her very physicality figures a procreative triumph over death—now with Shumann, later with some other. Life is all. She figures too the demi-urge. When she jumps, harnessed and without pants, her skirt up to her shoulders, she triggers the life fury of the crowd below. They go mad and maul her when she lands, until the police rescue and arrest her. Shumann sees the mind of the mob in one of the younger police officers, "a man besotted and satiated by his triumphs over abased human flesh . . . seeing now and without forewarning the ultimate shape of his jaded desires fall upon him out of the sky, not merely naked but clothed in the very traditional symbology —the ruined dress with which she was trying wildly to cover her loins, and the parachute harness—of female bondage." Later Shumann sees in another madman's face the same "terror and wild protest against bereavement" that Shumann had seen in Laverne's own face as she looked at him in the plane before her jump. The man screams, "I'll pay you! I'll pay her! I'll pay either of you! Name it! Let me . . . her once and you can cut me if you want." Laverne's sexuality, then, figures the full gamut of human vitality, its power and fear, its desire and frustration. She is infinite sexuality. Where Shumann's phallus, after orgasm, is "bereaved," Laverne takes on the whole universe with her sex. The screaming man, too, will be "bereaved." But not Laverne; she is the figural life energy that survives and prevails. As pornographic image she punctuates the vision with which Faulkner probes moral ambiguity and prospects for the Blakean marriage of heaven and hell.

The Hamlet is a much more complex novel, but it too explores the moral ambivalence of human vitality. Central to the novel is the emergence of the Snopes family from the Calibanic Mink Snopes to the phlegmatic machinations of Flem Snopes. The Snopes family, like Laverne's stunt-flying team, figures the brute crouch from which man pulls himself to something like his full height. But Faulkner makes it clear that even in his brutishness there is the faint preview of human "glory." Sexuality has great importance in the novel, but its most distinctively pornographic character is in the ironic *ro-*

mance of Mink Snopes. Mink is murderous, animalistic, greedy, and ominously pervasive. But, minklike as he is, he is nevertheless a man, and his moral being is an analogue of at least one dimension of all moral being. His pornographic romance defines both the animal and spiritual potentials of man. It is in every way a moral inversion of chivalric romance and its correlative moral idealism. The virtuous knight is an animalistic tramp. The lady fair is a promiscuous lesbian on horseback who surrounds herself with sado-masochistic paraphernalia—razors with which her eunuchs cut her hair, the "big rangy, well-kept horse" she rides, a quadroon procurer, and so forth. Purity is the theme of romance, but the lady— who selects her studs from among the work force of her father's lumber camp—is tupped by "the nameless, the identical, highwayman, murderer, thief." There is even an ironic virgin worship, of which Mink is celebrant: "He had been bred by generations to believe invincibly that to every man, whatever his past actions, whatever depths he might have reached, there was reserved one virgin, at least for him to marry; one maidenhead, if only for him to deflower and destroy." But even this demonic union, fitted out with all the trappings of pornography, has offspring and becomes part of the domestic culture. And not only does it survive, but for a time at least it even prevails, when Mink bushwhacks a man who has impounded his half-wild, unfenced cattle. But the metaphorical point of the pornographic parody of ideal love is summed up in this judgment by Mink's wife: "I've had a hundred men, but I never had a wasp before. That stuff comes out of you is rank poison. It's too hot. It burns itself and my seed both up. It'll never make a kid." There is danger in this man's very being. The same frustration, indefatigability, energy, and failure that makes us sympathize with him, also threatens our humanity. He is a killer, by will and by nature. He pornographically figures the brute in us that cannot transcend itself. He is the Caliban attracted, not to the beautiful Miranda, to the tradition of his humane glory, but to the female counterpart of himself—abortive and perverted.

105

In *Pylon* pornography imagistically enforces an ironic moral counter-argument to anemic conventions of good and evil. In *The Hamlet* pornography metaphors the bestial backdrop against which man's moral image must always be projected. In both novels pornography functions negatively. In *Pylon* it negates a sentimental morality; in *The Hamlet* it negates moral idealism. Faulkner is quite "consciously" using sexuality as figural enforcement of moral statement. His consciousness is verified, I think, by the fact that in such a novel as *Light in August,* where there is both pornographic and allegorical sexuality, he avoids pornography in the development of Lena Grove, whose character constitutes the novel's final comic affirmation. In this sense of profound affirmation the other two novels are not comic. At the most they accept life rather than affirm it. And their pornographic naturalism prefigures or prophesies the deep well of moral contradiction—fire and ice —that is the heritage of human nature. In *Light in August* there is some pornographic treatment of the affair between Joe Christmas and Joanna Burden, but it is altogether transcended by the allegorical treatment of Lena. Lena is alpha and omega; she begins the novel and she ends it. Like Laverne, she is fecund, but unlike Laverne, she is untainted. There is that touch of the holy virgin about her which she maintains to the end, when she denies the comforts of the bed to Byron Bunch. Here, by Faulkner's conscious denial of pornographic treatment, she becomes an allegorical statement of both transcendent fertility and that humanly sullied purity which alone is available to the good man. Comic transcendence, for Faulkner, goes the allegorical way traditional to the literature of transcendental statement. But his naturalistic statements, perhaps his most morally profound for their capacity to make judgments without passing judgment, are highly suggestive examples of the artistic possibilities for using sexuality to explore moral actuality.

The polarities of religious eroticism and sexual naturalism confirm the centrality of archetypal sexuality's moral meaning —both in the acts of and the impulse to sex. The imagery of sex has a coherent significance comparable to that of pastoral nature imagery. Indeed the pastoral itself was the model for St. John of the Cross's verses. Where the pastoral image as a statement of the good derives from transcendental morality, the sexual image as moral statement derives from naturalistic morality. Early pornography, such as *Fanny Hill,* affected a kind of pastoral quality in its stylistic presentation of sex. But, as naturalism became increasingly available to the imagination, pornography developed its own dissident identity as a moral phenomenon. Thus in de Sade sexuality becomes a complete morality and metaphysics—a world view. Such a view is not comprehensive, limited as it is by polemics and special pleading, and more balanced imaginations have used sexuality in less hyperbolical ways, however crucially they may conceive it as a sign or cause of human behavior and the natural order. Faulkner, of course, is one of these. But the pervasiveness of sexuality in imaginative confrontations with both the behavorial and mythical order of things testifies to the morality of sexual being and consequently of pornography, the literature about sexual being. For the artist pornography is a figural device which enables him to visualize his perception of sexual causality in human and even cosmic nature. For the audience pornography provides the imagery with which it may be instructed in the artist's vision of moral possibility. For both artist and audience, then, pornography can be a rhetorical agency of moral understanding.

107

5.

Tragedy and Pornography: Toward a Naturalistic Ethos

I.

I HAVE been arguing that pornography has the potential for both moral and mythic knowledge. It seems fitting therefore to examine the kinetic relationship between pornography and tragedy, the literature traditionally articulating the most profound problems of both morality and mythology. Because pornography as a genre has not developed sufficiently to have its own tragic literature, as the sentimental genre has for example, its relationship to tragedy must be qualified as kinetic. Besides which modern tragedy is so gingerly regarded by critics as to perhaps itself be properly termed kinetic. But, to avoid that quagmire, we can assume that, however it may modify tradition, there is such a thing as modern tragedy. And there is a connection, an important one, between it and pornography. In proposing such a relationship it should be implicitly clear that we are considering tragedy as a poetic quality rather than a dramatic form. In this context tragedy refers to that serious, usually fearful, poetic vision in which human affairs are dominated by ubiquitous and more or less incomprehensible pain and destruction. Such a vision may, of course, manifest itself in any form, but its principle ones are literature, myth, and religion, with considerable overlapping. Pornography, especially its basic mythos of animality, has a

108

logical though not conventional association with tragic mythoi. The most predominant motifs of tragedy are war and violence, both analogues of the mythos of animality. Plato in fact suggests that the art of war was mythically given to man to put him at parity with the rest of animal nature. Later, he says, the concepts of *shame* and *right* were given man to counteract his animal character and permit social organization. And the act of sex, throughout the history of both erotic and pornographic literature, has been figuratively depicted as an act of war. Sex and violence, as symbols of great passion, are then in the logic of symbolism unequivocally connected with tragedy. I want in this chapter to explore some of the artistic potential of that relationship. We must first look at some aesthetic history, and then look at pornography's place in the aesthetic movement toward a naturalistic ethos.

First, to suggest the significance of tragedy's transition from what it was to what it is. Tragedy has been traditionally regarded as the highest mode of western wisdom literature, and if we are sceptical about the possibilities of modern tragedy it is perhaps only because we are sceptical about the nature of modern wisdom. But for classical cultures wisdom was, if no less difficult than now of application, at least capable of confident articulation. And tragedy was its way, providing formulation and reflection of the highest levels of cultural imagination. It shaped, as well as being shaped by, the cultural ethos. It gave coherent formulation to religion, myth, and ethics. Tragedy—recall that Aristotle regarded the *Iliad,* the *Odyssey,* and other epics as tragedies—is a principal source of our knowledge of classical religion, myth, and ethics. And Socrates' objection to the tragedians was precisely that their formulations of such wisdom were not only erroneous but far too influential. As things worked out, Greek popular culture obviously thought Homer was closer to where it was all at than was Socrates, and dispatched him accordingly, as a troublemaker. Aristophanes and the Athenian people, as Hegel so brilliantly notes in *The Philosophy of History,* recognized in Socratic thought a revolutionary threat to the celebrated

109

"middle way," to in other words the fundamental complaisancy, coherence, and clarity of the mythic formulations of Greek law and order. So, though with characteristic civility, they put him up against the wall, preferring the ethics of religion and myth to the ethics of "truth." Hegel sums up that pivotal moment in tragic moral history thus:

He taught that man has to discover and recognize in himself what is the Right and Good, and that this Right and Good is in its nature universal. Socrates is celebrated as a Teacher of Morality, but we should rather call him the *Inventor of Morality.* The Greeks had a *customary* morality; but Socrates undertook to teach them what moral virtues, duties, etc. were. The moral man is not he who merely wills and does that which is right—not the merely innocent man—but he who has the consciousness of what he is doing.

Socrates—in assigning to insight, to conviction, the determination of men's actions—posited the Individual as capable of a final moral decision, in contraposition to Country and to Customary Morality, and thus made himself an Oracle, in the Greek sense. He said that he had a δαιμόνιον within him, which counselled him what to do, and revealed to him what was advantageous to his friends. The rise of the inner world of Subjectivity was the rupture with the existing Reality.

But the Athenians learned, or at least *we* learned from their demise, that, as a freshmen coed at Northwestern University once put it, "mental health is better than art." Freud and modern psychology are the somewhat belated vindication of Socrates' (though he has always been the sentimental favorite of the learned) insistence on self-knowledge. This knowledge —that, as Milton said, the mind is its own place, creating, as Milton could *not* say, heaven and hell—is that which modern tragedy has been pressing on an audience which, until rather recently with Sartre and the existentialists, was not capable of its assimilation.

The ego, we have discovered since Socrates, is sovereign. It feels itself the arbiter of reality, however much it is reminded of a larger reality. Establishing a harmony between the personal and universal metaphysical senses is the chief problem of not only psychic but social and cultural health. It is also the starting point of tragedy. The ego at its best sees all fates as relevant to itself and is interested in fates other than itself in proportion to its recognition of that relevance. Once out of the infancy vacuum, where the universe is accommodated to infant wants and needs, the personality is confronted with an antithesis, self and other. From there on life pretty much consists in working out in increasingly sophisticated ways a balance that resembles the infant stage of cosmic accommodation. The expanding sophistication of wants and needs, which expand at a rate much faster than one's consciousness or knowledge of them, makes this a constantly frustrated process. Thus the dynamics of human affairs, predicated largely on need, desire, and ignorance.

Tragedy, to articulate this process and its components, constructs a symbolic or ideal self and pits it against the cosmos, however any given tragedy's purposes may define it (as a society, nature, the gods, and so forth). It necessarily therefore refers man to myth, that is, to a fictive and symbolic representation of his relation to things. Because the other, the forces and rhythms of life outside himself, is most obscure to him, it is given patterns and comprehended as myth. But because man is obscure to himself as well, he too is given mythic character, as a hero. Thus the vehicle by which he is to understand himself and his relation to the universe is unavoidably a vehicle of distortion, presenting life and man as they are not in order to articulate what they are. Tragic mythoi, then, are as susceptible to obfuscation as they are to revelation. Knowledge depends on individual interpretation and always runs the risk of self-service. As myths are interpreted so are they created and evolved. Whatever man's preoccupations are find their way into his mythology. Tragedy is the most profound mythic representation because it confronts the most universal truth and human preoccupation, that of death and its analogues, pain and destruction. For though everyone *may not* be happy in life, everyone will surely die. Or, though one may be happy at a particular moment, so much so even that his consciousness

111

may seem to be filled with it, that happiness (the comic sense) is circumscribed by the conscious or unconscious knowledge of death. Happiness is a temporal condition, and, Christian rebirth not excepted, it is a condition that must end in the form that we know it. Christian comedy may let us transcend death, but even there we have to face it. Comedy presents what we are capable of on earth, that is, within the context of what we know how to achieve—a sense of being happy. And it has therefore a profound ethical meaning. But tragedy deals with man in the clutches of the dark powers, those beyond human ken and control, and it is the most profound of our mythic sensibilities for that reason, that it wants to help us accommodate ourselves to what is unknown but always with us. The ethos of tragedy is therefore essential to an exploration of the intimidating forces of which we are ignorant but to which we are subject; and in so doing, as Aristotle says of its effects, it relieves us of personal fear by uniting us with humanity, and thereby also makes possible the compassion necessary for human understanding and survival.

To serve the needs and wants, then, of human personality, tragedy developed as an art of religious mythology, relating man to the cosmic forces, which it represented as gods modeled on a frequently compromised (Socrates' objection) but nonetheless ideal human scale. Tragedy in effect humanized the cosmic forces by putting them, however reverentially, into the context of human motivation, that man might understand their ethical significance by analogy. Thus, by his construction of mythic form and substance, man himself became the creator (decadence rides again) of what it was he sought to know. He created an art form to represent his religious ethos, honing his will to meet the cosmic necessities he imagined as well as the ones he knew. But it is important to remember that the vehicle by which man understood his relation to himself and nature was the product of his own making. Thus it is logical that as his understanding evolves, so too will that art form that most closely reflects his understanding. The history of tragedy's transition to modernity is essentially the history

112

of the transition from a religious ethos to a naturalistic one.

Tragedy was the highest spiritual art, according to such profound students of it as Aristotle, Hegel, and Nietzsche; because it most thoroughly synthesized the personal and universal truths. It presented human life in the context of an ideal—that is, a heroic image of human want and need, of human energy in consort and conflict with cosmic energy—and *affirmed* an operative justice in *what is*. It presented man in his nearest proximity to the ideal, presented him, however pathetic, in his nobility. His nobility consisted in his aspiration to unity with the cosmic forces, his aspiration to godhood. Wisdom, the lesson of tragedy, consisted in knowing the limits of aspiration—Creon must remind Oedipus, after the sky has fallen on him and he yet seeks to impose conditions on his exile, that he cannot seek to be master in all things; he must go into exile alone. For classical man operated within a framework of divine necessity, subject to the often whimsical but nevertheless just powers of the gods. Ethical wisdom came with knowing the terms of that necessity and acting accordingly. Usually, as in the *Antigone* or the *Orestia,* the hero is like man himself in an inescapable dilemma. His choice consists, not of salvation or destruction, but of the manner of his destruction. In some ways Oedipus's choices are atypical because, although he should know better than to spar with the gods, he acts in immediate ignorance. The profundity of the drama lies in its hero's proximity to the human condition. He seeks to manifest his personhood—he does not want to murder his father and marry his mother—but he must do so in ignorance, for how can he know that they who seem to be his parents are not. Antigone, Orestes, and Medea have more clear-cut ethical choices. They know at every minute what they are doing. They seek to manifest personhood, as all self-respecting men must, with full knowledge of consequences. In fact their personhood demands the consequences. Medea *must,* to be Medea, destroy her humane and maternal self. That is the tragic dilemma. But tragic wisdom lies in proper understanding and interpretation of the dilemma. The

113

audience knows what Medea, in her heroic passion, forgot, that the violation of human and natural laws leads to destruction. Medea, like all tragic heroes, serves as example. Men should rather want to see than be one. The pleasure in tragedy consists, not in man's destruction (the source of fear), but in the knowledge that there is a predictable justice in the scheme of things and that men can get in harmony with it by moderating their passions, those energies that defy god and nature. Thus tragedy presents the mythoi of passion, and the tragic ethos articulates the dangers and temptations of men acting, passionately, beyond their ken. Classical tragic wisdom tells man three things: that the pressures of realizing his personhood will tempt him to overreach himself, that such ambitions will threaten natural and divine law, and that to maintain themselves these laws (in the form of the gods) will destroy him or see to it that he destroys himself.

The main theme of tragedy is that man lives in the circumference of necessity and that knowledge of it is the crux of human survival. The difficulty, as Plato saw, was that knowledge of the ethics of that necessity was as much obscured by the tragic mythoi as it was clarified. Specifically he objected to the implicit approval of the passions in tragedy, to the tragedians' acquiesence in the power of passion. Tragedians were persuasive imagists but imperfect philosophers. Caught between the roles of formulator and reflector, poets too brilliantly perpetuated mythic misconceptions—especially of *passion* as the principal heroic virtue. Thus men, inspired to emulate the heroes, were provided the wrong paradigm for imitation. To counteract the passions Plato proposed an environment— his Republic—in which men could get in harmony with their rational natures and thus avoid the tragic consequences of overwhelming passion. But, as even he realized, this was a utopian project unlikely to be realized—precisely because men *are* more "passionate" than rational. The tragedians may have given bad moral example by their representation of passion as ethical catalyst, but they were nevertheless telling an existential truth. Plato wanted to expand the existential potential of ethics by making men more conscious of the mythical (or decadent) basis of their values. Knowing the force of myth in formulating man's knowledge, he wanted to expand the moral archetypes on which myths are based to include rational analysis. He wanted, in other words, to "improve" the conscious values of Athenian culture by expanding the ethical basis of the mythic unconscious—represented by poetry, especially tragedy—from which they were derived. And it is on the pivot of this conflict—between in effect the conscious and unconscious self—that the transition from classical to modern tragedy begins.

Hegel, in the *Philosophy of Fine Art,* describes the problem so:

In this sense the Greek nation has also, in the representation of its gods, made its spirit visible to the perceptions and the imaginative consciousness, and bestowed on them by means of art a determinate existence, which is entirely conformable with their true content. By virtue of this homogeneous form, which is alike consistent with the fundamental notion of Greek art and Greek mythology, art became in Greece the highest expression for the Absolute, and Greek religion is the religion of art itself, whereas romantic art, which appeared later, although it is undoubtedly art, suggests a more exalted form of consciousness than art is in a position to supply.

In establishing the position, as we have just done, on the one hand, that essentially free individuality is the content of classical art, and, on the other, that a like freedom is the equally requisite determinant of the form, we have already assumed that the entire blending of both together, however much it may be presented in the immediate form, is nevertheless no original unity such as Nature's, but is necessarily an *artificial* association made possible by the subjective spirit. Classical art, in so far as its content and its form is spontaneity, originates in the freedom of the Spirit that is clear to itself. And for this reason also we may say that in the *third* place the artist occupies a position different from that of his predecessors.

Schiller, as we have noted earlier, says that the difference between classical and sentimental or modern sensibility is essentially that while classical men felt themselves of necessity in the rhythm of nature that modern men have found themselves increasingly out of touch with it. This alienation is natural enough. Electricity alone, for example, would have been sufficient, disobliging man as it does to regulate his activities by the sun, and thus revolutionizing both labor and leisure. Once the processes of science and technology start, the changes in man's behavior compound geometrically. Coordinately with greater knowledge of the universe and its provision of idle time came increasing "scientific" knowledge of the self. Modern men have become less dependent on nature and more so on themselves. And, as they have assumed responsibility, they have reasonably enough sought to discover still more about human nature and its potentials. Until by our time it has become axiomatic that man himself, not the gods, holds the key to his survival. And, as men have recognized the extent to which they alone have the power and responsibility for their own survival, they have felt a more and more urgent need for self knowledge. The rich crop of sensitivity groups in America in the past few years is just one, perhaps slightly desperate, index of that urgency.

Man has got out of touch with nature because his knowledge has in effect changed its shape. He is at once arrogant and humble before it. Arrogant because he is more in control of it than ever before, humble because he is still fumbling with this power. But more and more he sees himself as the answer. Perhaps because, now that God is dead, there isn't anybody else. Increasingly the cosmos is being revealed to him through his own efforts. What to "the ancients" was an inscrutable nature often represented as an angry or propitiated god, a nature whose ambivalence to man could only be explained mythically, a mysteriously dangerous nature, has been depersonalized and made accessible to calculation and prediction. Increasingly he is being uneasily revealed to himself. He finds his history in common with nature, its rhythms and urges still rooted deeply in spite of the camoflouge of civilization. He finds that fire was not a gift from the Titans but a discovery, his own discovery. There may be magic in

116

his universe, but if so he himself is the magician—as fraudulent and convincing as any. In short, wisdom to the modern mind is the recognition that knowledge of man and nature is not static but dynamic, and that on all levels of experience, from the scientific to the ethical, it is wise to remain open, simply because the truth keeps demonstrating itself to be never closed.

As is usually the case, knowledge breeds humility. In respect to tragedy, for example, man has stopped making himself over into an idealized hero. Having given up the idea of gods, he has stopped challenging them. He wrestles now with gravity and inertia both physical and moral. Win or lose, there is small occasion for pride, except now and then in the irrelevant chauvinistic sense. Problems have proliferated faster than his answers. And having seen enough of nature to know that he must be his own answer-man, he also sees that he has now more work to do than ever. But what he has lost in heroes, gods, and epiphenomena, he has gained in respect for and knowledge of phenomena. After a long look at himself and the nature of things, modern man has become an existentialist. Being out of touch with an ideal, he sees little of the heroic in himself, little analogy between himself and the gods. Thus, little nobility, much failure. Or, more accurately, more absurdity. For all his knowledge, vast areas of ignorance. But now his failures are measured against his existential potential rather than divine necessity. The sky's the limit, but in reaching modern man keeps losing his footing. Going to the moon, he slips on the banana peels of poverty and starvation and war. Thus he is pathetic, pathetic by virtue of his failure to deliver on the large existential potential promised by science and "democracy." Man has great ethical promise, but is victimized by the dark powers still lurking in his soul, the dark powers of ignorance within him that continually frustrate his knowledge. Thus he is perhaps more tragic than his ancestors because he has greater ethical expectations. In the classical tragic ethos, as Hegel sugests, the audience always knew what its hero *should do*—as with Oedipus—or at least knew his alternatives clearly—as with Antigone. It was therefore purged by a moral and ethical knowledge the mythical coherence and clarity of which made the audience superior to the hero. His failure re-enforced their sense of justice. But in the modern tragic ethos the audience shares the "hero's" confusion. It does not know any more than he what he should do. Thus the audience—as, for example, in *Waiting for Godot*—is not superior to the protagonists, but rather shares their lack of wisdom. What *is* there to do? With no mythic pantheon of gods to depend on, for either wrath or benevolence, with nothing in fact to depend on but himself, man is left to his own pathetic devices. Stay? Or leave? What's the difference? Beckett's curtain falls on that dilemma. Somehow with all his knowledge man ought to know what he ought to do. But, morally, his knowledge is chimerical. For all the spectrum of choices it gives, he is powerless to choose with any confidence. Predictable as things are, the uncertainty principle reigns. Classical tragedy elevated its audience to an ideal ethos that promised deliverance from the dark powers. Modern tragedy, dispossessed of a common belief, simply appeals to the compassion necessary for man to stay in the trenches and slog it out.

In classical Greek culture a fixed mythology provided a fixed and static vision of the moral and physical cosmos. Which is why Aristophanes could have such good, if fatal, fun with Socrates in *The Clouds*. Philosophers may have known about motion and flux, and they may have suspected an uncertainty principle, but they could not transpose that knowledge into a moral sphere. Moral knowledge was in the province of religion and art, where a closed mythology provided a coherent and therefore comforting *sense* of scheme in which a man always knew his place and knew what to expect if he stepped out of it. When Socrates attempted the transposition, attempted to question among many things the mythic assumptions of tragedians, he was dispatched according to the short and easy way with dissenters. The tragic tradition, from which the Greeks gained their moral and ethical confidence, was a tradition of affirmation not interrogation. Socrates was the victim of a cultural antagonism that plagues us yet today, that between a philosophical inquiry into the nature of reality and the cultural affirmation of its mythic configurations. But Socrates, the Socratic role, lives in a way that Sophocles does not. Socrates lives, often crude and nearly unrecognizable, in modern guerrilla literature, and as well in the streets and demonstrations and jails. In the Chicago Conspiracy trial. Sophocles only lives in the classroom, with an occasional culture hour on television. Cocteau and others have, perhaps as a political ruse, tried to bring him back. But there is a universe of difference between *The Infernal Machine* and *Oedipus Rex*. The large issues—man and morality—may be the same. But the specific differences of moral vision and ethical responsibility are vast. For Sophocles' Oedipus affirms the justice inherent in a system of necessity that Cocteau's Oedipus probes and connives against.

Probing and conniving are almost paradigmatic characteristics of the modern imagination. In this sense perhaps Marlowe's *Dr. Faust* is the first modern tragedy, rooted as it is in medieval and classical conventions. For it shows man willful and unrepentent in his probing and conniving against God, the ultimate synthesis of cosmic forces. Faust, in going to hell unrepentent, the taste of Helen on his lips, marks the end of man's fear, not only of damnation, but of knowledge. For knowledge, the devil's doing, brings him that sweetness and power in life the experience of which is worth the everlasting death that man, as man, has always secretly suspected to be his fate anyway. Right there, or nearabout, is the beginning of the death of God. It is, at any rate, a sign of the end of the domination of classical tragic motifs. For Faust is no idealized hero endowed with stupendous passion like Achilles or Medea, he is a bookish man, a cloistered scholar who desires merely to know and experience the world. He is, for all the supernatural paraphernalia, a kinetically existential hero. Even to the extent of being slightly absurd, a *schlep* transporting himself by knowledge—super-knowledge to be sure, but sym-

119

bolically knowledge nevertheless—to the courts of princes, sporting with the lips of Helen.

But it took the modern imagination a while to find itself and "escape" its religious trappings. The eighteenth century was the time of its most discernible realization, in the development of what Schiller called "sentimental" and Hegel sometimes "romantic" and sometimes "symbolic" art. By the eighteenth century large cracks had appeared in the monolith of religious mythologizing, aided and abetted by the new philosophy represented in such figures as Kant, Hume, and Descartes. The religious order was waning, the secular coming on. Naturally the influence of religion on literature diminished, changed character. Its role became less dogmatic and more implicit. Whereas, in the case of English literature, Spenser and Milton felt compelled to wrestle out religious dogma, Sterne and Richardson attempted to probe its ethos, discover and isolate those qualities in it that could articulate the good life. This shift in emphasis also had to do, as we have observed earlier, with the "democratizing" of the arts. As literature (the novel, for example) was increasingly made for a middle class or "common" audience, it naturally opted for a "popular" ethic. As its education was limited so too was the new audience's understanding and appreciation of the refinements of religious dogma and philosophical disquisition. But literature, as usual, not only formulated and reflected the cultural imagination, it was as well the mediator between the common man and philosophy and religion. And it fused two of the most complementary concepts, Christian *charity* and philosophical *sentiment,* modified them and made them the basis for a democratic ethos.

The great comic paradigm of this ethos is Sterne's *Tristram Shandy*. Two great tragic paradigms are Richardson's *Clarissa* and Marquis de Sade's *Justine*. We shall shortly look at de Sade in some detail. For the moment some general observations on the sentimental tragic mode must suffice to indicate the transition such works signify in the movement of tragedy toward modernity, pornography, and a naturalistic ethos. De

120

Sade's treatment of the sentimental tragedy is parodic, which is to say that he uses that convention to make another, more ironic, statement. But Richardson's use of the motif is real, that is, it reflects in itself a moral vision. In the classical imagination calamity fit into a pattern of more or less coherent cause and effect. Good things resulted from good behavior, bad things from bad. The Greek heroes, in keeping with their character, act out great passions—pride, vengeance, love. And, as their passion is excessive, they suffer for it. However sympathetic the audience may be with their motives (as with Antigone), or however much the poet celebrates the magnitude of their passion ("Sing, muse, of the wrath of Achilles"), the heroes act "wrongly," and their suffering is a clear effect of a clear cause. Necessity, in other words, is always clearly in mind. The result is a highly formal sense of what is tragic. Not so with sentimental tragedy. Necessity, for the romantic (and probably for the modern) mind, is present—because, as we have observed, its archetype, death, is always present— but it is undefined logically. It exists in nature, but its causes are not formally located. It is to be found at the sign of suffering, on Pathos Street. And its effect is highly unformal; it is in fact pretty sloppy. "Virtuous" people do a lot of it because suffering, in the sentimental ethos, is the sign of their virtue. "Bad" people cause it, though they can become virtuous by recanting, usually on their deathbed or in a letter discovered after their death. Tragedy here, unlike its classical antecedants, exists without the framework of a coherent ethos. Thus, because there is no dialectical cause, it focuses on effect—suffering. Both sentimental and modern tragedy, denied a clear knowledge of cause—denied, that is, a formal sense of what is tragic—have necessarily to represent tragic pathos as the universal imperative. Men suffer, and more's the pity. If men suffer without moral cause, a corrective, a way out, is difficult or impossible of discovery.

There are, of course, better and worse resolutions of this dilemma. The sentimental one tends to be rather weak. Richardson demonstrates its weakness, de Sade demonically attacked it. Clarissa, the tragic protagonist of Richardson's novel, is the prototype sentimental hero. Lovelace is the prototypical villain. Clarissa, all virtuous sentiments and "delicacy," is wooed and won (her tragic flaw) by Lovelace, all lace and fripery, without a decent respect for work, without sentiments of conscience (except of course touchingly at his demise). She is made, somewhat lasciviously in fact, to suffer, and then, because she is so steadfastly virtuous (she says, on her deathbed, "It is good for me that I was afflicted!" . . . and "Do you, sir, tell your friend [Lovelace] that I forgive him!—And I pray to God to forgive him!"), she is allowed pathetically to die. Lovelace also dies pathetically, from the avenging sword of Clarissa's cousin, after announcing that his death is expiation. There are causes for suffering here, but they are ethically trivial. Aside from the bourgeois Christian judgments implicit in Richardson's portrait of Lovelace, including Lovelace's somewhat anemic satanism, Lovelace as tragic cause is just undifferentiated badness. Richardson is not, in fact, really interested in causality at all. He is interested in the spectacle of suffering, the tragedy of which shall be suffused by Christian salvation. In his postscript to the novel, Richardson explains his purpose:

He [a third-person reference to himself as author] was resolved . . . to attempt something that never yet had been done. He considered that the tragic poets have as seldom made their heroes true objects of pity . . . and still more rarely have made them in their deaths look forward to a *future hope*. . . . The Author . . . is therefore well justified by the *Christian system*, in deferring to extricate suffering virtue to the time in which it will meet with the *completion* of its reward.

It is an index of the popular sentimental mind that Richardson is here defending himself against charges that his killing off Clarissa violated "poetic justice," a popular poetic doctrine apparently conceived for the preservation of happy endings. The point is that, to justify his plot, Richardson felt obliged to pull all stops. In defense of unhappy endings he enlists the support of Aristotle, Horace, Addison, Steele, Rapin, and the Psalms. Tame and sentimental as he seems now, in his time Richardson was leading his audience (at least the ancestors of our little old ladies in tennis shoes that comprised its bulk) toward a tragic sensibility based in what he thought was a naturalistic, though highly Christian, ethos:

And after all, what is the *poetical justice* so much contended for by some, as the generality of writers have managed it, but another sort of dispensation than that with which God, by revelation teaches us. He has thought fit to exercise mankind; whom placing here only in a state of probation, he hath so intermingled good and evil, as to necessitate us to look forward for a more equal dispensation of both.

But, bold as Richardson may have been for his time, and audience, his morality is too simple and categorical, too dependent on the spectacle of suffering (which, had he read his Aristotle a bit more vigorously, he might have known), to provide the foundation for a significant tragic ethos.

Though mythically profound, the psychic basis of the ethos of sentimentality is inadequate to anyone not sharing its faith in *feeling* as the ultimately potent moral force. This "doctrine" is more persuasive in a comic than a tragic vision. For it does not prepare us to cope with the dark destructive powers that ineluctably nudge and manipulate our feelings, making them often a good deal less than salvific. The pathos of powerlessness and suffering, as depicted in *Clarissa,* is not significantly counteracted by the instruction to do "good." Nor is it by a system of rewards and punishments, such as are worked out in *Clarissa.* Such devices are predicated on the existence of an ethical scheme in which all motivations are "flat" and distinctly recognizable, making it necessary for men to simply tap into the good ones and eschew the bad. This moral sense works in a comic vision like Sterne's, because in it all things— suffering included—are absurd. Calamity in Sterne's vision is the (decadent) invention of man's preposterous ratiocination. He simply refuses to take it seriously. Men, for example Wal-

123

ter or Toby Shandy, act absurdly and absurd things happen to them. But, his ethos insists, if men would rather consult their humane feelings, the model for which is Christian charity, they would recognize their absurdity and in so doing escape the morbidity of the indomitable human ego. But suffering is never ultimate in a comic vision; in tragic vision it is always ultimate. So a tragic vision must perforce have an ethos that accounts for the mind's capacity to make a hell of heaven and a heaven of hell. It must, in other words, either have access to a common, stylized morality, as the Athenians did, or it must have a naturalistic ethos to accommodate the full range of human vagary.

The classical tragedian found his material in a mythology to which there was general cultural assent, thus society enforced the substantive themes and the form of his art. Hegel sums up the necessary conditions for a classical art thus: ". . . the content must for the classic artist be presented him as something *already there* . . . as a thing essentially positive, as belief, popular opinion, or as an actual event either of myth or tradition." The sentimental imagination, the beginning of modern imagination, did not have access to an essentially positive public ethos, either naturalistic or mythic. Christian mythology, unlike classical mythology, was ethereal and allegorical. And the efforts of Aquinas and Dante to stabilize interpretation did not help. Dante's rather quixotic and arbitrary allegorical interpretations of his own poetry in the *Convivio* indicate how intractable Christian myth is to public formulation. Likewise, the "modern" mythologizing of Blake and Yeats show how Christian and modern myth tend to be private and interior intimations rather than cultural apocalypse. But the aesthetics of sentimentality were an approach to the naturalistic needs of a modern ethos. Even *Clarissa,* rooted as it is in an eighteenth-century bourgeois sensibility, gives some indication of what was to come—Clarissa's helpless fascination with Lovelace, perhaps as much with his evil as his charm, and Lovelace's kinetic demonism as well as his moral ambivalence (culminating in his "expiation") are a kind of prologue to the "Dionysiac" preoccupations of the modern imagination. For the modern tragedian is most into probing the paradoxes and contradictions that undermine the vestigial ethos that obliges us to act on it as if it were static and final when in fact it is still evolving and incomplete. And to do that he must explore the naturalistic contradictions and paradoxes of the human mind that are a vital part of shaping a modern ethos. The sentimental poetic was neither quite fish nor fowl. It has classical impulses without classical content. Hegel, with uncharacteristic succinctness, sums up the problem of a modern aesthetics in evolution:

Symbolic art remains the captive of its travail to bring to birth and make clear its form to its own vision, and this embodiment is itself only the original form, that is, on the one side Being in the immediate guise of Nature, and on the other the ideal abstraction of the universal, unity, conversion, change, becoming, origination, and passing away. In this original form of the artistic process, however, art does not come to its rightful possessions. Consequently, these representations of symbolic art, which should be expositions of content, remain still themselves riddles and problems, and merely testify to the struggle after clarity and the effort of Spirit, which on and on seeks to discover without obtaining the rest and repose of discovery.

For all his perspective on aesthetic transition, Hegel's view here is very much the product of the classicism in which he was so well schooled. His analysis of aesthetic history is for that very reason richly suggestive to any attempt at articulating a sense of modern aesthetics. His notion, for example, of art's "rightful possessions" presupposes either that there is an ideal to be "discovered" or that, supposing an ideal, it can and should be formulated in art. Neither supposition is "modern"; both make art's personal and cultural roles finite and closed; art always knows what it *should* be doing. But modern art, like modern culture, is in the *process* of discovery. Sometimes finding new things, sometimes interpreting old things. Its main drift is neither celebration, as with classical art, nor lamentation, as with sentimental art, but analytic naturalism, trying to find out what's "really" there. Its reality premise is,

125

as Hegel understood, subjective (the moral and metaphysical analogy of relativity), but the working out of subjectivity is not so sanguine as Hegel and his time would have had to suppose. If subjectivity is real, as Hegel agrees it is, then reality *must* be as fragmented as subjectivity makes it. Thus finding out what is "really" there will not necessarily lead to the comforts of a univocally ordered sense of nature. In any event, whether there is or is not an ideal yet to be discovered, modern art is in the position of being necessarily experimental and open— that is engaged in the process of *discovery*. Its uneasy forms and themes are therefore quite natural. In this sense, that is, according to even an Hegelian view of aesthetic history, an ethically experimental and open art is in fact the mainstream of modern artistic tradition.

The cultural role of modern tragedy, therefore, is complex to an unprecedented degree. For it must somehow fashion an objective image of life—of man and nature—out of a subjective theory of personal reality and a corresponding relativity in nature. It must, in other words, help formulate a convincing collective ethos out of the fragmented and disharmonious experience of its culture. It must give form to what is formless, make comprehensible what is incomprehensible. Unlike classical or sentimental tragedy, it has no persuasive mythology to draw on. Being analytic and naturalistic, it finds itself in fact suspicious of mythology, tending more to parody its humanistic fruitlessness, as Beckett does in *Waiting for Godot,* or satirizing its vicious absurdity, as Camus does in *The Stranger,* or exploring its pathological destructiveness, as Nabokov does in *Lolita,* or demonstrating its futility and wrongheadedness, as Miller does in *The Death of a Salesman.* Myth and the urge to mythologize are treated ironically in modern tragedy because of their tendency to obscure moral reality and thereby render impossible the formulation of the one kind of ethos, a naturalistic ethos, in which the modern mind can feel some ethical confidence. The role of modern tragedy, then, is Socratic rather than Sophoclean. It rejects mythologizing for its liability to cloud perceptions of reality, coercing men to ignorance of their individual and collective natures and resulting in ethical impotence and disaster.

The moral imperative of modern tragedy is that, although men do not have a universal talisman, they do have the capacity to recognize cause and effect. And, in ethical relativism, each individual act is ultimate, for which the actor must hold himself responsible. He cannot defer responsibility to death and the justice of divinity. He can be responsible only for what he knows, and, whereas he cannot know divine justice, he can know the ethical implications of his own actions. Knowledge, above all self-knowledge, is the key to this subjective ethos. Not only must men have hindsight about the ethical implications of their acts, they must work to understand the psyche, its motivations and vagaries, its sickness as well as its health, for they act under the influence of their total being. And if they are to have power over themselves they must know the forces with which they have to contend. Clear perceptions of reality are therefore crucial. Like Socrates, however, modern tragedians know that no perception is clear; no perception, therefore, is final. Consciousness is an open-ended and ongoing work, imperative to the moral knowledge for which all men are responsible. So modern tragedy is a gadfly to the consciousness, reminding men that a failure of consciousness, where men hold their fates in their own hands, is fatal. And reminding men, also, that their perceptions are vulnerable, that their conscious vigilance is *ethically* necessary, and that failure to distinguish the "real" from the chimerical is, potentially at least, a moral failure. In *Death of a Salesman,* for example, Willy Loman, an archetypal modern protagonist, destroys his sons, himself, and his wife through a failure of consciousness. He fails to recognize that the ethos to which he subscribes and which he imposes on his sons—the ethos of being well liked to achieve the myth of "success"—is not only in itself destructive of humanity (symbolized in the grotesque recurring vision of Willy's uncle Ben and Willy's tawdry infidelity to his wife), but that, ironically, it does not even work. One son, recognizing the wrongness of the ethos and the du-

127

plicity of Willy in proposing it, is nihilistically paralyzed. The other son blindly adopts Willy's ethos in the very face of its failure, committing himself to its destructive perpetuation. And Willy's wife is left emotionally and economically destitute by Willy's suicide. His life insurance, naturally, is invalidated by the suicide, so his wife's fidelity to Willy and his ethos is ultimately frustrated. Willy, by so pathetic a misreading of his own and everyone's humanity, by his failure of consciousness, fails in death as well as in life. That his ethos is obviously representative of our culture extends the tragedy to the failure of cultural mythology. Willy's consciousness symbolizes the cultural consciousness. Nabokov's *Lolita,* as we have observed in an earlier chapter, makes consciousness a collective cultural responsibility. The novel depicts a telescoping of tragic "demons." Humbert is Lolita's demon, Quilty is Humbert's demon, and Humbert's life story is society's demon. This last, especially, is what Humbert in his trial wants to establish with his audience, the "ladies and gentlemen of the jury." Humbert is purged from Lolita by her pregnancy, the "normal" product of relations with her young husband. The purgation is not soon enough, however, to prevent the dissipation of Lolita's vitality by the age of seventeen, part of the novel's tragic pathos. Quilty is purged from Humbert when Humbert murders him. But Humbert cannot be purged from the culture. That is the point of his defense. There being no question of his guilt and execution, he argues for the consciousness of the whole culture—new world and old—to recognize his existence and what it means to its ethos. We must know that he is a man much larger than he seems, a man beset by demons, demons that led him to debauch and murder. But he is also as small as he seems; so that we may recognize that his demons are ours. The mythic exorcism of trial and execution, therefore, will not suffice the commonweal. We must be conscious that Humbert's demons live in all of us. His demons are part of our nature. These tragedies, like most modern ones, are an attempt to articulate the naturalistic paradoxes out of which human conduct springs and to generate thereby the knowledge and compassion for our natures necessary for the formulation of an adequate ethos. Explicit in these, as in most, modern tragedies is the rebuttal of those mythic shadows (the myth of success, the myth of exorcising evil by fiat and so on) that cloud men's minds and perpetuate so many vestigial dimensions of the modern ethos.

II.

The evolution of tragic sensibility from a religious to a naturalistic ethos means that western man's most profound literary mode has effected a fundamental transition. Its change signifies an equally important change in our total cultural sensibility. I want to argue, now, that pornography has had a role in that development and to examine something of what it has been. In a previous chapter we analyzed the hypothesis of decadence and its influence on a poetics of obscenity. To get at pornography's relationship to a naturalistic ethos I want to use as example perhaps the world's most celebrated decadent and practitioner of obscene poetics, the Marquis de Sade. Because he is so enigmatic and fascinating a figure one is tempted to fuse his literary and personal histories in an attempt to assess the meaning of the de Sade charisma. But that work has been done already by Simone de Beauvoir in her magnificent long essay, "Must We Burn de Sade?" De Sade himself is at once a myth and a reality in our cultural imagination, and our long-standing repression of his works and revulsion at his name tell us much. For most of us he is the archetypal "sadist," the model for a disease. There is probably enough "sadism" in his biography at least partly to justify that. But the real models for that character of imagination we exorcise with the label "disease" are much more the literary documents of his imagination than the conduct of his life. In many ways his life *is* more interesting than his work, but without his extraordinary writings de Sade would be a historical curiosity rather a rich index of sub-cultural psychology and life. He is not, however, important only to psychology, but to the devel-

129

opment of literature and philosophy as well. He is not, as some of his enthusiasts claim, a great novelist, a great philosopher, or a great psychologist. But he is a prodigious figure in our cultural history nonetheless. Both as myth and reality he looms peripherally but inescapably on the path to cultural "modernity." And the key to de Sade's meaning for us is in his literary remains.

Quite rightly, Simone de Beauvoir says de Sade is most significant as a moralist. But, because his moral vision is "decadent" and often contradictory, we can get at his morality more clearly if we consider the artistic medium through which it is articulated. De Sade's artistic quality is vitiated by his compulsive personal apologetics—that is, his need to defend his personal behavior and his need to attack society nearly always overpower those personally disinterested perceptions necessary to artistic integrity and universality. But it must be remembered, first, that de Sade did nearly all of his writing while imprisoned (it is not insignificant to his political thinking that he was, as Jean Paulhan has noted, imprisoned at various times by all the forms of French government under which he lived—Monarchy, Republic, Consulate, and Empire), and, secondly, that the mythic force and durability of Sade-ism come from the very personality with which he represents his imagination. He is, then, an extraordinary artist, and we do ourselves disservice to dismiss his vision because we depreciate his manner. His vision is so present, so much larger than questions of art, that we are obliged to work through the obstacles presented by his artistic form.

Nor is the problem one of aesthetic simplicity or naïveté. Though one detects these in his work, the works themselves are constructed with a peculiar complexity and sophistication of perception, so much so that we have only recently arrived at the aesthetic and moral attitudes necessary to comprehend what he was up to. Far too much so for his time, his aesthetic is distinctly modern. The key to it is decadence and the dialectical inversion of morality characteristic of it. We shall return to that. Now, let us look briefly at de Sade's ideas about

130

fiction, the form most important to presentation of his morality. In "idée sur les Romans," which prefaced a collection of his stories, de Sade reveals conventional enough notions of fiction, but not only are the conventions he prefers significant but also those few "original" perceptions on the nature of fiction with which the essay is spotted. Here, for example, is his designation of the basis of fiction: "Man is subject to two weaknesses which pervade his existence and characterize it. Everywhere he needs *to pray,* everywhere he needs to *love,* and those are the bases of all novels . . . since man *prayed* and *loved* everywhere . . . there were novels, that is to say, works of fiction which sometimes depicted the fabulous objects of his worship, sometimes the more real ones of his love." De Sade's own fictive motives start in these needs, but they are, in characteristic decadent fashion, inverted. Prayer is secularized in de Sade's fiction to celebration, and its object is demons rather than gods. Love is best translated in de Sade to mean *passion,* and is thus rendered exclusively mundane and naturalistic. His fiction is in effect a celebration of the demonic passions. To what end, we shall see further on. Nor, in appreciating de Sade, can one overlook the fact that man's *needs* are *weaknesses,* and that weakness is the basis of fiction. For de Sade, fiction was a dialectical vehicle for exploring the weaknesses of man and society, and its most ambitious end is analysis and refutation of the mythic superstitions by which man's weaknesses become idols of the mind. This anthropological notion of fictive utility also informs his theory of its origin and evolution.

Let us not be in any doubt about this: it was in the countries which first recognized the Gods that novels found their source, and consequently in Egypt, the undeniable cradle of all cults. Men had hardly *suspected* the existence of immortal beings before they made them act and speak; from then onwards we see metamorphoses, fables, parables, novels; in fact we see works of fiction, as soon as fiction seizes upon the mind of men. We see fabulous books, as soon as there is any question of fancies: when nations, led first by the priests, after having been sacrificed for their fantastic divinities,

131

finally took up arms for their king or their country, the homage offered to heroism counterbalances that of superstition. Not only are the heroes, and very wisely, put in the place of the Gods, but songs praise the sons of Mars just as they had celebrated those of heaven. The narrator embellishes the great actions of their lives, or weary of feeding upon them, creates characters who resemble them . . . who surpass them, and before long new novels appear, doubtless more probable, and created much more for man than those that only celebrated phantoms.

His sense of aesthetic history is acute, recognizing at an early time that fiction had moved from a religious to a naturalistic function. In noting that fiction has taken on an increasingly humanistic character he rightly observes that it must deal more precisely in probability, that is to say, it must give a more accurate accounting of cause and effect, an accounting as little confused as possible by phantoms. De Sade's interpretation of the history and function of fiction, then, was precociously responsive to the development of naturalism. It was, of course, his own peculiar version, rooted in his idea of the authenticity of the senses. In de Sade's dialectical apparatus naturalistic sensuality is the center of epistemology. Man can escape deceptive phantoms of the mind—"virtue," for instance—only by knowledge of the real meaning of the sensual. And fiction, in which that sensuality can be imaged in all its force, imaged working against the ineffectuality (in which its falseness is revealed) of virtue, fiction is the form through which that knowledge can be revealed.

What *good,* he asks rhetorically, are novels? ". . . they are good for painting you just as you are, vain individuals, who would like to escape the pen because you fear its effects. The novel being, if it is possible to define it thus, *the portrait of agelong customs,* is as essential as history to the philosopher who will understand man." For the philosopher must deal with man's actions, as man "makes himself seen," whereas the novelist "pierces his innermost thoughts." But de Sade clearly wants to fuse the philosophic and fictive roles to get at "the most essential knowledge that is demanded," which is the "understanding of the heart of man." Yet the novelist has over the philosopher the further advantage that he can, he must as an artist, according to even the most classical of artistic "rules," see and represent nature without the prism of dialectical predisposition. For a true perception of nature must take in all her variables and apparant contradictions and account for everything, high and low:

Nature, more bizarre than the moralists depict her to us, escapes at every moment from the confines that those gentlemen would like to prescribe for her. Uniform in her plans, irregular in her effects, her ever-stirring womb resembles the crater of some volcano from which in turn are cast up either precious stones which serve man's luxury or balls of fire which destroy him; magnificent when she peoples the earth with many an Antonius and a Titus, frightful when she vomits up an Andronicus or a Nero, but always sublime, always majestic, always worthy of our studies, our pens and our respectful admiration, because her designs are unknown to us, because, slaves as we are to her caprices and her needs, it is never upon what we are made to suffer that we should regulate our feelings for her, but upon her grandeur and her might, whatever their results may be.

And the role of art, being so attuned to nature, is to further the progress of enlightenment. The artist, being the freest of seers, being obliged to nothing but his perceptions, must extend the range and evolution of all men's perceptions:

As minds become corrupted and a nation grows old, by virtue of the fact that nature is studied more and analyzed better, that prejudices are better destroyed, it is necessary to get to know them further. This law is the same for all the arts, it is only by advancing that they become perfected, they only arrive at their goal by means of trying. Doubtless it was not necessary to go so far in those frightful times of ignorance when, crushed beneath the iron yoke of religion, those who wished to appraise them were punished with death, and the Inquisition's faggots were the rewards of talent. But in our present state, let us always set forth from this principle, when man has weighed up all the checks, when with an audacious glance he measures up his barriers, when with the example of the Titans he dares to lift his bold hand against the Heavens, and, armed with his

133

passions as the former were with the coals of Vesuvius, he no longer fears to declare war on those who formerly made him tremble, when even his delinquencies seem no more to him than errors justified by his studies, then should one not speak to him with the same force that he himself employs in his behavior? The man of the eighteenth century, in short, is he then the man of the eleventh?

The end of art, then, in de Sade's aesthetic is knowledge, knowledge of nature purged of the defensive machinery imposed on it by man's ambition and vanity, the weaknesses of his mind. On one level of vocabulary de Sade's aesthetic rings with the peal of conventional eighteenth-century attitudes. But on a deeper level—the level at which nature means *what is* rather than what is *theorized about,* the level at which nature is experienced and represented as experienced, the level at which natural history is described in terms of its changes rather than its constancy—at this analytical level of understanding de Sade is in profound disagreement with his time. Simone de Beauvoir points out, for example, that de Sade not only refuted the traditional theists but also the deists. De Sade, like some of the deists, knew that nature was not simply good. "But what distinguishes him from his predecessors," she says, "is the fact that they, after exposing the evil of nature, set up, in opposition to it, a morality which derived from God and society . . ." But de Sade, having, as we have just seen, a strict, almost Longinian confidence in nature's sublimity, was prepared to follow her ethos through no matter what paradoxes of experience. His faith in nature is religiously absolute, and the logical manipulations by which throughout his works he shores up that faith are themselves worthy of a Jesuit. This profound faith in nature and de Sade's often casuistic efforts to fashion an ethos out of it, in all its complexity and contradiction, define the recurring motifs through which he so extensively anticipated and influenced the development of a naturalistic ethos.

De Sade's theory of fiction tells us that to understand the human heart and nature an artist must have both misfortune and extensive travel. Travel of course will inform man of ethical relativity; he will discover that different societies manifest different—sometimes antithetical—moral values. But misfortune is the central thesis of de Sade's ethical vision. The plot of *Justine* is designed, however hyperbolically, to demonstrate that good or bad fortune (in *Justine* the good perish, the bad prosper) is a decadent invention of man, and nature is without intrinsic concern for man's affairs. He is here obviously refuting the simplistic Christian ethic that good behavior will bring good fortune. At any rate, making misfortune central to fictive epistemology means that tragedy is the paradigmatic mode of his aesthetic. Further, de Sade greatly admired Richardson, especially *Clarissa*.

It is Richardson and Fielding who have taught us that only the profound study of the heart of man, that veritable labyrinth of nature, can inspire the novelist, whose work must make us see man not only for what he is or what he shows of himself (that is the duty of the historian), but for what he may become, for what he may be made by the modifications of vice and the blows of passion. It is necessary therefore to know them all and to employ them all if you wish to work this field. We learnt also that it is not always by making virtue triumph that interest is maintained; that it is quite certainly necessary to aim at it as far as possible, but that this rule, existing neither in nature nor in Aristotle, but being only one to which we would wish that all men subjected themselves for the sake of our happiness, is by no means at all essential in the novel, and is not even one which must compel interest. For when virtue triumphs, things being what they should be, our tears dry up before they begin to flow; but if after the severest afflictions we at last see virtue crushed down by vice, our souls cannot escape harrowing, and the work, having moved us exceedingly, having, as Diderot said, *steeped our hearts throughout in blood,* must indubitably evoke interest, which is the only surety of fame.

Let us ask this question: if after twelve or fifteen volumes the immortal Richardson had ended *virtuously* by converting Lovelace, and making him marry Clarissa *quietly*, would we, reading this novel taken in the reversed fashion, have shed the delicious tears that it draws from every sensitive creature? It is therefore nature that we must grapple with when working in this sphere, it is the heart of

135

man, the most remarkable of all his works, and not virtue at all, because virtue, however beautiful and necessary it may be, is nevertheless but one of the moods of this astonishing heart, the profound study of which is so necessary to the novelist, and every twist of which the novel, that faithful mirror of this heart, must necessarily plot.

De Sade's appreciation of *Clarissa* and his own aesthetic and moral vision suggest that his highest fictive model is the sentimental tragedy. *Justine* is, for example, clearly modeled on the example of *Clarissa,* and it is the single work that perhaps most comprehensively presents de Sade's moral vision. But the fundamental differences between his vision and Richardson's explain why de Sade, in using the mode of sentimental tragedy, had to parody it. For de Sade was neither sentimentalist nor Christian. It is true that there is a kind of decadent theme in *Clarissa.* Her family, acting according to what they *think* are the facts, and acting on what they therefore *suppose* to be an ethical good, are in fact mistaken both about the facts of Clarissa's liaison with Lovelace and the ethic upon which they act. A cloudy perception of the facts, therefore, forces them to cause evil by doing what they assume is good. But the ethical force of this theme is vitiated by the sentimental tone of the novel and its concern to balance bad with good. Richardson's aesthetic is a synthesis of Christian sentimentalism, bourgeois ethics, and popular fiction forms. It is able, as we said earlier, to deal convincingly only with moral effects. De Sade had a much stronger dialectical impulse, a much greater faith in nature, and total indifference to (if not contempt for) popular moral opinion. And de Sade's aesthetic is *symbolic,* partly in Hegel's sense of that term and partly in Arthur Symon's later sense. But what that meant for de Sade was that he could be more reductive in representing a "true" image of human life than Richardson. Richardson, being a popular writer, was obliged to represent life as his audience expected it, though there was some dispute about what it expected, as we have seen. The checks and balances of his characterization and plot are in the democratic tradition. De

Sade, writing for himself, obliged to his vision alone was concerned only to give himself full rein in depicting his demonically microscopic image of moral reality. His image of life represents exclusively his private vision. And the audacious insistence that that image, private as it is, is universally true signifies the symbolic character of his tragic sense. This being so, he would have had to parody a form that required philosophical assumptions so radically different from his own.

Though both de Sade and Richardson explore the misfortunes to which virtue is subject, Richardson's purpose was to celebrate virtue's ultimate triumph over evil, while de Sade's purpose is to demonstrate that good and evil form an ineluctable rhythm in nature that remains indifferent to and unaffected by the passage through it of decadent "virtue." Richardson, in short, was enforcing the myth of sentimentality, de Sade was refuting the illogicality of that popular mythology. Richardson's novel is, of course, a much better work of "art" than de Sade's. But it is not de Sade's artistic quality that is significant; what is significant is his dialectical restructuring of the myth of sentimentality. Richardson subsumes human "perversity" (de Sade would call it "diversity") by making Lovelace in effect repent his persecutions of Clarissa. Christian grace, thus, exorcises human perversity. No matter how pathetically potent it may be, it need not therefore be accounted for by the cultural ethos. Perversity, in simplified Aristotelian fashion, is purged by the pathos of its effects. But de Sade knew better. Not being a Christian, and seeing that much of the world (including Christendom) was not Christian, and seeing that the way of the world was much more warlike (de Sade also admired Hobbes) than benevolent, whatever Christian gloss it might assume, de Sade knew that Christian sentiment was incapable of establishing justice. He knew that by observing the warlike state of nature where men act more from their fears and self protectiveness than they do from charity. And they construct their social institutions accordingly. Thus he knew that the mythologically directed establishment ethos must necessarily suppress what he understood to be natural justice—the con-

137

dition in which all men are free to realize their particular "natural organization," however perverse it might be. Our difficulty in perceiving the ethical viability of de Sade's work comes from failing to see that each of his works is a tactical step toward the realization of his more comprehensive moral strategy, arguing for the completely tolerant ethos that he thought would reflect and help establish a state of natural justice.

This failure is compounded by the fact that the political analogue of his tolerant ethos is anarchy, and, responding as de Sade knew we must, our fear of that analogy intimidates our understanding, and so we categorically reject his ethic. The failure, of course, is not all ours. De Sade is a prodigiously inadequate novelist, and his own need to refute and reject his audience, to confuse it by invoking its blindnesses so skillfully (and furiously) as to dazzle it with its own sightlessness, indicates his own very real failure to communicate. Toward humanity he was highly ambivalent. He professes concern for human beings (in *The New Justine* he says, "To falsify such basic truths, regardless of their consequences, reveals a fundamental lack of concern for human beings."), and in his own conduct, though it was pretty much erratic, he was charitable. When, as a judge just before the Terror, he had opportunity to revenge himself on the mother-in-law he despised, he did not. And he in fact resigned his position rather than pronounce judgments of execution, appealing that such judgments were "inhumane." But toward *society*, toward, that is, the collective abstraction of institutions, he was hostile. And, having been imprisoned by four diverse kinds of social government, he was not without reason. Whatever the causes, which are not our concern here, the failure at communication is as much de Sade's doing as our own. But we shall only serve our ignorance if, at this date, we allow that failure to perpetuate itself.

De Sade was propagandist for an ethos still pretty much inaccessible to us, though now that his work is more completely available we can see something of his dialectical strategy. *Justine,* as we have observed, is central, adding the dimension of tragedy to what might otherwise be dismissed, as it has often been, as simply perverse. De Sade is perverse, of course. But not *simply;* as a writer perversity is his stock in trade. The persistent motif through all his work is his defense of perversity as a natural phenomenon. His point is not, as it is so frequently mistaken, that perversity is *good,* merely that it *is* and in such quantity and prosperity that its naturalness is undeniable. If, then, one is to know nature and act according to natural justice—that is, according to an ethos of tolerance —he must know the range of moral diversity under heaven. To confuse the desire for moral unity and coherence, for a univocal idealistic good, with its actuality is, for de Sade, necessarily to dispossess natural justice. "The very masterpiece of philosophy," he says at the beginning of *Justine,*

would be to develop the means Providence employs to arrive at the ends she designs for man, and from this construction to deduce some rules of conduct acquainting this wretched two-footed individual with the manner wherein he must proceed along life's thorny way, forewarned of the strange caprices of that fatality they denominate by twenty different titles, and all unavailingly, for it has not yet been scanned nor defined.

Here is the plan of not only *Justine,* but of all de Sade's work —forewarning of strange caprices and a fatality not yet scanned or defined. *Justine,* perhaps not a masterpiece of philosophy, nevertheless is designed to explore those rules of conduct on which life operates, rules sentimentally supposed to reflect Providential benevolence. But, as one of Justine's many persecutors tells her,

Become better acquainted with your Providence, my child, and be convinced that as soon as it places us in a situation where evil becomes necessary, and while at the same time it leaves us the possibility of doing it, this evil harmonizes quite as well with its decrees as does good, and Providence gains as much by the one as by the other; the state in which she has created us is equality: he who disturbs is no more guilty than he who seeks to re-establish the balance; both act in accordance with received impulses, both have to obey those impulses and enjoy them.

139

"Providence" is not what it is supposed; it is rather a balance of good and evil; more accurately, a composite of forces interacting to which we apply the labels of *good* or *evil*. One cannot therefore be guilty of violating nature, only of violating man's hypotheses about nature. More importantly, the dynamic rhythms of nature in which "good" and "evil" contend constitute a state of natural justice. In fact, given the ethos of society, plagued by such decadent idols of the mind as "virtue," de Sade proposes that "evil" will more often than not overpower "good," being more attuned to the machinations of what Darwin was to call natural selection. Justine is the heroine whose misfortunes articulate the fate of virtue in a world where the fittest survive best.

Justine sums up her 350 pages of misfortune thus:

During my childhood I meet a usurer; he seeks to induce me to commit a theft, I refuse, he becomes rich. I fall amongst a band of thieves, I escape from them with a man whose life I save; by way of thanks, he rapes me. I reach the property of an aristocratic debauchee who has me set upon and devoured by his dogs for not having wanted to poison his aunt. From there I go to the home of a murderous and incestuous surgeon whom I strive to spare from doing a horrible deed: the butcher brands me for a criminal; he doubtless consummates his atrocities, makes his fortune, whilst I am obliged to beg for my bread. I wish to have the sacraments made available to me, I wish fervently to implore the Supreme Being whence howbeit I receive so many ills, and the august tribunal, at which I hope to find purification in our most holy mysteries, becomes the bloody theater of my ignominy: the monster who abuses and plunders me is elevated to his order's highest honors and I fall back into the appalling abyss of misery. I attempt to preserve a woman from her husband's fury, the cruel one wishes to put me to death by draining away my blood drop by drop. I wish to relieve a poor woman, she robs me. I give aid to a man whom adversaries have struck down and left unconscious, the thankless creature makes me turn a wheel like an animal; he hangs me for his pleasure's sake; all fortune's blessings accrue to him, and I come within an ace of dying on the gallows for having been compelled to work for him. An unworthy woman seeks to seduce me for a new crime, a second time I lose the little I own in order to rescue her victim's treasure. A gentleman, a kind spirit, wishes to compensate me for all my sufferings by the offer of his hand, he dies in my arms before being able to do anything for me. I risk my life in a fire in order to snatch a child, who does not belong to me, from the flames; the infant's mother accuses and launches legal proceedings against me. I fall into my most mortal enemy's hands; she wishes to carry me off by force and take me to a man whose passion is to cut off heads: if I avoid that villain's sword it is so that I can trip and fall under Themis'. I implore the protection of a man whose life and fortune I once saved; I dare expect gratitude from him, he lures me to his house, he submits me to horrors, and there I find the iniquitous judge upon whom my case depends; both abuse me, both outrage me, both accelerate my doom; fortune overwhelms them with favors, I hasten on to death.

What fleshes out her history of course are the elaborately detailed pornographic descriptions of abuse to which she is put. We shall come back to that as we look into the tragic ethos of *Justine*.

The narrative structure of the novel introduces two sisters, Justine and Juliette, who are at an early age bereft of family and economic means of survival. Justine is a "virtuous" girl of sensibility and delicacy. Juliette is a pragmatist. She suggests that, being young and pretty, they make their way through the expedient of marketing their only commodities. Justine naturally declines so indelicate a life. They go their separate ways. Juliette, augmenting youth and beauty with guile, murder, and libertinage, makes her way handsomely, becoming a rich and powerful Lady. Justine, augmenting delicacy with innocence and good will, undergoes the horrors summarized above. When next the two meet—the occasion of Justine's narrative—Justine is on her way to execution, Juliette is lounging through the countryside. They meet, Justine tells her story, is recognized as the long-separated sister, her pardon is secured through Juliette's influence, and she retires to Juliette's country estate, where, what else, she is struck by lightening (". . . the lightning entered her right breast, found the heart, and after having consumed her chest

141

and face, burst out through her belly. The miserable thing was hideous to look upon . . ."). Juliette is moved by this "appalling stroke" to forfeit her fortune and become a Carmelite nun. The novel ends with a conventionally cursory (but significant) overture to "Providence": "May you be convinced with [Juliette], that true happiness is to be found nowhere but in Virtue's womb, and that if, in keeping with designs it is not for us to fathom, God permits that it be persecuted on Earth, it is so that Virtue may be compensated by Heaven's most dazzling rewards."

Such is the history of Justine. The "moral" of virtue's misfortunes is that it had best be its own reward and compensated hereafter, because on earth, that is, in the life of man, its value is problematic. Systematically, as Justine's summary suggests, virtue is corrupted or destroyed while vice marches prosperously on. That is the ethical dialectic of the novel. But its tragic ethos is far more sophisticated than that simplistic opposition. For the novel's moral vitality exists in the symbolic action of its pornography. The sentimental ethos which its use of the sentimental tragedy format invokes becomes the foil in which the naturalistic diamond is set. Richardson's straight use of the form was to reinforce belief in the idealistic sentimental mythos—that virtue is real, vice a sensual chimera. De Sade demonstrates, through the pornographically vivid imagery of sensuality, that vice is also *real,* more real in the workings of the world than virtue. And he who would deduce the "rules of conduct" by which man may realistically proceed along life's way—he, that is, who would construct a true ethos—had best know this. Virtue, by which de Sade designates the mythos of sentimentality, must be left to heaven. What man *can* know, though it is obscured to him by his desire for heaven, is nature. And if his ethos is to reflect *nature's* justice, rather than his sentimental myth of it, that ethos must be responsive to man's full complexity of motives rather than his sentimental evasion of them—his sublimation of human nature to a mythically configured moral idealism.

142

On earth, in the life we know as men, misfortune has authenticity. Like pain and pleasure its reality can be *felt*. Pathos is *real,* not the transcendental sign of a better life to come. The sentimental artist invokes vicarious emotions. When, for example, Richardson describes Clarissa's rape, the description is decorous, mythic; one's response therefore is removed to the level of impersonality. We have an analogous fear, which is to say that we can imagine what such a scene *would be like*. But de Sade wants his audience to experience *real* feelings, not analogous, artistic ones. The pathos of Justine's life is merely philosophical; it tells us something about the abstract relation of man to nature. It takes on human meaning—has, that is, the shock of recognition—only when it is experienced in the context of authentic feeling, the *revulsion* and *desire* one authentically *feels* in confronting de Sade's descriptions of sexual abuse:

I remove my mistress' simar, and when she was naked conducted her to her husband who had already taken his place in a large armchair: as part of the ritual she perched upon this armchair and herself presented to his kisses that favorite part over which he had made such a to-do with me and which, regardless of person or sex, seemed to affect him in the same way.

"And now spread them, Madame," the Count said brutally.

And for a long time he rollicked about with what he enjoyed the sight of; he had it assume various positions, he opened it, he snapped it shut; with tongue and fingertip he tickled the narrow aperture; and soon carried away by his passions' ferocity, he plucked up a pinch of flesh, squeezed it, scratched it. Immediately he produced a small wound he fastened his mouth to the spot. I held his unhappy victim during these preliminaries, the two boys, completely naked, toiled upon him in relays; now one, now the other knelt between Gernande's thighs and employed his mouth to excite him. It was then I noticed, not without astonishment, that this giant, this species of monster whose aspect alone was enough to strike terror, was howbeit barely a man; the most meager, the most minuscule excrescence of flesh or, to make a juster comparison, what one might find in a child of three was all one discovered upon this so very enormous and otherwise so corpulent individual; but its sensations were not for that the

143

less keen and each pleasurable vibration was as a spasmodic attack. After this prologue he stretched out upon a couch and wanted his wife, seated astride his chest, to keep him, by means of suckings, the same service he had just received from the youthful Ganymedes who were simultaneously, one to the left, one to the right, being excited by him; my hands meanwhile worked upon his behind: I titillated it, I polluted it in every sense; this phase of activities lasted more than a quarter of an hour but, producing no results, had to be given up for another; upon her husband's instructions I stretched the Countess upon a chaise longue: she lay on her back, her legs spread as wide as possible. The sight of what she exposed put her husband in a kind of rage, he dwelt upon the perspective . . . his eyes blaze, he curses; like one crazed he leaps upon his wife, with his scalpel pricks her in several places, but these were all superficial gashes, a drop or two of blood, no more, seeped from each. These minor cruelties came to an end at last; others began.

He seizes her ferociously, places her as I was placed, arms suspended by two black straps; mine is the task of securing the bands; he inspects the knots: finding them too loose, he tightens them, "So that," he says, "the blood will spurt out under greater pressure"; he feels the veins, and lances them, on each arm, at almost the same moment. Blood leaps far: he is in an ecstacy; and adjusting himself so that he has a clear view of these two fountains, he has me kneel between his legs so I can suck him; he does as much for first one and then the other of his little friends, incessantly eyeing the jets of blood which inflame him. For my part, certain the instant at which the hoped for crisis occurs will bring a conclusion to the Countess' torments, I bring all my efforts to bear upon precipitating this *dénouement,* and I become, as, Madame, you observe, I become a whore from kindness, a libertine through virtue. The much awaited moment arrives at last; I am not familiar with its dangers or violence, for the last time it had taken place I had been unconscious. . . . Oh, Madame! what extravagance! Gernande remained delirious for ten minutes, flailing his arms, staggering, reeling like one falling in a fit of epilepsy, and uttering screams which must have been audible for a league around; his oaths were excessive; lashing out at everyone at hand, his strugglings were dreadful. The two little ones are sent tumbling head over heels; he wishes to fly at his wife, I restrain him: I pump the last drop from him, his need of me makes him respect me; at last I bring him to his senses by ridding him of that fiery

liquid, whose heat, whose viscosity, and above all whose abundance puts him in such a frenzy I believe he is going to expire; seven or eight tablespoons would scarcely have contained the discharge, and the thickest gruel would hardly give a notion of its consistency. . . .
[*Justine*]

MADAME DE MISTIVAL, *screaming like a banshee*—Aïë! aïë! aïë!

DOLMANCÉ, *driving the needle deep into her flesh*—Silence, bitch! or I'll make a hash of your buttocks. . . . Eugénie, frig me . . .

EUGÉNIE—Willingly, but upon condition you prick her more energetically, for, you must admit, you are proceeding with strange forbearance. (*She frigs him.*)

MADAME DE SAINT-ANGE—Work upon those two great cheeks for me!

DOLMANCÉ—Patience, I'll soon have her carved like a shank of beef; Eugénie, you are forgetting your lessons: you capped my prick!

EUGÉNIE—'Tis because this bitch's sufferings are inflaming my imagination to the point I no longer know exactly what I am doing.

DOLMANCÉ—Sweet fucking God! I'm beginning to go out of my mind! Saint-Ange, have Augustin bugger you in front of my eyes while your brother flies into your cunt, and above all dress me a panorama of asses: the picture will finish me. (*He stabs Madame de Mistival's buttocks while the posture he has called for is arranged.*) Here, Mamma dear, take this . . . and again that! '. . . (*He drives his needle into at least twenty places.*)

MADAME DE MISTIVAL—Oh pardon me, Monsieur, I beg your pardon a thousand times over . . . you are killing me . . .

DOLMANCÉ, *wild with pleasure*—I should like to . . . 'tis an age since I have had such an erection; never would I have thought it possible after so many consecutive ejaculations.

MADAME DE SAINT-ANGE, *executing the called-for attitude*—Are we as we should be, Dolmancé?

DOLMANCÉ—Augustin, turn a little to the right; I don't see enough ass; have him lean forward: I must see the hole.

EUGÉNIE—Ah fuck! look at the bugger bleed!

DOLMANCÉ—Rather a good deal of blood, isn't there? Well, are the rest of you ready? As for myself, one minute more and I'll spray life's very balm upon the wounds I have just opened.

MADAME DE SAINT-ANGE—Yes, my heart, yes . . . I am coming . . . we arrive at the end at the same time . . .

145

DOLMANCÉ, *who has finished his task, does nothing but increase his stabbing of the victim's buttocks as he discharges*—Ah triple bloody fucking God! . . . my sperm flows . . . 'tis lost, by bleeding little Jesus! . . . Eugénie, direct it upon the flanks I have just mutilated . . . oh fuck! fuck! 'tis done . . . over . . . I've no more . . . oh, why must weakness succeed passions so alive? . . . MADAME DE SAINT-ANGE—Fuck! fuck me, brother, I discharge! . . . (*To Augustin:*) Stir yourself, great fucking-john! Don't you know that it is when I come that you've got to sink your tool deepest into my ass? . . . Ah, sacred name of God! how sweet it is, thus to be fucked by two men . . . (*The group disperses.*) [*Philosophy in the Bedroom*]

He is bound hand and foot, as if he were a wild beast and he is dressed in a tiger's skin. When thus readied, he is excited, irritated, whipped, beaten, his ass is frigged; opposite him is a plump young girl, nude and tied by her feet to the floor, by her neck to the ceiling, in such a manner she cannot stir. When the roué is all asweat, his captors free him, he leaps upon the girl, bites her everywhere and above all her clitoris and her nipples which, usually he manages to remove with his teeth. He roars and cries like a ferocious animal, and discharges while shrieking. The girl must shit, he eats her turd upon the floor. [*The One Hundred Twenty Days of Sodom*]

An artist, like Richardson, would manipulate our feelings, that we might have them more piquantly. Clarissa's rape is elaborately prepared for, and happens more in the anticipation than in the event. She herself is drugged and *feels* nothing. And when she dies, she dies of so abstract a thing as *shame*. But de Sade is not really interested in art or exquisitely conceived emotions. He wants a thump in the gut. Revulsion and desire. He wants us to *feel* those passions that make life tragic. If we will not be revolted at the perhaps subliminal knowledge we have of viciousness in our daily conduct—as he knows we will not be, having practiced and disguised it for so long we are blind to it—maybe we will be revolted at his pornographic descriptions, and if not at those then he will so describe them that we will be sexually aroused. If we are able to suppress that, we must certainly be revolted at the desire we have had to suppress. Or, at their brutality, we will feel fear. We will, by God, feel something. And in the feeling know those passions which motivate men in the conduct of their tragic lives.

This is why pornography is so crucial to de Sade's tragic vision. He not only had a spontaneous kinship with it, but pornographic rhetoric was, he knew, the one kind capable of generating a *real* effect. And it was the one kind of rhetoric able to elicit both revulsion and desire, the precise passions upon which de Sade's tragic ethos turns. Father Clement, one of Justine's persecutors (de Sade seems to have stamped the idea of the debauched priest indelibly into pornographic convention), after a prolonged flagellation scene (". . . the whip's long and supple strands, penetrating [the vagina] with much more facility than could withes or ferules, leave deep traces of his rage . . . his eyes glitter, foam flecks his lips . . . the villain brings us to blood . . . the blows are redoubled: the unhappy Armande receives one upon the breast which staggers her, this last horror determines his ecstasy. . . ."), the foam-flecked priest tells Justine:

> . . . one never tires of this mania notwithstanding the fact it is a very pale image of what one should really like to do; ah, dear girl! you have no idea to what lengths this depravity leads us, you cannot imagine the drunkenness into which it plunges us, the violent commotion in the electrical fluid which results from the irritation produced by the suffering of the object that serves our passions; how one is needled by its agonies! The desire to increase them . . . 'tis, I know, the reef upon which the fantasy is doomed to wreck, but is this peril to be dreaded by him who cares not a damn for anything?

Clement, like all of de Sade's spokesmen for perversity, may be hyperbolic in fictive representation (de Sade's conclusion apologizes for the "perhaps too heavy brushstrokes" in his portrayal of life), but he argues a truth that subsequent psychology has demonstrated about all human nature, a truth that explains the orgies of the Roman Coliseum, the French Terror, the Nazi experiments, the Japanese atrocities in the Philippines, the American festival at My Lai, not to mention the civilization-long history of pornography itself. Practiced to the extremes of de Sade's characters, or perhaps in de Sade's own life, sadism is doubtless a derangement, but referred to its power in man's imagination Clement's perception is unerring. Nor, as de Sade knew, is it buried in the "normal" imagination. Its normal manifestation is in such social institutions as the public execution, reaching a maniacal pitch in the Terror, repeating itself at Buchenwald, the search and destroy missions in Vietnam, on and on. One never tires of this mania notwithstanding the fact that it is a very pale image of what one should really like to do. Pain, pleasure, and sex. De Sade knew the myth of animality well. He knew how it *felt,* boiling as it was within him. He saw others feeling it, acting on it, and denying it—with myths of sentimentality, idealism, civilization, what have you. And he wanted to confront man with an image of himself that could not fail to revolt him, and in the very revulsion arouse his desire. He wanted man to see himself face to face.

This is not a sick vision of man. It is rather a vision of man's sickness. But normal enough for all of that, as Freud later saw. And natural; Clement goes on:

Will it never be understood that there is no variety of taste, however bizarre, however outlandish, however criminal it may be supposed, which does not derive directly from and depend upon the kind of organization we have individually received from Nature? . . . Have we the power to remake ourselves? Can we become other than what we are? Would you demand the same thing from some one born a cripple? and is this inconformity of our tastes anything in the moral sphere but what the ill-made man's imperfection is in the physical?

All men, thus, are crippled, restricted in their movements by the range of their imaginations. Man's desire, his passion, to move beyond that range is what makes for tragedy. That, and his passion to assert *that* and *what* he is. This tragic rhythm is nature's basic motif. The dynamics of this condition are the movements by which man's tragic life is defined. De Sade's vision is the vision of one of the few men in literary history who have actually *believed* in tragedy as the truest statement of human life. The state of nature, for him, is a state of tragedy, filled with pain and ending indifferently in destruction. And the tragedy is compounded by man's pleasure in pain and destruction, making them all the more inescapable. We aspire to them, both the giving and the getting. We nurture them, as Clement says, in our fantasies, even though the fantasies themselves are doomed, incapable of their own realization, spurring us on to further rhythms of pain and pleasure. The mind is indeed its own place and, as de Sade knew, it controls us. Our tragedy is its power.

The ethos of such a vision, a vision of absolute tragedy, cannot be transcendental. We cannot be relieved of what is inescapable. The act of love, says the saint, is on the arm. Indeed, all acts are on the arm. Man became man when he was made flesh. Before that he was an idea. The mind then can act only through the flesh. The body, for man, is inescapable. Thus de Sade, like all morally serious pornographers, makes the flesh the figural sign of the tragic rhythms of pain and pleasure. Thus, too, the flesh symbolizes the spirit. As the flesh is raped, tortured, destroyed, so symbolically is the human spirit. Clement, one of de Sade's most profound fictive spokesmen, is not accidentally a wolf in shepherd's clothing. False priest that he is, he is the answer to his own question, have we the power to remake ourselves. The answer is no, and so to survive man disguises himself, assuming the signs of Virtue to mask the workings of Vice. For the idealistic "prejudices" of human morality preclude an honest representation of human nature. Given the choice of criminality or hypocrisy, men will naturally choose hypocrisy. Hypocrisy, therefore, is the gearwheel of social action in de Sade's vision. Society, like Clement, masks its true nature behind the formal guise of Virtue, constructing false values and institutions designed to perpetuate the hypocrisy and thus keep man's true nature underground. When it pops up, as it persists in doing, it is simply rendered criminal by virtue of its honesty. Society, like Clement, keeps the sacrament of Hypocrisy, and thereby the human spirit is defiled. How figuratively appropriate to such a theme that Justine's flesh should systematically be defiled by the priest

149

and his social analogues—the aristocrats, the shopkeepers, the doctors, the judges—the good citizens. Social prejudice and superstition, the bases of the myth of sentimentality, are, in de Sade's vision, defilements of nature. And that relationship can best be articulated in the pornographic depiction of innocence debased by the canny guardians of hypocrisy.

Hypocrisy is of course rooted in egoism. And egoism is the root of de Sade's theory of man, and as well of his pornographic representation of human nature. Clement observes that "If egoism is Nature's fundamental commandment, it is very surely most of all during our lubricous delights that this celestial Mother desires us to be most absolutely under its rule." Pleasure, then, takes one into the self and its intensity corresponds proportionally to the degree that nothing interferes with selfishness. Somebody else's pleasure, that of the sex partner, is an interference and diminishes one's own. Therefore it is expendable. Indeed, Clement continues, somebody else's pain may heighten one's own sense of pleasure, and he proposes therefore an ethic of pain and cruelty to restore a natural balance upset by the myth of sentimentality:

. . . the more the deed seems appalling to us, the more it is in contradiction with our manners and customs, the more it runs headlong against restraints and shatters them, the more it conflicts with social conventions and affronts them, the more it clashes with what we mistake for Nature's laws, then the more, on the contrary, it is useful to the same Nature. It is never but by way of crimes that she regains possession of the rights Virtue incessantly steals away from her.

Again, we must remember to interpret Clement, as we must interpret all de Sade's spokesmen for perversity, in the fictive context of symbolic hyperbole where he lives. De Sade did not expect that his audience would conclude, with Clement, that "the vaster the crime, the better it will serve Nature." Clement's ethic, after all, *is* perverse. And de Sade did not intend to argue that perversity is *good,* only that it *is.* At another point, for example, Clement observes, by way of a Sadean modification, that "The man endowed with uncommon tastes is

150

sick." The ethic of cruelty is not an ethic to be emulated; but it is an ethic that the world knows and uses, and it indisputably exists in nature. It articulates nature's tragic rhythms: witness Oedipus and his "complex." Justine says of the man who subscribes to such an ethic, "But the man you describe is a monster." Clement replies, "The man I describe is in tune with Nature." Justine's response is more ironic than she knows, "He is a savage beast." Yes, Clement allows, savagery is elemental to nature. Say what you will, says Justine, "I shall never accept this destructive lubricity." "Because," says Clement, "you are afraid of becoming its object—there you have it: egoism." And, of course, for de Sade's dialectical purposes, he has her. Characteristically, an ethic is the product of one's desires and fears. An ethic of abstinence, then, such as a fundamentalist Christian ethic, is not necessarily or naturally better than an ethic of indulgence. It is the product of weakness, the inability to indulge. Here is Clement's explanation of Christian ethics:

The doctrine of brotherly love is a fiction we owe to Christianity and not to Nature; the exponent of the Nazarene's cult, tormented, wretched and consequently in an enfeebled state which prompted him to cry out for tolerance and compassion, had no choice but to allege this fabulous relationship between one person and another; by gaining acceptance for the notion he was able to save his life.

Even docility, then, has its naturalistic cause, egoistic fear. But, of course, Clement's arguments are, as we have noted, purposely exaggerated to emphasize the naturalistic basis of even the most exalted idealism. What de Sade is after here, as elsewhere, is the recognition that an ethos not rooted in nature, and not taking account of those passions that are undeniably in nature, must be false and designed to serve, again, the social sacrament of hypocrisy.

But the flesh is inescapable. The starting point of all sensation, the proof that man is alive. And de Sade of all men knew man's need to *feel* alive. Moreover, he knew that if man did not feel, he was dead, ambulatory but decaying matter. Zom-

151

bies with political power are dangerous, for their moral imaginations are unreal; dissociated from sensation, they administer pain and death abstractly, under the guise of political, or social, or some kind of chimerical *necessity*. Zombies with political power are dehumanized, and so are the institutions they conceive and administer. De Sade saw it in the Terror, and he resigned his role in the revolution, at considerable risk to his own life, because he would not do what was "inhumane" —kill human beings in cold blood. A rational modification of the demonic hyperbole of de Sade's ethos of pain and pleasure (which is what de Sade expected of his readers, knowing, as he said, that few of them would manage it) tells us not only that pain and destruction are tragically inevitable facts of life, but that pleasure and temporal happiness are also possible. *If* we honor the flesh. If we honor its sensations for what they are, an index of man's capacity for life. Clement offers a demonically brilliant exegesis of this capacity:

Voluptuous emotion is nothing but a kind of vibration produced in our soul by shocks which the imagination, inflamed by the remembrance of a lubricious object, registers upon our senses, either through this object's presence, or better still by this object's being exposed to that particular kind of irritation which most profoundly stirs us; thus, our voluptuous transport—this indescribable convulsive needling which drives us wild, which lifts us to the highest pitch of happiness at which man is able to arrive—is never ignited save by two causes: either by the perception in the object we use of a real or imaginary beauty, the beauty in which we delight the most, or by the sight of that object undergoing the strongest possible sensation: now, there is no more lively sensation than that of pain; its impressions are certain and dependable, they never deceive as may those of the pleasure women perpetually feign and almost never experience; and, furthermore, how much self-confidence, youth, vigor, health are not needed in order to be sure of producing this dubious and hardly very satisfying impression of pleasure in a woman. To produce the painful impression, on the contrary, requires no virtues at all: the more defects a man may have, the older he is, the less lovable, the more resounding his success. With what regards the objective, it will be far more certainly attained since we are establishing the fact that one never better touches, I wish to say, that one never better irritates one's senses than when the greatest possible impression has been produced in the employed object, by no matter what devices; therefore, he who will cause the most tumultuous impression to be born in a woman, he who will most thoroughly convulse this woman's entire frame, very decidedly will have managed to procure himself the heaviest possible dose of voluptuousness, because the shock resultant upon us by the impressions others experience, which shock in turn is necessitated by the impression we have of those others, will necessarily be more vigorous if the impression these others receive be painful, than if the impression they receive be sweet and mild; and it follows that the voluptuous egoist, who is persuaded his pleasures will be keen only insofar as they are entire, will therefore impose, when he has it in his power to do so, the strongest possible dose of pain upon the employed object, fully certain that what by way of voluptuous pleasure he extracts will be his only by dint of the very lively impression he has produced.

We must read this, of course, with an eye to de Sade's dialectical determination to make the worse appear the better cause, to the end of forcing men simply to recognize its reality, its power in the lives of men. Clement is not only a fictive example of social hypocrisy, he represents also the desperation of man to feel alive within the confines of moral prejudice. Like nearly all of de Sade's pornographic "heroes," Clement is *impotent* without the application of gross and violent stimulants. Having been cut off from sensation by its suppression in moral idealism, it can only be realized through the excessive modes of "irritation" that de Sade so tirelessly invents and describes.

Assuming, like Clement, the mantle of Virtue, the social animal becomes increasingly social and decreasingly animal. He becomes, in other words, an abstraction defined by the context in which he lives rather than what is intrinsically his, passion. Soon the guise becomes second nature, satisfying his political needs perhaps but violating psychic ones in the process, obscuring and suppressing the animal dimension of human nature. But the body is inescapable. Man's animal nature, willy-nilly, manifests itself. The more it is suppressed the

153

more devious it becomes. It wages a guerrilla war with his public sentimental nature. Rendered impotent, threatened with extinction, it slashes out in a desperate and devious fury, asserting its life violently because it is left no other means. Having been outlawed, it plays the outlaw's role. But, being animal, it will have its pleasure. And the sign of pleasure, like that of love, is on the arm. Animal vitality, then, the reassurance that man is man and not an idea, asserts itself through voluptuousness, the pleasure of the body, "the strongest possible sensation." Thus, again, since "one never better irritates one's senses than when the greatest possible impression has been produced. . . , he who will most thoroughly convulse this woman's entire frame, very decidedly will have managed to procure himself the heaviest possible dose of voluptuousness." And because woman's pleasure, still more than man's, has been vitiated by the sentimentalities of Virtue, because women more even than men have been superstitiously dissociated from their bodies, the agency of convulsion, perversely, is pain. Thus the ethic of cruelty, at once hyperbole and truth. It is the truth that de Sade indefatigably expounds, the terrible, tragic, insatiable human rhythm of pleasure and pain.

Pornography, then, the hyperbolic representation of the pleasure-pain syndrome in the sexual life of man, is de Sade's rhetoric of naturalism. It represents the entrapment of man inside his skin and the volcano of his fevered brain. But it is more than rhetoric, too; for the rhetoric is itself an assault on the sensibilities of the audience, a symbolic confrontation between de Sade and his fellow man. "I am about to put forward some major ideas," de Sade says in "Yet Another Effort, Frenchman, if You Would Become Republicans." "If not all of them please, surely a few will; in some sort, then, I shall have contributed to the progress of our age, and shall be content." This parenthetical essay in *Philosophy in the Bedroom* presents de Sade's political naturalism. He presents here, with clear self-consciousness and social purpose, the metaphysics of republicanism, in which form of government he thought personal freedom and idiosyncracy would be maximal. But even here, in direct philosophical disquisition, he wanted his argument bracketed by pornographic authenticity, the reality of the senses substantiating abstract ideas. "Yet Another Effort" articulates the necessity of republicanism to extend the revolution to religion and manners, but, again not accidentally, it is presented in the middle of a dialogue pornographically attacking chastity, simple heterosexuality, and motherhood. It ends with the debauched "ingenue" professing hatred for her mother, assisting at her torture and sodomization, and sewing up her mother's vagina, "so that you'll give me no more little brothers and sisters." The hyperbolic ethic of cruelty. Here again is de Sade's demonic dialectic at work, not simply informing or persuading but assaulting his audience. And the self-consciously fluid juxtaposition of rhetorical and real arguments: "If not all of them please, surely a few will."

De Sade knew how little his pornographic naturalism would please, and that was its utility. For he wanted to "convulse" *society's* "entire frame." Perhaps he was serving his own voluptuousness, but we need not grudge a man his pleasures. Especially when his larger purposes and his vision are so astute, so precociously committed to a finally healthy evolution of morality and manners.

In this age, when we are convinced that morals must be the basis of religion, and not religion of morals, we need a body of beliefs in keeping with our customs and habits, something that would be their necessary consequence, and that could, by lifting up the spirit, maintain it perpetually at the high level of this precious liberty, which today the spirit has made its unique idol.

He is speaking to the French Revolution, at once the greatest and most terrifying in history. De Sade knew its terror firsthand. But he also knew its greatness, its humanistic spirit. He saw the revolution as one of the great cyclic events in the establishment of natural justice, the rhythmic recurrence of the "have nots" wrenching power and authority from the "haves." And, as with the sensual body so with the body politic, the agency of convulsion is pain, the shock of recognition. Spirit,

155

for de Sade, was not a mystical infusion. It was the manifestation of the strongest of passions, the desire for personal liberty. Thus his pornographic analogy between the body personal and the body politic. Religion, because it institutionalizes the idols of superstition and prejudice that paralyze man's mind and body, was de Sade's primary enemy; he warns the revolution that if it does not solidify its work by abolishing religion:

Before ten years are out—utilizing the Christian religion, its superstitions, its prejudices—your priests, their pledges notwithstanding and though despoiled of their riches, are sure to reassert their empire over the souls they shall have undermined and captured; they shall restore the monarchy, because the power of kings has always reinforced that of the church; and your republican edifice, its foundations eaten away, shall collapse. . . .

Be persuaded that . . . people, a good deal wiser than you suppose them, once rid of tyranny's irons, will soon also be rid of superstition's. You are afraid of the people unrestrained—how ridiculous! Ah, believe me, citizens, the man not to be checked by the material sword of justice will hardly be halted by the moral fear of hell's torments, at which he has laughed since childhood; in a word, many crimes have been committed as a consequence of your theism, but never has it prevented a single one.

The people unrestrained: responsive to the rhythms of their bodies, the rhythms of nature, that is the positive dimension of de Sade's political and moral ethos. It will not preclude man's tragic nature, but it will maximize the pleasure and temporal happiness that are available to man. And he was wise enough to know the need, given human savagery, for education:

Frenchmen, only strike the initial blows; your State education will then see to the rest. Get promptly to the task of training the youth, it must be amongst your most important concerns; *above all, build their education upon a sound ethical basis,* the ethical basis that was so neglected in your religious education. Rather than fatigue your children's young organs with deific stupidities, replace them with excellent social principles; instead of teaching them futile prayers which, by the time they are sixteen, they will glory in having forgotten, let them be instructed in their duties toward society; train

156

them to cherish the virtues you scarcely ever mentioned in former times and which, without your religious fables, are sufficient for their individual happiness; make them sense that this happiness consists in rendering others as fortunate as we desire to be ourselves. If you repose these truths upon Christian chimeras, as you so foolishly used to do, scarcely will your pupils have detected the absurd futility of its foundations than they will overthrow the entire edifice, and they will become bandits for the simple reason they believe the religion they have toppled forbids them to be bandits. On the other hand, if you make them sense the necessity of virtue, uniquely because their happiness depends upon it, egoism will turn them into honest people, and this law which dictates their behavior to men will always be the surest, the soundest of all.

De Sade at his best, at his least bedeviled, knew the revolutionary need for construction. And he had, at his best, a humanistic faith in man's capacity to achieve at least so much happiness as is available to him. And he knew, for better or worse, that the body is inescapable. And he knew that a true ethos would have to account for its rhythms—its desire for pain and pleasure, its desire for liberty, its desire to feel its own vitality.

Nor, regardless of his rhetorical ethic of cruelty, did he contradict the principle of maximal freedom even when it came to enforcing the abolition of religion:

I do not, however, propose either massacres or expulsions. Such dreadful things have no place in the enlightened mind. No, do not assassinate at all, do not expel at all; these are royal atrocities, or the brigands' who imitate kings; it is not at all by acting as they that you will force men to look with horror upon them who practiced those crimes. Let us reserve the employment of force for the idols; ridicule alone will suffice for those who serve them: Julian's sarcasm wrought greater damage to Christianity than all Nero's tortures.

Liberty, political and moral liberty, is de Sade's theme. Liberty rooted in a naturalistic ethic. Thus libertinage, a freely pornographic life style, is his symbol of the free life. It is, as he acknowledges, an exaggerated statement. But he knew to whom he was talking, and that they were few and perhaps some way off in time. He knew he must be misunderstood, that his vision authentically presented would have to be incomprehensible to minds molded by the very sentimentality he refuted:

. . . let no one say that by my writings I seek to blunt the remorse in evildoers' hearts, that my humane ethics are wicked because they augment those same evildoers' penchant for crime. I wish formally to certify here and now, that I have none of these perverse intentions; I set forth the ideas which since the age when I first began to reason, have identified themselves in me, and to whose expression and realization the infamous despotism of tyrants has been opposed for uncounted centuries. . . . I address myself only to people capable of hearing me out, and they will read me without any danger.

De Sade knew that somewhere, sometime there was an audience capable of handling his extravagantly obscene manner. And he knew that that audience would be able to assimilate his vision and give it its proper relation to that progress of enlightenment to which he so feverishly wanted to contribute.

His philosophical, logical, and stylistic lapses result from his furious need, in prison, to write and exorcise the fantasies his sensual deprivation manufactured in his brain. They are nonetheless faults. His fury diminished his art, but it also made possible the writing out of his vision. De Sade's faulty work exhibits the difficulty of articulating the mythos of animality. No pornography before or since has had his significance or vitality because no serious writer has worked so exclusively in the genre. Perhaps one needs to be as possessed as de Sade was to do it. Or as persecuted. If mad Ireland hurt Yeats into poetry, surely mad humanity hurt de Sade into pornography. In spite of the infamy of his life, as Simone de Beauvoir suggests, de Sade's Humbertian eroticism reached its truest dimension in literature. In life it was merely criminal. His vision fastened on the fundamental inconsistency in the morality of western culture—that economic rape is legal while sexual rape is not. De Sade simply raped the logic of that fact and forced the dialectic to its logical conclusion, one way or the other.

De Sade's own mythic battle with the forces of civilization

recalls the mythic battle between the Titans and the new Greek gods. The old gods, Prometheus for example, showed man how to use the powers of nature, as Prometheus gave him the gift of fire. The new gods, for example Apollo, the god of wisdom, introduced spiritual values to man. As the new subdued the old, spirituality prevailed over nature. De Sade is a parable of the old gods; in him the natural powers raise their heads again, and find their celebrant. In this parable de Sade saw that the new gods—and their analogue, the Judeo-Christian God—had gone berserk. In their zeal to bring man the benefits of the new message they suppressed his ineluctable animal origins, the natural roots from which his detachment is fatal. So, in his pornographic mythos of animality, de Sade reminded man of the inescapable facts of his nature. He reminded man that the old gods may be subdued but not destroyed. De Sade's pornography tells us that the old gods live and that, however much they be forced underground, they have powerful sway still in the life of man.

6.

Pornography and Moral Anarchy

In raising the spectre of the mythic battle between the old and the new gods, de Sade invokes the concomitant spirit of moral anarchy—the humanistic equivalent of both natural and religious rhythms of death and resurrection. Moral anarchy means simply the denial of any univocal ethical authority, and it follows quite logically from a naturalistic ethos, especially as represented in the aesthetic of pornography for which de Sade is paradigm. Anarchy in this sense, then, is positive, depending not only on a sustained interrogation of moral assumptions but also on the capacity of the human mind to progressively reintegrate itself in the face of continuously expanding knowledge of nature and the resulting moral ambiguity. In this sense de Sade saw the French Revolution as a naturally anarchical event at once destroying an anachronistic order and preparing for the birth of a new one. His arguments against religion and conventional morality in *Philosophy in the Bedroom* show his awareness that the Revolution in his time was dilemmatically strung out between the monolithic morality represented by the church, on the one hand, and the relativistic subjective ethos of naturalism, on the other. He was rightly afraid that this unresolved antagonism would vitiate the positive possibilities of moral anarchy by a mindlessly confused focus on revolutionary destruction. The murderous destructiveness of the Terror confirmed his fear. Consequently he urged, as we have seen, the Revolution to complete the cycle it had begun by recognizing

160

the constructive anarchy implicit in a thoroughly naturalistic ethos.

Though de Sade's own ideas on this are not sufficiently systematic or complete to make it clear, his choice of a pornographic dialectic to illustrate the constructiveness of moral anarchy is not without religious and symbolic support. To see this we may refer briefly to the sacred orgiastic traditions modern anthropologists have discovered to be endemic in both primitive and civilized societies. De Sade's own use of the orgy, most elaborately sustained in his *120 Days of Sodom,* is of course vehemently profane. But his conception of the orgy derives, nevertheless, from the sacred communal sexuality of agricultural societies. And there is of course a tendency of the sacred orgiastic rituals to profane themselves as time and cultural evolution dissociate them from their religious origins. But, sacred or profane, the orgiastic tradition is rooted in the anarchic impulse to destroy the old to make way for the new.

The orgy seems to have originated as part of what Mircea Eliade calls, in *Patterns in Comparative Religion,* the "seasonal ritual drama" of fertility:

Unbounded sexual frenzy on earth corresponds to the union of the divine couple. As young couples re-enact that sacred marriage on the ploughed fields, all the forces of the community are supposed to increase to their highest point. . . . Men cannot do better than imitate the example of the gods, particularly if the prosperity of the whole world and, above all, the course of animal and vegetable life, depends on their doing so. Their excesses fulfil a definite and useful role in the economy of the sacred. They break down the barriers between man, society, nature and the gods; they help force, life and the seeds of things to move from one level to another, from one zone of reality to the rest. What was emptied of substance is replenished; what was shattered into fragments becomes one again; what was in isolation merges into the great womb of all things. The orgy sets flowing the sacred energy of life.

The orgiastic impulse, then, is clearly religious, symbolically serving to bring man, natural powers, and the cosmos into the harmony necessary for the preservation of life. The orgy is at

161

once agricultural and mythic, inducing not only productive and reproductive generation but also a unity of human spirit. On the human level the orgy is magic, a talismanic metaphysics, a symbolic synthesis of the mythos of animality and the mythos of love. In the orgy man is his own husbandman; he recognizes the natural analogy between himself and his crops, his flocks. He augments his animal state with spiritual hope and recognition of forces larger than himself, to which he is subject. And the orgy signifies that he knows these forces are simultaneously within him and without, psychic and cosmic. The orgy therefore serves to unify man with himself by unifying him with natural rhythms. Significantly, man sees in the orgy a more comprehensive morality than his quotidian ethic permits; so, in honor of that higher morality, and to remind himself of his ultimate responsibility to it, the orgy is the ritual drama through which he violates his petty ethic in order to harmonize with the cosmos. Eliade observes of the *Holi* Indian vegetation rites that "All decency was forgotten, for the matter was far more serious than mere respect for norms and customs; it was a question of ensuring that life should go on." The celebrants, men and children, paraded through the streets, and when they saw a woman, either on the street or through a window, "tradition required them to hurl the most appalling obscenities and insults." It is of course this verbal aspect of the orgiastic ritual drama that is of particular interest to the cultural meaning of pornography, and we shall get back to it.

Orgiastic regeneration also had a specifically social dimension. Eliade comments that not only is the orgy important to agricultural mystique but that it is also "a way of expressing the life of the community as a whole." He cites the orgiastic rationale of an Indian sect, that through the year men and women accumulated and harbored vicious impulses and the orgy satisfied these and so served the equilibrium of community life. Thus, again, the quotidian ethic, usually reflected in civil laws, is violated with cultural sanction in order to harmonize with the higher natural law. In such situations animality, by virtue of social acknowledgement, is harnessed

162

to serve rather than bedevil the individual and society. Scholars of such divergent interests as J. J. Meyer, a cultural anthropologist, and E. K. Chambers, a literary historian, have observed the pagan new year saturnalias common in medieval European churches, and which survive still in some places. Though the Church naturally tried to suppress these practices, they tended rather to be absorbed into Christian new year celebrations, where they survive now in such muted forms as mummers and the like. But in their early orgiastic vitality these traditions were anarchical, reversing the order of things, reversing normative relations—both in sexual behavior, where debauch became the norm, and in administrative hierarchy, where custodians became priests and priests custodians, and so on—to the end of regenerating community life. Thus the cycles of community life were regarded as analogues to those of natural life. Eliade sums up the intent of the sacred communal orgy thus:

Like seeds that lose their shape in the great underground merging, disintegrating and becoming something different (germination), so men lose their individuality in the orgy, combining into a single living unity. They effect thus a total fusion of emotions in which neither "form" nor "law" is observed. . . . And further, by bringing back the mythical chaos that existed before the creation, the orgy makes it possible for creation to be repeated. For a time man goes back to the amorphous, nocturnal state of chaos that he may be reborn, more vigorous than ever in his daylight self. Like immersion in water, the orgy destroys creation while at the same time regenerating it; man hopes, by identifying himself with formless, pre-cosmic existence, to return to himself restored and regenerated, in a word, "a new man."

In the orgy, then, man merged with his mythic past, the processes of nature around him, and with his own natural impulses to transcend social restrictions and harmonize himself symbolically with a naturalistic ethos. The orgy was a sacred act, attempting, as Eliade says, to renew the sacred act of creation annually, to sustain a communal sense of the ubiquitous presence of sacred time and life.

163

The rhythm of the orgy, then, like that of moral anarchy, is the rhythm of death and regeneration, destroying creation while at the same time regenerating it. It signifies man's unity with nature. However, that unity requires the disordering of social authority, for society is constructed to protect man from nature and therefore stands between him and it. The orgy, in its various manifestations, did precisely this, dissolve the normal order of society. Slave and master, king and subject, whore and lady, priest and janitor, all hierarchical structures were toppled, reversed. Eliade, again, sums up the object of orgiastic anarchy:

Licence is let loose, all commands are violated, all contraries are brought together, and all this is simply to effect the dissolution of the world—of which the community is a copy—and restore the primeval *illud tempus* which is obviously the mythical moment of the *beginning* (chaos) and the end (flood or *ekpyrosis,* apocalypse).

The orgy is not only consciously hypersexual, it is conscious disorder, the denial of any univocal ethical authority. The ultimate moral authority is natural energy, the symbolic representation of which is sexual license, both verbal and physical. The subordination of all things to that is thus represented in the orgy. But it is not simply a purge of disorder; it is, with each repetition, the beginning of a new order modeled on creation, which is to say closer to nature than social ordering permits. Orgiastic chaos is a way of exorcising social decadence and revitalizing man's cognizance of his natural self, the cell around which can grow the body of a naturalistic ethos.

Keeping in mind the verbal role of obscenity in the sacred orgy, we may see pornography as a kind of profane ancestor. The orgy flourished in either "primitive" (that is, non-urban and non-industrial) or non-Christian cultures. As western culture became urban and Christian, ritual fertility dramas dropped the sexual orgy and masked its anarchy in allegory. Inasmuch as cultural norms forbad acting out the ritual, it is reasonable to regard pornography as the symbolic acting out

164

(in Kenneth Burke's sense) of the ritual orgy, at its most artistically ambitious the searching after unity with nature. In *Love's Body* Norman O. Brown postulates an erotic symbolism that provides us with a new consciousness, of "an erotic sense of reality." This suggests how close the modern erotic imagination is in its concerns to those of the orgy. Brown reminds us of Freud's observation that "symbolism is on the track of a former identity, a lost unity." Brown goes on to say that "It is the erotic sense of reality that discovers the inadequacy of fraternity, or brotherhood . . . we must be either far more deeply unified, or not at all. The true form of unification . . . is: 'we are all members of one body.'" He notes, with Freud, that "The tendency of the sexual instinct is to restore an earlier state of things, an earlier state of unity," and goes on to say that modern egoism, with its emphasis on individuation, has broken with "the Dionysian, or drunken, principle of union, or communion, between man and man and between man and nature. The integration of the psyche is the integration of the human race, and the integration of the work with which we are inseparably connected." Brown is here describing, though at a highly sublimated level, the principle of the sexual orgy. The level of sublimation at which he is tells us something of how removed the modern erotic imagination is from its orgiastic ancestors. Nevertheless, its basic concern, as represented in such theorists as Freud and Brown or in such pornographers as de Sade or D. H. Lawrence or Jean Genet, is much the same—the regenerative possibilities of moral anarchy.

Pornographic anarchy reaches its most comprehensive and sustained development in Genet. But it is used to greater or lesser degree by many of the most significant modern and contemporary writers. And it proliferates, for better or worse, in the hundreds of minor writers. D. H. Lawrence, of course, was one of the first to not only use it, but to attempt constructing a social and moral dialectic from it. It is at its most pornographic, that is, its most sexually exclusive, in *Lady Chatterley's Lover.*

165

There he articulates sexual anarchy, the refutation of what is humanly divisive. Of Mellors, Lady Chatterly's lover, Lawrence says:

And he realized as he went in to her that this was the thing he had to do, to come into tender touch, without losing his pride or his dignity or his integrity as a man. After all, if she had money and means, and he had none, he should be too proud and honorable to hold back his tenderness from her on that account. "I stand for the touch of bodily awareness between human beings," he said to himself, "and the touch of tenderness. And she is my mate. And it is a battle against the money, and the machine, and the insentient ideal monkeyishness of the world."

Lawrence and Genet are antithetical on many things, but on the necessity and moral viability of sexuality they are one. It is there, in the spiritual orgy, that the straight and queer worlds can recognize a common humanity. Lawrence, like Genet, celebrates the regeneration of orgy:

In the short summer night she learnt so much. She would have thought a woman would have died of shame. Instead of which, the shame died. Shame, which is fear: the deep organic shame, the old, old physical fear which crouches in the bodily roots of us, and can only be chased away by the sensual fire, at last it was roused up and routed by the phallic hunt of the man, and she came to the very heart of the jungle of herself. She felt, now, she had come to the real bedrock of her nature, and was essentially shameless. She was her sensual self, naked and unashamed. She felt a triumph, almost a vainglory. So! That was how it was! That was life! That was how oneself really was! There was nothing left to disguise or be ashamed of. She shared her ultimate nakedness with a man, another being.

Lawrence develops these themes more subtly and comprehensively in other novels, *The Rainbow* and *Women in Love,* for instance, and they are his major themes. But *Lady Chatterly's Lover* was specifically intended as a work of confrontation, a disruption, a declaration of orgiastic anarchy. It was a work to clear the air, so that the works of his more comprehensive vision, and the works of others as well, might breathe the better.

Genet is the quintessential anarchist, more "dangerous" than de Sade because less mad, more dangerous because, unlike the self-destructive de Sade, he is existentially, homicidally, free from his own indomitable ego, more dangerous therefore because he is free to see into the cauldron of social and private self and *sing,* celebrating its obscene reality. In *The Thief's Journal,* commenting on a beggarly sojourn through Andalousia, he says:

I dared not even notice the beauty of that part of the world—unless it were to look for the secret of that beauty, the imposture behind it, of which one will be a victim if he trusts it. By rejecting it, I discovered poetry.

The very basis of Genet's aesthetic is anarchic, rejecting beauty as imposture, dangerous to him who becomes its victim. Which is to say that to respond to beauty is to respond to idealism, and to make idealism your metaphysic is to make believe— make believe that reality is the good, the true, and the beautiful. Genet counters: plumb the depths of your desires, storm the heavens and steal the fires. Like de Sade, Genet has been made a criminal—bastard, thief, murderer, homosexual—and, like Edmund, he cries, *Now gods, stand up for bastards.* What gods will do so? The shadow knows; speaking directly to us, the solid citizens, Genet says:

It seemed to me to be definitely settled that I was to dwell in shame, . . . I made up my mind to live with my head bowed and to pursue my destiny toward darkness, in an opposite direction to yours, and to exploit the underside of your beauty.

What gods? The dark gods living on the underside of beauty. And, ironically, Genet's destiny has been well served by his commitment to the obscene, to the underarm of idealistic reality. For the genius of his vision he was pardoned and his life sentence commuted. He tells us in *The Thief's Journal* that "I am writing this book in an elegant hotel in one of the most fashionable cities in the world, where I am rich . . ." Not only is he rich, he regrets not being able to flaunt his riches be-

167

fore the poor with "more ostentation and insolence." Here of course he surpasses de Sade again in anarchical example. Not only does crime pay, but one need not even be humble or repentant about it. And what more convincing proof of the truth of Genet's vision than that we will handsomely subsidize his trip to the nether world. We want a report that badly. Being the archetypal con-man, Genet must have known all along—even hopelessly imprisoned, writing *Our Lady of the Flowers* on the paper sheets he was to make bags of—through all that he must have known how hungry we were for what he knew. And knowing that, his faith in his destiny must have been reinforced. So, too, his faith in the obscene backside of beauty. Like Moses, Genet saw God's hinder parts and lived profitably to tell the tale. Genet, unlike de Sade or Al Capone, who were too hysterically anarchists, is the living proof of the social viability of moral anarchy.

Moral inversion and orgy are the *sine qua non* of Genet's dialectic. *Our Lady of the Flowers* begins with a catalogue of public enemies, three murderers and a traitor; the list is punctuated by Genet's dedication: "And it is in honor of their crimes that I am writing my book." Murder bespeaks, he says, their secret and future glory. The criminal, in Genet, is sanctified, the more so as his crime is more debased, degrading, and profitless. For then his life articulates the "motiveless malignancy" of humanity and he becomes an exemplum of man's dark reality, an upside down saint. *The Thief's Journal* begins:

Convicts' garb is striped pink and white. Though it was at my heart's bidding that I chose the universe wherein I delight, I at least have the power of finding therein the many meanings I wish to find: *there is a close relationship between flowers and convicts*. The fragility and delicacy of the former are of the same nature as the brutal insensitivity of the latter. Should I have to portray a convict—or a criminal—I shall so bedeck him with flowers that, as he disappears beneath them, he will himself become a flower, a gigantic and new one.

Fleurs de mal. A single unity, humanity, devised and represented from the antipodes of fragility and brutality, delicacy and insensitivity. Genet's passion to synthesize moral antitheses, to reveal "the man in the god," is at one with the orgiastic passion. Like Freud or Norman O. Brown or the pagan naturalisms before them, Genet sees the fusion of man and god, man and nature, man and man in erotic reality; and his linking criminality with sexuality brilliantly illuminates a dehumanizing cultural association inherited from sentimental idealism:

. . . men doomed to evil possess the manly virtues. Of their own volition, or owing to an accident which has been chosen for them, they plunge lucidly and without complaining into a reproachful, ignominious element, like that into which love, if it is profound, hurls human beings. Erotic play discloses a nameless world which is revealed by the nocturnal language of lovers. Such language is not written down. It is whispered into the ear at night in a hoarse voice. At dawn it is forgotten. Repudiating the virtues of your world, criminals hopelessly agree to organize a forbidden universe. They agree to live in it. The air there is nauseating: they can breathe it. But—criminals are remote from you—as in love, they turn away and turn me away from the world and its laws. Theirs smells of sweat, sperm, and blood. In short, to my body and my thirsty soul it offers devotion.

Love, as the Greeks knew from Medea, Clytemnestra, Antigone, can make men outlaws. Sex, the sign of love, can also, as Christ and Augustine and de Sade knew. This mythic dichotomy between man's private and public order, rooted in anarchical antithesis, is the heart of Genet's vision. Genet, outlawed by his terrible loves—love of men, criminals, evil, obscenity—says of *The Thief's Journal* that it is "a song of love," that his life was preparation for "erotic adventures," and that of what he has to tell "only this book of love will be real." Love and sexuality, then, the love of evil and homosexuality, are Genet's reality. *The Thief's Journal* (does the title recall Christ's fellows in crucifixion?) is Genet's anarchical Bible. He brings a new testament of love and squalor, refuting the singular authority of beauty with a vision of its underside. Evil, he says, be thou my good. And he seeks, from us, the consecration of his perverse law, the old testament: "my book, which

169

has become my genesis, contains—should contain—the commandments which I cannot transgress."

What better vehicle for this mission of moral anarchy than orgiastic celebration. He turns the moral universe on its ear to show *all* of what is there. For if he can persuade us of a "sanctity" in the underworld, persuade us that a man may reject all our prejudices, live in a world we consign to madness, embrace what we find repulsive, if he can do all this and still persuade us that he is in touch with reality, then we must acknowledge more dimensions of reality than we suspected. This is precisely what he attempts in *Our Lady of the Flowers*. It is the inspired word, inspired by his vision of public enemies transformed to saints by the creative energy, the orgiastic regeneration, achieved in his nightly prison-cell masturbation fantasies. The criminals whose crimes his book honors—Weidmann, Angel Sun, Pilorge—are made over into the saints of Genet's black liturgy. They are given appropriately allegorical names: Divine, Our Lady of the Flowers. Naturally the protagonists are men in moral drag, emphasizing the moral inversion of Genet's dialectic. Nightly Genet masturbates. He mimes the creation. From the mud of earth ("Made of mud and mist," he says in *The Thief's Journal*, "Stilitano was indeed a divinity to whom I could sacrifice myself"), he creates his perverse universe:

At night I love them, and my love endows them with life. During the day I go about my petty concerns. I am the housekeeper, watchful lest a bread crumb or a speck of ash fall on the floor. But at night! Fear of the guard who may suddenly flick on the light and stick his head through the grating compels me to take sordid precautions lest the rustling of the sheets draw attention to my pleasure; but though my gesture may be less noble, by becoming secret it heightens my pleasure. I dawdle. Beneath the sheet, my right hand stops to caress the absent face, and then the whole body, of the outlaw I have chosen for that evening's delight. The left hand closes, then arranges its fingers in the form of a hollow organ which tries to resist, then offers itself, opens up, and a vigorous body, a wardrobe, emerges from the wall, advances, and falls upon me, crushes me against my straw mattress, which has already been stained by more

170

than a hundred prisoners, while I think of the happiness into which I sink at a time when God and His angels exist.

And having made his world of mud and mist, Genet saw that it was good: "It was a good thing that I raised egoistic masturbation to the dignity of a cult!" The isolation of his cell is repeated in the egoistic isolation of masturbation. He creates the world that society had made available to him—night after night. Being a criminal, having his *being* in crime, having no other being than crime, he naturally generates a criminal world. He creates the world of sweat, sperm, and blood, and in the creation, a creation drawn from his descent into that underworld, he testifies to its reality. And not only to its reality, but, in the anarchy of his vision, he argues for its sublimity. "I wanted," he says in *The Thief's Journal,* to affirm it in its exact sordidness, and the most sordid signs became for me signs of grandeur." In that solitary world, sordid and obscene, he finds love. Through the orgy of masturbation he regenerates his life; through it he makes communion with man, with nature, with cosmic spirit. He affirms it with the life material at his disposal, affirms it deliberately with the materials the normal world negates. And in so doing he existentially refutes the univocal authority of normality. And, he reminds us, marvelling that we take such trouble to keep him in his cell ("My good, my gentle friend, my cell! My sweet retreat, mine alone, I love you so!"), we are his accomplices, for he, a prisoner in prison, is subsidized in the maintenance of his world by society. We help him cultivate the anarchy of his antipathetic reality. He knows what we want. He does his part.

He shares with us his orgiastic vision, complete with real sexuality, symbolic sexuality, ritual sexuality. And, like the archetypal orgy, sexuality is magic; Genet's sperm and pornographic fantasy fertilize his otherwise barren world. Through them he comes to love his cell, the prison, his isolation, and above all the criminality that is their catalyst. As in the orgy, in Genet's onanistic vision all things are inverted. Having been born and grown up a criminal, first a bastard, then a thief, he

171

recreates the furtive sexuality he has known—masturbation and homosexuality. Nor, if such chroniclers as Stephen Spender are to be believed, is the juvenile penal colony appreciably different in this respect from the British public school and its international counterparts. But it is not sufficient, real sexuality, and he needs to expand it, interpret it in the context of natural and social forces. Again, his world, expanded now to include more unequivocally our own, provides the model. The common denominator of imprisoning and warring societies is power. Orgiastic power is the power of growth and procreation; but war and imprisonment are barren, and this is total anarchy after all, the underside of normality. Thus the barrenness of homosex and masturbation are raised to a symbolic level, articulating the ironic barrenness, criminality, and violence of the larger frame of reality:

Darling is a giant whose curved feet cover half the globe as he stands with his legs apart in baggy, sky-blue silk underpants. He rams it in. So hard and calmly that anuses and vaginas slip onto his member like rings on a finger. He rams it in. So hard and calmly that his virility, observed by the heavens, has the penetrating force of the battalions of blond warriors who on June 14, 1940, buggered us soberly and seriously, though their eyes were elsewhere as they marched in the dust and sun. But they are the image of only the tensed, buttressed Darling. Their granite prevents them from being slithering pimps.

Police, both as sexual and official objects, naturally fascinate the thief: "Criminals and the police are the most virile emanation of this world. You cast a veil over them. They are your shameful parts, which, however, I call, as you do, noble parts." But the Germans of *der Führer* (Genet's characters pray to "Our *Mother* who art in heaven"), like their latter-day counterparts in Russia and America, certified on the large symbolic scale the nobility of crime; they ripped off the veil we try now with decadent discretion to replace:

It was no longer a social institution but a sacred power, acting directly upon my soul and troubling me. Only the German police, in

Hitler's time, succeeded in being both Police and Crime. This masterly synthesis of opposites, this block of truth, was frightful, charged with a magnetism that will continue to perturb us for a long, long time.

The inversion, thus, of heaven and hell, or rather its synthesis. Our history feeds with such blocks of truth the orgiastic anarchy of Genet's morality. In full pornographic truth, the lion and the lamb lie together. Finally, then, the orgy becomes ritual, a celebration of the obscenely sacred anarchy of sexual energy:

I close my eyes. Divine and Darling . . . Darling's penis is in itself all of Darling: the object of her pure luxury, an object of pure luxury. If Divine is willing to see in her man anything other than a hot, purplish member, it is because she can follow its stiffness, which extends to the anus, and can sense that it goes farther into his body, that it is this very body of Darling erect and terminating in a pale, tired face . . .

I close my eyes beneath the lice-infested blankets. Divine has opened the fly and arranged this mysterious area of her man. Has beribboned the bush and penis, stuck flowers into the buttonholes of the fly. . . . The result is that to Divine, Darling is only the magnificent delegation on earth, the physical expression, in short, the symbol of a being (perhaps God), of an idea that remains in heaven.

Genet closes his eyes. He masturbates. He conjures. He invokes his dark reality. Denied, reviled, and hid away, he creates a "beautiful" life out of obscenity. He worships, and his worship unveils the aesthetic potential of shame. A life reduced to shame finds there the stuff not only of survival but of affirmation. And the affirmation of our shame is the anarchic refutation of our idealistic nobility.

For Genet all things are charged with the eroticism and inversion of orgy. He tells us, in *The Thief's Journal,* that the *"pursuit* of traitors and treason was only one of the forms of eroticism." Likewise his pursuit of theft, murder, fraud, crime of any sort. Crime destroys the illusion of purity and righteousness, and prepares him for acceptance of himself in all his shame. With the strength of that acceptance he is empowered

173

to construct an ethos. That ethos is at once antisocial and authentic. Its very existential authenticity calls in question the wisdom of the normal ethos that expends its energy denying the natural authenticity and even, witness the murderous virtuousness of democracy in Asia, the *efficaciousness* of evil. To enforce our consciousness of that paradox Genet turns crime into a sacrament—his books, remember, *should* contain "the commandments which I cannot transgress." He builds an ethos on those commandments of evil:

> . . . the theft I had committed became in my eyes a very hard, very pure, almost luminous act, which only the diamond can symbolize. I had, in achieving it, destroyed once again—and I thought to myself once and for all—the dear bonds of brotherhood.
>
> "After that, after this crime, what kind of moral perfection can I hope for?"
>
> As the theft was indestructible, I decided to make it the origin of a state of moral perfection.
>
> "It's cowardly, weak, dirty, low . . . (I shall define it only with words expressing shame). None of the elements composing it leaves me a chance to magnify it. Yet I do not deny this most monstrous of my sons. I want to fill the world with its loathsome progeny."

This ethos becomes the basis for sanctification of Divine and Our Lady. To fill the world with such progeny is to fill the world with the consciousness of evil's vitality, and with the consciousness that though evil may be repented it cannot be undone. An evil act, like any other, is discrete, eternal. There is here of course the refutation of Christian grace, a concept, latterly distorted by sentimentalism, whereby evil is exorcised and the consequence of which is that its vitality is denied.

But Genet knows, as many of the Christian fathers knew, that evil is vital, that it exists simultaneously with good, and that it is an indelible fact of human life. Any true ethos, then, must acknowledge and genuinely cope with its reality. Our Lady's orgiastic sanctification comes about when he strangles an old man, a friend, to commit theft. After doing so, he cannot find the money and, as he is about to leave, he accidentally knocks over a vase, "The vase falls down and twenty thousand francs scatter graciously at his feet." God's grace indeed works in strange ways. Like de Sade, Genet's life and dialectic tell us that crime pays. Evil has vitality. After the murder, itself an orgiastic creation of Genet's onanistic dream, "the murderer's hand seeks his penis, which is erect. He strokes it through the sheet, gently at first, with the lightness of a fluttering bird, then grips it, squeezes it hard; finally he discharges into the toothless mouth of the strangled old man." Then he falls asleep. To dream, of course, is to regenerate. The destruction of the old to regenerate the new. Divine's sanctification is still more perverse. He unscrews a railing so that a child will fall to its death. After watching the fall, he gently scoops together the mangled remains, respectful of the means of his beatitude. "Divine's goodness was dead. For: 'What good would it do me to be a thousand times good now? How could this inexpiable crime ever be redeemed?" The irretrievable act is irretrievable. The straight world, the world of sentimental comedy, denies humanistic value by making its violation redeemable, and thus its morality denies its ethics. The queer world knows better. What is done is never undone by metaphysical magic. Thus Genet's plot refutes the authority of a deceptively casuistic ethos. Evil has vitality. He articulates our moral absurdity with the image of orgy working out in human life. And we are reminded that his perverse fantasies have their origin in real life, the lives of his honored public enemies.

And he knows that we need and want such reminders of our own dark reality. Our Lady's murder trial is reminiscent of that in Camus' *The Stranger*. Our Lady's defense advocate, representing the sentimental ethic of redemption, pleads for rehabilitation. He invokes poverty, hardship, Our Lady's youth. But Our Lady has more mythic sensibility than that: "Ah no, not the Corrida, it ain't worth it. I'd rather croak right away." And when Our Lady is asked what he has to say in his own defense, this is the scene Genet describes:

The old tramp who was his cellmate . . . had prepared a few suitable words for him to say to the Court. He looked for them but was unable to find them. The phrase "I didn't do it on purpose" took

175

shape on his lips. . . . Nobody would have been surprised. Everyone expected the worst. . . . He had to be natural. To be natural, at that moment, was to be theatrical, but his maladroitness saved him from ridicule and lopped off his head. He was truly great. He said:

"The old guy was washed up. He couldn't even get a hard-on."

Luckily, for Our Lady's beatitude if not his survival, the jury too recognizes his mythic meaning. "The Court felt that it had to sanctify this young man." Neither the defense attorney nor the judge, committed to their sentimental justice, can prevent Our Lady's sainthood. The jurymen, his peers, know that they live in him, that they must honor his evil as their own, that they must canonize it by executing him. Unlike the official guardians of sentimentality, they can perceive the necessary truth of moral anarchy.

At the end of *Our Lady of the Flowers* Genet tells us that the hearing for his pardon looms on the morrow. He considers the meaning of freedom.

Free, in other words, exiled among the living, I have made myself a soul to fit my dwelling. My cell is so sweet. Free: to drink wine, to smoke, to see ordinary people. And tomorrow, what will the jury be like? I have anticipated the stiffest possible sentence it can inflict. I have prepared myself for it with great care, for I have chosen my horoscope (according to what I can read of it from past events) as a figure of fatality. Now that I can obey it, my grief is less great. It is annihilated in the face of the irremediable. It is my hopelessness, and what will be, will be. I have given up my desires. I too am "already far beyond that" (Weidmann). Let me therefore live between these walls for a man's lifetime. Who will be judged tomorrow? Some stranger bearing a name that was once my name. I can continue to die, until my death, amidst all these widowers. Lamp, washbasin, regulations, broom. And the straw mattress, my spouse.

He affirms here the reality he has pictured for us; he asserts its irremedial authenticity. The judgment of society is too late to free him. It is irrelevant to his being. To free him is to rather postulate another being. Genet is after all Our Lady, and like him/her he knows his mythic utility to mankind. And he knows that his life metaphors, hyperbolically but nonetheless authentically, our own. Life consists in each man being exiled to himself. Throughout Genet's work is the emphasis on solitude and isolation, the inviolability and persistence of the imagination to formulate its own reality. Prison figures the human condition. To be free is merely to exchange one mode of exile for another. To be released from his cell is simply to have access to different materials for his construction of reality. Criminal or citizen, the pattern is the same. Faced with the possibility of a new life, he continues to affirm the values of the old life. He will not renounce that truth. For to do so would be to deny the authenticity of the underworld, to deny his own being, to forfeit the mythic significance that he knows perfectly well he has. And, as it turns out, we know it as well. After all, we honor it. Sartre calls him "Saint Genet" not because he embraces a new faith but because, faced with burning at the stake of liberty, he insists on the truth of his awful vision. That, precisely, is his mission.

Genet's homosexual pornography, then, seeks to inform us of man's spiritual determination to be at one with himself and his environment, whatever its degradation or hopelessness. The spirit of orgy he sees in man *is* in fact spiritual. Isolated, man must love himself. And, as the act of love is on the arm, he masturbates. If a man has only the company of other men, he must love them—homosexually. How he manifests his need and determination to love is of petty consequence. Genet's books —all of them thief's journals—are books of love, and they document the insistence of man to tear down what stands between him and it. Heterosexuality is an accident of time, place, opportunity. Its normality cannot and will not stand between man and love. Genet tears down its monolithic imperatives to regenerate himself, to make life possible in his peculiar circumstances. In so doing he discovers a reality he had not hoped for. He finds life in the environs of death. With wonder, he tells us that, depraved, shameful, and evil as he and his fellow criminals may be, they are *alive*. And the very vitality of their being testifies to the authentic moral reality of their mode of life.

177

The moral object of modern literature is the same with that of the whole history of literature, to represent reality according to the philosophical possibilities of its representation at a given time in history. It is no accident that pornography began to appear in significant quantity at about the same time that naturalistic philosophy was developing, in the eighteenth century. But formal aesthetics tend to lag behind both philosophical speculation and poetic practice. At roughly the same time neo-classical aesthetics were declaring that "the first Almighty Cause / Acts not by partial but by general laws," John Cleland was writing *Fanny Hill* and Defoe had already written *Moll Flanders,* both of them books about aberrational life, that is, depicting "partial" laws in operation. And the philosophers too were referring man to nature rather than the "first Almighty Cause." As the naturalistic possibilities of representing nature opened up, literature assimilated them. And pornography, being one of those possibilities, began developing accordingly. It began to take itself more seriously. What was fun for Casanova and profit for Cleland became philosophical necessity for de Sade. In the embattled development of naturalism pornography became the logical genre for the extreme affirmation of the mythos of animality. As naturalism gained the strength and authority necessary to challenge idealism, pornography became a phenomenological vehicle of refutation, howevermuch underground. In our time it has emerged and has become more distinctly the principal agent of moral confrontation.

The essential quality of all pornography, its orgiastic anarchy, began in serious or artistic pornography to take on moral significance. It became, to greater or lesser degree, a phenomenological statement of naturalism documenting the existence of animal energy as a positive rather than negative force in man's life. Like the orgy, it seeks now to reunite man with the mythic sacredness of creative energy most recognizable in his sexuality. This refutes the main line of western philosophy, which, since Plato, has emphasized reason as an echo of divine harmony, and which has feared and suppressed the passions as disruptive. Pornography, being the literature of orgiastic sexuality, is particularly suited for the confrontation with idealism, especially in its latter day deterioration into sentimentalism. For sentimentalism is an attempt to idealize the passions and thereby deny the natural and moral significance of their physicality, and often to deny their physicality altogether. By denying the passions to the point of ignoring their physical and moral viability, idealism has become morally vestigial. It recommends an ethos that is based on only half of human nature. The murderous chaos of contemporary world culture is evidence of how that ethos is failing us. Pornography has become, therefore, the principal rhetoric of attack on this ethos. Its physicality *is* disruptive, disruptive of the serene ignorance of moral establishmentarianism. The insistent, loin shaking beat of its physicality refutes the human authority of sentimental idealism. As that beat urges us to dance we are forced, in our dancing, to acknowledge its viability. And, as it makes us dance *better,* we are forced to acknowledge its moral potential.

7.

Pornography as Comic Catharsis

TRAGEDY, in exploring cosmic mythoi, has the cultural function of defining the range of moral possibility. However symbolically, anarchical literature "politicizes" the moral imagination and informs it of the mythic rhythm of death and rebirth; its emphasis, as we have seen, is on the destruction of the old, from the ashes of which the new can be regenerated. Comedy represents the spirit of the new. Synthesizing the tragic and anarchic visions, it traditionally augments them with the celebratory confidence that, through regeneration, the "golden age" can be restored. As Northrop Frye points out in his essay, "The Argument of Comedy," tragedy and comedy grew out of the same ritual and each presents merely a different focus on the cycle of life and death, and each is therefore contained in the other: "for in the ritual the tragic story has a comic sequel. Divine men do not die: they die and rise again. The ritual pattern behind the catharsis of comedy is the resurrection that follows the death, the epiphany or manifestation of the risen hero." Tragedy, in this sense, is "uncompleted comedy," and comedy, being —whatever the extent of its affirmation—about life, contains within itself the potential of tragedy. Moral anarchy tells man that he must exert his own energy to effect the passing from destruction to a New Jerusalem. Hope being endemic to human nature, we tend to think of the comic as the highest vision. And perhaps philosophically it is. But in its artistic representation, especially for the modern imagination, comedy is most

180

persuasive—which is perhaps to say instructive—when put in the morally realistic context of tragic potential. Thus, much of what is called "black humor" (and its attendant obscenity) derives from the recognition that the truest fiction requires fusion of both the tragic and the comic. Wisdom consists in knowing that cosmically neither happiness, the condition of comedy, nor pathos, the condition of tragedy, is final. But man learns slowly, and, as the biblical lessons of The Flood and threat of The Fire Next Time attest, man seems best to learn of the good life through the pedagogy of destruction. To understand the connection between comedy and pornography, therefore, we do well to begin by considering this tension in the argument of comedy.

Satire, standing between comedy and tragedy, synthesizes the concerns of both, though its resolutions tend to be comic. Frye says that "Old" or Aristophanic comedy was essentially dated before Aristophanes died. Perhaps, but the satiric dimension of Aristophanes, the serio-comic spirit which frequently takes for its subject topical morality—such as, for example, the Spartan war—has never died, and it has in modern comedy become something very like a paradigm. Whereas "New Comedy" developed into elaborate plotting of confused romantic situations which would eventually resolve themselves happily, as in *A Midsummer Night's Dream,* "Old Comedy" developed into such mythic critique and affirmation as is developed in *The Tempest.* For there not only is the state righted, true love triumphant, moral generosity manifest, but nature and the elements are restored to proper order. *A Midsummer Night's Dream* may make us *feel* happy, but *The Tempest* gives us happiness with an ethical basis. Prospero provides man with a vision of moral possibility and a happiness with not only personal but social and even cosmic significance. Its comic affirmation develops out of potential tragedy. Prospero might very well have been the hero of a vengeance tragedy. The comedy, in fact, depends on Prospero's overcoming tragic passion. When he gives up power, magic, he surrenders to the human virtues— love and charity. In so doing, he restores man and nature to equilibrium. He provides, therefore, the comic moral model, the man who knows himself well enough to escape the destructiveness of passion and who knows the necessity of cosmic balance. Thus the most ethically instructive comedy is that which is morally naturalistic rather than fantastic or sentimental. It is that sort which advises us that happiness is accessible as a consequence of moral action based on moral knowledge. Ethical comedy presents man emerging positively, however bedraggled, from the humanly necessary confrontation with tragic destructiveness.

Prospero, a moral anarchist, turns things on their ear in order to prepare for their ultimate righting. In this way *The Tempest* represents a kind of paradigmatic structure for ethical comedy. The force of its comic affirmation comes from its potential tragedy. But the tragedy is modified to anarchy and prepares its world for a moral regeneration, the resolution of which is comic. Anarchy, then, is central. It tells us that, if anyone does, man has the power to make, at least proximately, his own happiness. Such a premise is, in the sense that we have been discussing it, naturalistic. Naturalism is of course at the heart of pornographic comedy. The prodigious erect phalluses of Aristophanes' *Lysistrata* have been more recently unsheathed in an Off Off Broadway production of Ronald Tavel's *Indira Ghandi*, indicating how closely the history of comedy has been and continues to be not only naturalistic but pornographic. As in tragedy, the comic use of pornography is to explore the potential of an existential ethos.

When, in the Preface to his *Memoirs,* Casanova says, "Man is free; yet we must not suppose that he is at liberty to do everything he pleases, for he becomes a slave the moment he allows his actions to be ruled by passion," he underscores the essential theme of ethical comedy. For comedy characteristically presents the mythos of enslavement overcome. *A Funny Thing Happened on the Way to the Forum,* a modern musical pastiche from Plautus, exemplifies this fact, on a parodic level. The slave becomes master, though, as is often the case in this sort of comedy, when he gets too big for his britches he gets his comeuppance and order is restored. In more profound naturalistic treatments of the theme, such as Joyce's *Ulysses* or Lawrence's *The Rainbow,* man works through his "enslavement" to the passions to reach a knowledge and love of himself and thus achieve, or at least approach, moral freedom. Casanova's *Memoirs* are a kind of comic biographical novel, a comedy of manners; largely erotic manners, for much of its interest centers on Casanova's considerable sex life (love life if you prefer, though it is sexually explicit even in the decorousness of its style). From the comfort of his well-provided "retirement" he says of his adventures that:

They are the follies inherent to youth; I make sport of them, and, if you are kind, you will not yourself refuse them a good-natured smile. You will be amused when you see that I have more than once deceived, without the slightest qualm of conscience, both knaves and fools. As to the deceit perpetrated upon women, let it pass, for, when love is in the way, men and women as a general rule dupe each other. But on the score of fools, it is a very different matter . . . for fools generally are insolent and so self-conceited that they challenge wit. We avenge intellect when we dupe a fool, and it is a victory not to be despised . . .

He invokes the virtues of eighteenth-century gentility; they feature the dispassionate exercise of intelligence. For it is in the reasonable life that Casanova, like his century, saw human dignity and freedom from "enslavement." Be not too passionate in judgment; be not too passionate in love; do not suffer fools gladly. Accepting the world and its mores, indeed using them so brilliantly to his advantage, he is the comic answer to de Sade. He is complacent in the face of life, recognizing his own responsibility for its conduct:

As for myself, I always willingly acknowledge my own self as the principal cause of every good or evil which may befall me; therefore I have always found myself capable of being my own pupil, and ready to love my teacher.

He is, however, also naturalistic in his sense of fortune:

183

I have often met with happiness after some imprudent step which ought to have brought ruin upon me, and . . . dire misfortune has befallen me in consequence of actions prompted by the most cautious wisdom.

He recognizes that accident and chance rather than moral desert describe the pattern of human affairs. But such things do not sway him from his pragmatic sanguineness or his orthodox Christian faith. He is at peace with the world, free from the obsessive "enslavement" of a de Sade. He is a comic hero, picaresquely wandering through life's good fortune and vicissitude with perfect tranquility. Nor, to maintain that posture, does he deny the "ugly" or the "obscene." He professes not only a liking for strong tasting and smelling food but also for body odors and the like; "I have always," he says, "found the odour of my beloved ones exceedingly pleasant":

"What depraved tastes!" some people will exclaim. "Are you not ashamed to confess such inclinations without blushing?" Dear critics, you make me laugh heartily! Thanks to my coarse tastes, I believe myself happier than other men, because I am convinced that they enhance my enjoyment. Happy are those who know how to obtain pleasures without injury to anyone; insane are those who fancy that the Almighty can enjoy the sufferings, the pains, the fasts and abstinences which they offer to Him as a sacrifice, and that His love is granted only to those who tax themselves so foolishly. God can demand from His creatures only the practice of virtues the seed of which He has sown in their soul, and all He has given unto us has been intended for our happiness: self-love, thirst for praise, emulation, strength, courage and a power of which nothing can deprive us—the power of self-destruction if, after due calculation, whether false or just, we unfortunately reckon death to be advantageous. This is the strongest proof of our moral freedom so much attacked by sophists. Yet this power of self-destruction is repugnant to nature and has been rightly opposed by every religion.

Casanova is, then, the most amiable of anarchists, arguing by word and deed for man's liberation from *all* enslavement, even life if it should be so construed. He is a prototype of naturalistic comedy, intent, like Bacon, on liberating men from idols of the mind, knowing that such idolatry makes men slaves. And, being a rational sensualist, he articulates the smiling dimensions of existential naturalism for the balanced mind capable of turning all things to the ultimate in humanistic pleasure—the canny enjoyment of what life *does* have to offer. "The really virtuous," he says, "are those persons who can practice virtue without the slightest trouble; such persons are always full of toleration; and it is to them that my *Memoirs* are addressed." Because his is a pragmatically comprehensive and highly social vision, an eighteenth-century handbook on how to succeed in life without working up a sweat, Casanova presents in his *Memoirs* a kind of sentimental or soft core pornographic version of Cleland's hard-core pornographic comedy, *Fanny Hill.* Cleland presents an exclusively sexual and non-social ethic of happiness. Casanova augments Cleland's sexuality with aristocratic sociability, in effect advising men to learn the ropes and let life work for them. He is, however, more than the original *Playboy,* for his *Memoirs* mark an important step toward naturalistic erotic comedy.

Henry Miller is the democratic extension of Casanova's pornographic comedy. In a 1966 interview Miller said that he thought he had made the erotic novel meaningful to "the man on the street." Casanova retired to the patronage of a Count's castle. Miller has retired to a solid middle-class neighborhood in Los Angeles. So goes history. But, though Miller is probably not yet so accessible to the man on the street as he hoped, he is a popular writer, and his significance to, especially, pornographic comedy is immense. His work combines the relaxed intellectual graciousness of Casanova and the demonic Sadean insistance on the complete animalistic "truth." Miller's is ethical comedy, concerned at once with representing the possibility of the common man emerging from life destructiveness, usually taking the form of social convention, with his head bloody but unbowed and with representing human energy, usually taking the Dionysian form of sexual activity, as a mode of affirmation. Unlike Genet or Lawrence, Miller is not dialectically oriented. His comic vision is rather figural than logical. Using his own life

185

to figure the possibilities of freedom and happiness he becomes
himself the comic hero, documenting the viability of liberation
from bourgeois enslavement with his own, perhaps partly fanta-
sized, life.

The Rosy Crucifixion, a trilogy consisting of *Sexus, Plexus,*
and *Nexus,* depicts Miller working through his own personal
anarchy—an analogue and effect of the destructiveness of the
American environment—eventually to free himself and leave
the country for a new life. The plot of the trilogy constitutes a
comic exorcism of bourgeois enslavement to profit, self, and the
varieties—from sex to fraud—of moral debauch. It is, in other
words, an exorcism of the living death Miller finds in American
culture. The concluding sequence of events in *Nexus* show him
routing the enemy. The day before he is to leave for Europe he
is walking the streets of New York, and he has a reminiscent
vision of death. After reading to his grandfather, he dreams, he
looks through a smokehouse fence and sees "Rows and rows
of stiff, blackened fish. . . . They're hanging by the gills, these
rigid, frightened fish." He asks his grandfather why dead things
are always so stiff: "Because there's no joy in them anymore."
Joy, in Miller, is the vehicle of life, and his vision of American
culture shows him its deadness:

By day the graveyard of senseless sweat and toil; by night the ceme-
tery of love and despair. And these creatures who had so faithfully
learned to run, to beg, to sell themselves and their fellow men, to
dance like bears or perform like trained poodles, ever and always
belying their own nature, these same wretched creatures broke down
now and then, wept like fountains of misery, crawled like snakes,
uttered sounds which only wounded animals are thought to emit.

Miller is escaping that death, and to do it he needs a final liturgical gesture, the exorcism of the symbol of death, the exorcism
of the Yankee Dollar. Conveniently, a panhandler asks him for
a dime. Miller offers him a dollar instead. The panhandler,
among the living dead, unliberated even by his poverty, is
suspicious. "All I need is a quarter . . . two bits. That'll do.
And I'll thank you kindly." Miller offers him up to five dollars,

"Five's the maximum." He only wants two bits. But, when Miller hands it to him, he drops it and it rolls into the gutter. Miller tells him to let it stay there, for "the other fellow." He gives him another. The panhandler asks, can he not have the other one too. Miller counters, giving him a dollar bill:

Imagine, if you can, that it's tomorrow and that you're passing the same spot, wondering who'll give you a dime. I won't be here, you see. I'll be on the *Ile de France*. Now then, your throat's parched and all that, and who comes along but a well-dressed guy with nothing to do—like me—and he flops down . . . right here on this same bench. Now what do you do? You go up to him, same as always, and you say—"Spare a dime, mister?" And he'll shake his head. No! Now then, here's the surprise, here's the thought I had for you. Don't run away with your tail between your legs. Stand firm and smile . . . a kindly smile. Then say: "Mister, I was only joking. I don't need no dime. Here's a buck for you, and may God protect you always!" *See?* Won't that be jolly?

The panhandler panics, running off waving the bill, shouting, "You crazy bugger! You dirty cocksucker! Piss on you, you goon!" Thus, the power of the dollar is exorcised. "There you are," Miller muses to himself, "couldn't take a little joke." Even the panhandlers are zombies, programmed for the usual. Everyone knows his miserable place. Miller, to build anew, destroys the confidence of that place. And, naturally, for his efforts he is condemned as mad. But he, at any rate, is ready for the new life. If humor and joy are "crazy," if palsied panhandlers are part of the mortuary establishment, it's damn well time to get out.

The way out is not easy. Given the psychic and social repressiveness of the life we define for ourselves, it takes heroic action and persistence to reach the point of freedom. Miller, as comic hero, has two keys to human joy that seem imperative to making it. He is at once a con-man and a sex-artist. Both of these qualities become figural antitheses of establishmentarianism. They are the anarchic means the comic hero has of weakening the cultural strangle hold. And it is clearly imperative to break that hold if one is to get free. Characteristically,

187

the con-man manifests the free enterprise virtue of wanting to get rich. Only his *means,* being vaguely criminal, are objectionable. His ends are laudable, in capitalistic context. He mirrors the capitalistic ethos. Which is why, in the criminal code, he is the aristocrat of criminals. But Miller's use of the motif contradicts the ethos from which it derives. He does not want to get rich. His con-artistry is used to make life accessible to himself. The figural implication is that we should all have the access to life that the rich have—the access to good food, good wine, good women, good homes, security—without having to suffer the spiritual corruption, the surrender to living death, necessary to getting and spending in a capitalistic ethos. As with Casanova, when Miller cons men out of their money to give himself or someone else (he as often cons for someone else's benefit as for his own) vitality, he strikes a blow against folly, the folly of materialism, and for life. This is rather simply illustrated when, in an episode in *Nexus,* he and a friend con a speakeasy out of an extravagant evening by paying the bill with a check to which they sign the name of a rich friend who died the day before. This episode not only pools the straight and underground worlds in their common corruption, it celebrates con-artistry as the proper weapon of the true moral anarchist. For not only does he give himself joy but turns as well the decay of the culture against itself.

But the con-game has a larger and more fundamental significance. Even an ethos where fraud is the norm has something to teach us. There is a metaphysics of fraud; the decadent notion that reality is what we say it is, that it is distorted by the medium of its articulation, has also a positive character. If reality is largely a product of consciousness, then a "better" consciousness will make a better reality, both psychically and morally. Reality, then, is a con-game. A game in which, when the rules become oppressive, we can change them, make them accord more truly with our needs. Miller discovers this metaphysic when, in *Sexus,* he undertakes the role of analyst with a doctor friend who himself aspires to being an analyst. At first the doctor introduces Miller to some of his patients as a psychoanalyst, and Miller "treats" them, though he has no formal training. The patients are pleased with his services, and show improvement. It works so well that the doctor himself decides to become Miller's patient. Miller plays the role strictly, and sustains it. In doing so, he discovers the metaphysics of fraud and the moral freedom that is its corollary. First he discovers that everyone, with infinite time and patience, could be saved. The art of healing, which he discovers through his con-artistry, comes to this:

. . . *everybody becomes a healer the moment he forgets about himself.* The sickness which we see everywhere, the bitterness and disgust which life inspires in so many of us, is only the reflection of the sickness which we carry within us. Prophylactics will never secure us against the world disease, because we bear the world within.

This moral recognition is the ultimate moral anarchy, bringing with it the possibility of regeneration and the triumph of a new life. Bearing in ourselves moral and psychic reality we have the power to shape a new life. "We must," says Miller, "die as egos and be born again in the swarm, not separate and self-hypnotized, but individual and related." We must, then, reject an ethos of false self-denial, the effect of which is to force the ego underground for its gratification. We must discover the *processes* of life and have confidence in their efficacy, their ability to direct us in keeping with our nature. This is the theme of the naturalistic comic ethos, that nature in its full complexity is the only way out. "The way of life," Miller says, "is toward fulfillment, however, wherever it may lead. . . . The process is everything . . . the way . . . the Tao . . . And so the analyst says 'Adapt yourself!' He does not mean, as some wish to think—adapt yourself to this rotten state of affairs! He means: adapt yourself to life! *Become an adept!*" And one must *learn* to do it well. It is a beginning to recognize the moral potential of fraud, the utility of the con-game. And to do that one must have confidence in his ability to redefine reality. Miller offers God as an existential example, for God is, after all, the ultimate comic hero:

We are all guilty of crime, the great crime of not living life to the full. But we are all potentially free. We can stop thinking of what we have failed to do and do whatever lies within our power. What these powers that are in us may be no one has truly dared to imagine. That they are infinite we will realize the day we admit to ourselves that imagination is everything. Imagination is the voice of daring. If there is anything God-like about God it is that. He dared to imagine everything.

Imagination is the basis of the con-game. It provides the context, the reason and meaning, for conning one's way to freedom, to life. God is the archetype and the example. One can do no better than to imitate him. Miller's ethos, therefore, advises us to imagine more than the prison we already know: "The prisoner is not the one who has committed a crime, but the one who clings to his crime and lives it over and over." Imagine the way out, the way to freedom. This is Miller's moral imperative, sine qua non.

Equally important to his exorcism of enslavement is Miller's use of sexuality. For if the body is, as the Christian fathers teach, a prison, it is the more so if we imprison ourselves within it in our own minds. If, in other words, we make an ethos that inspires fear, suspicion, and compulsive privateness about the body, as we have done, then the body becomes more than ever a prison. Miller bursts these bonds, and in so doing extends sexuality to symbolize the way of shattering so humanly destructive an idol of the mind. Sexual freedom signifies human freedom to be human, the freedom to take pleasure in being a human animal. The *process* of being human is everything, and to deny a part of that process is to deny it all. This theme is exemplified in the story of Maude, Miller's first wife in *Sexus.* As the novel opens Miller is already alienated from her and has just discovered Mona, his second wife, with whom he has a tortuous relationship throughout the trilogy. He is alienated from Maude because she is alienated from herself. Her jealousy, pettiness, and morose self-indulgence are incompatible with Miller's restless, large-spirited need to live. After he has left her to live with Mona, he takes Maude and his daughter on an outing to the country. While there, Miller fondles Maude, not averse, though they are divorced, to giving and getting sexual affection. Maude poutingly puts him off, playing out her dehumanized role flatly. Later, however, back at her house, after they have been caught in a rain storm and soaked so that they take off their clothes to dry them out, she engages Miller in what turns out to be an orgy. It begins thus:

I'm standing in front of the big mirror admiring my quivering cock when Maude trips in. She's as frisky as a hare and all decked out in tulle and mousseline. She seems not at all frightened by what she sees in the mirror. She comes over and stands beside me. "Open it up!" I urge. "Are you hungry?" she says, undoing herself leisurely. I turn her around and press her to me. She raises a leg to let me get it in. We look at each other in the mirror. She's fascinated. I pull the wrap up over her ass so that she can have a better look. I lift her up and she twines her legs around me. "Yes, do it," she begs. "Fuck me! Fuck me!" Suddenly she untwines her legs, unhitches. She grabs the big arm chair and turns it around, resting her hands on the back of it. Her ass is stuck out invitingly. She doesn't wait for me to put it in—she grabs it and places it herself, watching all the time through the mirror. I push it back and forth slowly, holding my skirts up like a bedraggled hussy. She likes to see it coming out—how far will it come before it falls out. She reaches under with one hand and plays with my balls. She's completely unleashed now, as brazen as a pot. I withdraw as far as I can without letting it slip out and she rolls her ass around, sinking down on it now and then and clutching it with a feathery beak. Finally she's had enough of that. She wants to lie down on the floor and put her legs around my neck. "Get it in all the way," she begs. "Don't be afraid of hurting me . . . I want it. I want you to do everything." I got it in so deep it felt as though I were buried in a bed of mussels. She was quivering and slithering in every ream. I bent over and sucked her breasts; the nipples were taut as nails. Suddenly she pulled my head down and began to bite me wildly—lips, ears, cheeks, neck. "You want it, don't you?" she hissed. "You want it, you want it . . ." Her lips twisted obscenely.

191

"You want it . . . you want it!" And she fairly lifted herself off the floor in her abandon. Then a groan, a spasm, a wild, tortured look as if her face were under a mirror pounded by a hammer. "Don't take it out yet," she grunted. She lay there, her legs still slung around my neck, and the little flag inside her began twitching and fluttering. "God," she said, "I can't stop it!" My prick was still firm. It hung obedient on her wet lips, as though receiving the sacrament from a lascivious angel. She came again, like an accordeon collapsing in a bag of milk. I got hornier and hornier. I pulled her legs down and lay them flat alongside my own. "Now don't move, damn you," I said. "I'm going to give it to you straight." Slowly and furiously I moved in and out. "Ah, ah . . . Oh!" she hissed, sucking her breath in. I kept it up like a Juggernaut. Moloch fucking a piece of bombazine. Organza Friganza. The bolero in straight jabs. Her eyes were going wild; she looked like an elephant walking the ball. All she needed was a trunk to trumpet with. It was a fuck to a standstill. I fell on top of her and chewed her lips to a frazzle.

The sexuality of this scene is uncompromised. It is pure sexuality, unmitigated with pretence to love. But it has an almost miraculous regenerating effect on Maude, who has heretofore been spiteful, vicious, and mean. Miller asks her if she hates him still. She answers, "I don't hate anyone. I'm sorry it's turned out the way it has. Now I'll have to share you . . . with her." As she goes about fixing them something to eat, Miller notices that "She looked a thousand times better than I had ever seen her look. She was like a bright voracious animal. . . . Jesus, it was quite wonderful. It was like getting to know one another all over again." Maude recognizes the difference herself. Their sexuality takes on more affection as they play erotically. Maude asks if it was her fault that they had not done this before. "Was I such a squeamish creature?"

Then, as if consciously consecrating her new humanity, her regeneration, she turns the affair more formally into an orgy, bringing down a girl friend from upstairs. "I want to celebrate," she says. They light candles, drink wine, play music, and dance. It is a Dionysian orgy. As their sexuality becomes more involved, Maude's humanity expands. "Maude looked on with a pleasant smile of satisfaction. I leaned forward and

kissed Elsie's cunt. 'It's wonderful not to be jealous any more,'
said Maude very simply." They arrange themselves in an elaborately entwined sexual trinity. Miller brings both the women
and himself to a climax. Maude says, "I've never been so
happy." And so it goes. Maude is given a new life through the
specific agency of sexuality. Following Miller's rule of thumb,
she becomes a healer, of herself, when she forgets about herself, when she releases herself from the prison of her body.
Through sexual orgy she takes on a new, improved personality
and humanity.

But, though sexuality is consistently a figure of liberation in
Miller's work, it does not exist in isolation, however purely
physical he represents such scenes. For the trick is not to be
enslaved, either, to sexuality if one is going to achieve human
liberation. "The moment you stop having a good time you
grow melancholy. You don't regulate your life—you let your
cunt do it for you. You're at the mercy of a stiff prick . . ."
The good, the human, life requires something far more complex than sex, even though free and joyous sex are signs. One
must have the desire to live, what Miller calls "hunger." Life
requires *going after* even more than gratification. Hunger is the
naturalistic counterpart of transcendental sublimation:

Food is poison to the spirit. Food doesn't satisfy hunger, nor drink
thirst. Food, sexual or otherwise, is only satisfying to the appetites.
Hunger is something else. Nobody can satisfy hunger. Hunger is the
soul's barometer. Ecstasy is the norm. Serenity is the freedom from
weather conditions—the permanent climate of the stratosphere.
That's where we're all headed . . . towards the stratosphere.

This is hunger for life, living, the avoidance of the great crime
of not living life to the full. Hunger is a product, not of the
belly, but of the imagination. When Maude gets hungry she
comes to life. It is so throughout Miller's work. His hunger is
what makes him the comic hero. It is what sets him apart
from other men.

Sex, being a complete act, cannot of course satisfy hunger.
It rather feeds hunger. It is a symbol of the serenity available

193

to men: Elsie, the third person of the orgiastic trinity, says in the throes of orgasm, "This is heaven." It is not; but it is the figural basis by which men might believe in heaven. It is also the source of the most intense physical feeling, by which men may know that they *are* and *want to be* alive. "Nobody," says Miller, "is altogether dead." Wherever he goes, he sees people trying to come alive, too often failing. Sex, being available to all men, a part of the processes of life, becomes therefore the way, the Tao. Its value to the body is that it certifies the possibility of life. Its value to the soul is that it feeds hunger, the will to live. Miller, then, is the comic celebrant of the mythos of animality. A naturalist, a kind of latter day deistic naturalist, he embraces the positiveness of what is, professing love for all things under the sun, excepting *work* and *flies*. "Of course," he says, "I don't feel that way every day—but I'd like to. And I do when I'm normal, when I'm myself. Everybody does, if given a chance. It's the natural state of the heart . . . but . . . we terrorize ourselves." Get free, then, free from terror. Liberate body and soul from the system, by fraud if necessary, since that's the pattern established by the system. "Woof, woof, woof, woof," is how Miller ends *Plexus* and begins *Nexus*. It is the cry of the animal in us trying to get free, to help us get free from ourselves, from the great, morose, depressed mind-rape perpetrated on humanity by its vestigial institutions. "I know," says Miller, "that underneath the mess everything is marvelous. I'm sure of it. I know it because I feel so marvelous myself most of the time. And when I feel that way everybody seems marvelous . . . everybody and everything. . . . That's what I want to write about. . . ." That is his comic message. If we can get in touch with ourselves, really in touch, as in the act of sex, then perhaps we can route the downhead meanies and find the joy endemic to life.

Miller approaches life-joy, in sex as in all things, with heroic capacities. There is, consequently, in his work a defiance; you, he tells the establishment, may detour me, you may slow me down, you may depress me occasionally, but you will never defeat me. All of his work radiates the confidence of his vision. There is something of the superman about him. And it does not matter much whether the Miller of life is the same Miller of the novels. Whoever he is, we feel in him the triumph of the comic hero. But, for that very reason, there is also something austere and unapproachable about him. We may acknowledge his truth; we may even use him as an ideal—as to large extent the Beats and the Hippies have done—but the fusion of fiction and fact in his work make it at once too lifelike and too much larger than life for most of us. We do not have the heroic capacity, by and large, to say, as he does at the beginning of *Tropic of Cancer,* "I have no money, no resources, no hopes. I am the happiest man alive." Somehow when Merseult, in Camus' *The Stranger,* comes to the same recognition in a work that is unequivocally fictive, we are better able to assimilate it. Perhaps we are embarrassed at our personal timidity. Perhaps we are afraid of failing at life, precisely what Miller's point is. Perhaps we do not have the genius he has demonstrated for defying the cultural mores and emerging, after all, on top. For, as with Casanova and Genet, and as ironic as it might be, Miller's life has paid off, in coin. In short, there is something too challenging in Miller, too direct. His ethos is somehow too much like Elsie's orgasm, it's heaven. To adopt it we would have to immerse ourselves completely in his, for most of us, inaccessible comic world. To translate his ethos we need a more fictive context, a context into which we might ease ourselves more obliquely. This is not to say that Miller is not hugely valuable; it is only to say that we also need other, perhaps less heroic, perspectives on the comic ethos he represents.

Lawrence and Joyce, for all their "artistic" complexity, are more easily assimilable into the "normal" man's morality. And they represent an ethos essentially similar to Miller's. They too celebrate the life force as the means of man's emergence from the enslavement imposed by the ignorance and denial of human animality. And sexuality, especially with Lawrence, is their symbol of liberation. Lawrence, in his essay "A Propos of *Lady Chatterley's Lover,*" says:

195

. . . the greatest need of man is the renewal forever of the complete rhythm of life and death, the rhythm of the sun's year, the body's year of a lifetime, and the greater year of the stars, the soul's year of immortality. This is our need, our imperative need. It is a need of the mind and soul, body, spirit and sex: all. . . .

It means a return to ancient forms. But we shall have to create these forms again. . . . We have to go back, a long way, before the idealist conceptions began, before Plato, before the tragic idea of life arose, to get on our feet again. For the gospel of salvation through the Ideals and escape from the body coincided with the tragic conception of human life. Salvation and tragedy are the same thing, and they are now both beside the point. . . .

Now we have to re-establish the great relationships which the grand idealists, with their underlying pessimism, their belief that life is nothing but futile conflict, to be avoided even unto death, destroyed for us. . . . The Christian religion lost, in Protestantism finally, the togetherness with the universe, the togetherness of the body, the sex, the emotions, the passions, with the earth and sun and stars.

But relationship is threefold. First, there is the relation to the living universe. Then comes the relation of man to woman. Then comes the relation of man to man. And each is a blood-relationship, not mere spirit or mind. We have abstracted the universe. . . . So that all three great relationships are bodiless, dead.

Here, in brief, is the essential argument of this book. Lawrence wrote *Lady Chatterly's Lover* specifically to articulate in fiction this theme. Though it contains the tragic potential of paralysis and death, it is a comic theme finally, affirming the possibility of life's triumph over death, and its symbol is the sexual and emotional liaison of Lady Chatterly with her gamekeeper. The theme takes on a more archetypally mythic character in *The Rainbow*, where three generations of a family wrestle with it.

In that novel Lawrence explores the Jungian implications of love and sex, and, in the novel's final image, celebrates the liberation of the third generation. Through the novel a dialectical tension is developed between the female *animus*, which Lawrence sees characterized by the impulse to vision and spirit,

196

and the male *anima,* which he sees trapped into work and pragmatism and resistant therefore to spiritual vision. In this psycho-mythic sense, all mankind is hermaphroditic. Two generations are subdued by the *anima,* but Ursula, of the third generation, works her way through the suppression of male domination and reaches the apocalyptic vision by affirming her option for life. The apocalypse begins when she takes her lover, in a desperate and demonic consummation, beneath the light of a full moon. The emotional failure of their love-making signifies the failure of their "relationship." Later, thinking she is pregnant, Ursula goes for a walk in the country to decide if she should marry her lover. She is caught in a thunderstorm in a pasture, where a herd of horses is made wild by the storm. The scene takes on the mythic quality of Lear's madness on the heath. The threat of the horses, a time-honored erotic symbol, takes on a distinctly masculine and sexual character: "She knew the heaviness in her heart. It was the weight of the horses. But she would circumvent them. She would bear the weight steadily, and so escape." But the horses draw nearer and cut her off,

But the horses had burst before her. In a sort of lightning of knowledge their movement travelled through her, the quiver and strain and thrust of their powerful flanks, as they burst before her and drew on, beyond.

. . . She was aware of their breasts gripped, clenched narrow in a hold that never relaxed, she was aware of their red nostrils flaming with long endurance, and of their haunches, so rounded, so massive, pressing, pressing, pressing to burst the grip upon their breasts, pressing for ever till they went mad, running against the walls of time, and never bursting free. Their great haunches were smoothed and darkened with rain. But the darkness and wetness of rain could not put out the hard, urgent, massive fire that was locked within these flanks, never, never.

She has then a clearly orgasmic image, "Like circles of lightning came the flash of hoofs from out of the powerful flanks." And the flanks of the horses, as if with one purpose, "were up against her." But she escapes, and in so doing she is liber-

197

ated from their power and terror: "They were almost pathetic, now. Her will alone carried her, till, trembling, she climbed the fence . . ." This apocalyptic experience helps her interpret her relationship to her lover: "Must she belong to him . . . Something compelled her, and yet it was not real. Always the ache, the ache of unreality, of her belonging to Skrebensky. . . . Why must she be bound, aching and cramped with the bondage, to Skrebensky's world? . . . Anton and Anton's world, not the Anton she possessed, but the Anton she did not possess, that which was owned by some other influence, by the world." She struggles with this tension, until she sees herself as a natural object, "the naked, clear kernel thrusting forth the clear, powerful shoot, and the world was a bygone winter." She is a natural thing, with her own power of being, not dependent on what is clearly seen to be the conventionally crippling enslavement of marriage, the forfeiture of self demanded by the world. "The kernel was free and naked and striving to take new root, to create a new knowledge of Eternity in the flux of Time. And the kernel was the only reality; the rest was cast off into oblivion." The child, then, need not be a prison gate. Nothing need be a prison gate. Through her sexual being, in all its complexity, she comes to a knowledge of the freedom of choice she has as a human being. And her choice is confirmed by the final apocalyptic vision, that of the rainbow, in which, as in herself, there is a new cosmic "archtecture," a communion of relationships—of man to nature, of man to woman, of man to man.

Lawrence's sexual dialectic is at once epistemological and metaphysical. There are, he says, many ways of knowing and many kinds of knowledge. "But the two ways of knowing, for man, are knowing in terms of apartness, which is mental, rational, scientific, and knowing in terms of togetherness, which is religious and poetic." Metaphysically, reality confronts unreality at the level of individual consciousness of self and the possibilities self has for communion with man and nature. Lawrence's now much sentimentalized concept of "togetherness," then, is the key. So sexuality is its natural and spontaneous symbolism. Highly ritualistic and mythisized as it is, its physicality is emphasized in *Lady Chatterley's Lover;* its racial mythos is emphasized in *The Rainbow.* Other works, such as *Women in Love* and *Sons and Lovers,* continue the exploration of the sexual mythos. But *Lady Chatterley* was intended not only as an exploration of Lawrence's basic theme, but also as a wedge into public acceptance of that theme as a serious poetic statement. He wanted, in effect, to exorcise the whole concept of "pornography" by a direct and healthy representation of sexuality. His hostility to masturbation and homosexuality is well known. He despised them as he despised "pornography," because all of them, he thought, contributed to making sex "secret" and "dirty." As such they separated man from his body, from the rhythms of nature. Their "dirt" makes for fear and rejection; their "secrecy" makes for isolation, the separation of man from nature and himself. Nor is his dialectic harmlessly stratospheric. He saw political consequences from such isolation and fear.

The sense of isolation, followed by the sense of menace and of fear, is bound to arise as the feeling of oneness and community with our fellow-men declines, and the feeling of individualism and personality, which is existence in isolation, increases. The so-called "cultured" classes are the first to develop "personality" and individualism, and the first to fall into this state of unconscious menace and fear. The working-classes retain the old blood-warmth of oneness and togetherness some decades longer. Then they lose it too. And then class-consciousness becomes rampant, and class-hate. Class-hate and class-consciousness are only a sign that the old togetherness, the old blood-warmth has collapsed, and every man is really aware of himself in apartness. Then we have these hostile groupings of men for the sake of opposition, strife. Civil strife becomes a necessary condition of self-assertion.

Thus, Lawrentian pornography, in both its physical and mythic configurations, is designed to affirm human community. It is a comic vision that transcends Henry Miller's defiance. It lives at a figural level that permits us to absorb and learn from it without being made to feel inadequate to its ethos. While its

199

imaginative challenge may be greater than Miller's, its personal challenge is not so great. It enfolds us, and we feel a part of its morality even as we fail it. And we are thereby the more liberated from our failure.

Liberation from failure is even more pronounced in Joyce. *Ulysses,* for example, is finally a comedy of failure. Certainly Leopold Bloom, Joyce's comic answer to the Homeric Ulysses, is a "failure" in many ways, as a businessman, as a husband, as a father, as a lover. Molly Bloom's partly affectionate, partly contemptuous diminutive, "Poldy," indicates something of his failure at achieving dignity. Molly herself is only slightly less a failure. Though professionally and sexually "successful," she too is a failure as a wife and mother. Nor is Blazes Boylan, Molly's lover, much more successful. He cuckolds Bloom, and ridicules him in the bars, and has the appearance of typically florid, loquacious, Irish, "masculine" success. But even as lover he is something of a failure, failing for all his virility (Molly, in her soliloquy, says of him, "he must have come 3 or 4 times with that tremendous big red brute of a thing he has I thought the vein or whatever the dickens they call it was going to burst . . . it like iron or some kind of a thick crowbar standing all the time he must have eaten oysters I think a few dozen . . . no I never in all my life felt anyone had one the size of that to make you feel full up") to earn more than Molly's amazement, and even with that she concludes, by way of comparison, "but I don't know Poldy has more spunk in him." And being, in spite of her promiscuity, a profoundly religious person, Molly is contemptuous of Boylan's arrogance: "he says your soul you have no soul inside only grey matter because he doesn't know what it is to have one." Human failure, then, is one of the basic themes in *Ulysses.*

Molly's consciousness, her soliloquy, is the interpretive center of the novel. It is also the pornographic center. Like Lawrence, Joyce sees the dichotomy of the masculine and feminine worlds represented in terms of the tension between materialism and spirituality. Unlike Lawrence, and here is where Joyce's celebrated genius in creating point of view is

200

significant, he does not impose a dialectical reality on the feminine *animus*. Nor, through ritual or myth, does he sublimate the naturalism of that point of view. It may be possible, with Molly lying in bed recounting her erotic life, to find in her a mythic earth-mother figure. But that seems to be fetching pretty far. For Joyce goes to some trouble to make her consciousness distinct and personal rather than archetypal. And if, as it has been suggested, her soliloquy is an extended masturbation fantasy, then that reduces the likelihood of her archetypicality still more. Earth-mothers do not masturbate. Unlike human beings, they do not have such neurotic needs. Molly is above all a human being, with all the weaknesses, needs, and failures of human beings. But she also has the spiritual dignity of humanity at its best. She is, in that sense, the most comprehensive kind of feminist, conscious of the need and superiority of femaleness in the world,

I dont care what anybody says itd be much better for the world to be governed by the women in it you wouldnt see women going and killing one another and slaughtering when do you ever see women rolling around drunk like they do or gambling every penny they have and losing it on horses yes because a woman whatever she does she knows where to stop sure they wouldnt be in the world at all only for us they dont know what it is to be a woman and a mother how could they where would they all of them be if they hadnt all a mother to look after them.

These are clichés, yet coming from the mind of a woman who is also conscious of herself as an adultress and conscious of her sexuality and its indulgence and conscious also of masculine sexuality and its vagaries and conscious, through all, of human spiritual dignity, the cliches take on profound meaning. Above all they exemplify the spiritual generosity necessary to love not only mankind but oneself.

Spiritual generosity in the face of human failure is the crux of Joyce's comic vision, and Molly is its spokesman. One thinks of its antithesis in the terrifying, obscene, and spiritually mean retreat sermon Joyce describes in *A Portrait of the Artist as a*

201

Young Man. Molly, conversely, affirms everything human. The word "yes" recurs throughout her soliloquy like a liturgical incantation. "Yes," she begins, "because he never did a thing like that before as ask to get his breakfast in bed," and we know she is affirming Bloom, her "Poldy." She affirms Bloom not simply because, after ten years of impotence, he asserts himself as a man, but because that assertion confirms what she has perceived in him through all of his indignity and depravity, the presence of spiritual generosity and self-consciousness in the best epistemological sense. Bloom, unlike Boylan, has been on an odyssey in search of himself. Kinetically at least, he finds the image of that self when he befriends Stephen Dedalus, in whom he finds an analogue to his dead son, Rudy. Bloom, like Ulysses, has at last come home to his "faithful" Penelope. And Molly affirms even that sad relationship, her infidelity and his impotence; she affirms it by finding a way for them to "make it," however abnormal it may have to be:

. . . its all his own fault if Im an adulteress . . . if thats all the harm ever we did in this vale of tears God knows its not much doesnt everybody only they hide it I suppose thats what a woman is supposed to be there for or He wouldnt have made us the way He did so attractive to men then if he wants to kiss my bottom Ill drag open my drawers and bulge it right out in his face as large as life he can stick his tongue 7 miles up my hole . . . Ill let him do it off me behind provided he doesn't smear all my good drawers O I suppose that cant be helped . . . I know every turn in him Ill tighten my bottom well and let out a few smutty words smellrump or lick my shit or the first mad thing comes in my head . . .

Shortly after this passage, Molly begins the crescendo of affirmation with which the novel and her soliloquy end. She too, like Lawrence's Ursula, has a vision of apocalypse. But rather than co-joining earth and sky as the rainbow does, Molly's vision is altogether earthy, a reminiscence of Bloom's proposal of marriage. In the remembering, punctuated with the rhythmic incantation of "yes," she affirms what happened then and all that has happened since:

I gave him the bit of seedcake out of my mouth and it was leapyear
like now yes 16 years ago my God after that long kiss I near lost my
breath yes he said I was a flower of the mountain yes so we are
flowers all a womans body yes that was one true thing he said in his
life and the sun shines for you today yes that was why I liked him
because I saw he understood or felt what a woman is . . . and then
I asked him with my eyes to ask again yes and then he asked me
would I yes to say yes my mountain flower and first I put my arms
around him yes and drew him down to me so he could feel my
breasts all perfume yes and his heart was going like mad and yes I
said yes I will Yes.

And so the novel ends, with existential celebration, regretting
nothing. Bloom's "triumph" derives from his moral hermaph-
roditism, his fusion of the masculine and feminine worlds; he
may only be a man, but he strives, however bunglingly, to be
more. And Molly, the voice of Joyce's comic ethos, honors both
Bloom and herself as existential models. What we are is what
one can expect—"doesn't everybody only they hide it"—and
we must love ourselves and one another nonetheless, in all the
failure of our nature. We find some beauty, as Joyce says we
must, in the very grossness of earth.

We have been considering pornographic rhetoric in the structure of high or philosophical comedy. It also has a role in satire.
There too it works to exorcise mental idols. Sex itself, or fear
of sex, has become a bogey. It has become, in fact, almost a
cultural mania. Popular magazines, newspapers, and books are
filled with sexual advice columns and articles. Schools are bad-
gered by proponents and opponents of sex education. The
relation between sexuality and society has itself reached something like burlesque proportions. This does not mean that the
problem is not serious. It is. But the hysteria it causes is frequently pretty funny. Satirical pornography has picked up this
mood, and uses it to mock the seriousness with which we regard
sex, and because of which we tend to be controlled by it. The
popular media, such as *Playboy,* and the recent pornography
tabloids, have particular fun with it. The cultural need to have
some fun with sex, and relieve the oppressiveness of our pre-

occupation with it, has made *Candy,* which might otherwise have been an amusing trifle, an international sensation. The conception of the novel, the sexual adventures into which a simple, beautiful, ingenue is thrust by her innocence, offers marvellous possibilities for satirical allegory. The movie version seems to have pursued them even more imaginatively, if in less physiological detail. What the novel ridicules is the notion that something so natural and ubiquitous as sex is reasonably compatible with moral and religious traditions of innocence as a moral virtue and as well the sentimental idealism which is its philosophical basis. Candy Christian, motivated by the great sentimental ideals of self-sacrifice and good deeds, of as she puts it (in the words of Professor Mephisto, her great teacher of contemporary ethics, who turns out, alas, to be a lascivious queer and lecher *extraordinaire*), the "privilege and duty of giving oneself fully to those who have great need," has her succulent honey pot plundered by one needy (rhymes with greedy) dipper after another. The burlesque opportunities are obvious enough, and the novel exploits them well. What is ridiculous, our sublimation of natural impulses to transcendental virtues, is covered with ridicule. Nature and absurdity prevail. The idea is to exorcise the sullenness of sexual preoccupations and put it, through humor, into a reasonable perspective. For, as Lawrence's Ursula and Miller's Maude discover, carnal knowledge is not the end of the world, it is a new beginning.

Comedy overrides the anxiety caused by the mythos of animality by turning that myth to irony, playing off reason and passion against one another. Man's passions are ridiculed, and thus cut to size, because they are finally so puny. Joyce's Bloom is a puny hero with puny, abortive passions. In presenting him as a modern hero Joyce is at once banishing the mythology of heroics as morally useful for a modern ethos and telling us that an existential condition of whatever quotidian character has moral reality. Philip Roth continues the tradition of *schlep* as hero in *Portnoy's Complaint.* While the mythic heroes are moved to rape by their passions, Portnoy, the *schlep* hero, can only get it up for masturbation. Portnoy's complaint, "a disorder in which strongly felt ethical and altruistic impulses are perpetually warring with extreme sexual longings, often of a perverse nature," is the logical conclusion of the cultural ethos against which de Sade, Miller, and Lawrence raged. Man is made impotent by being put out of touch with his body. The narrative framework of the novel, in which Portnoy talks out his complaint to a mythical analyst (much the same way that Humbert talks out his defense to the mythical jury in *Lolita*), suggests the pathological consequences of levitating sex from the loins to the head.

Superficially, *Portnoy's Complaint* is the longest Jewish mother joke in history. But, like all such jokes, it taps into a much larger issue, the conflict between the new and the old, death and regeneration. It is therefore natural that the novel's chief symbol is the malfunction of the organ and imagination of regeneration. Portnoy's story, simply put, is that the compulsive care of his Jewish parents has given him a mania for masturbation. From self-abuse he expands to self-indulgence (". . . while all the other sons have been carrying forward the family name, what he has been doing is—chasing cunt. And *shikse* cunt, to boot Chasing it, sniffing it, lapping it, *shtupping* it, but above all, *thinking about it*"); from that to perversity (three in a bed), and finally in Israel, where other Jews find new life and potency, to impotence (as he tries to seduce a kibbutz girl, thus: "Licked her earholes, sucked at her unwashed neck, sank my teeth into the coiled braids of hair . . . and then, even as resistance may actually have begun to recede under my assault, I rolled off of her and came to rest, defeated, against the wall—on my back. 'It's no good,' I said, 'I can't get a hard-on in this place'"). In short, Portnoy is sexually ridiculous: " 'Then,' I pleaded, as she began to drag me by her powerful leg across toward the door, 'at least let me eat your pussy. I know I can still do that.' " And sexually ridiculous is humanly ridiculous.

The cause of the absurdity, again superficially, is the anal compulsiveness of the Jewish mother. More profoundly, however, it is the moral alienation of man from his body, enforced by the cultural emphasis of "success" and "cleanliness." It gets to Portnoy's father as constipation; he is an insurance agent, so much so that he cannot even let go of his waste. It gets to Portnoy in his compulsive masturbation. It is summed up in his cunt-chasing, "but above all, *thinking about it.*" The separation of mind and body, the separation of man from himself, from the rhythms of nature, as Lawrence lamented, diminishes man to self-mockery. When Portnoy sings "Impotent in Israel" to the tune of "Lullaby in Birdland," the kibbutz girl asks, "Another joke?" "And another," Portnoy replies, "and another. Why disclaim my life?" Roth, then, satirizes the ethos of impotence by making it a joke. A sick joke, but a joke nonetheless, because finally all there is to do is laugh at yourself, maybe a little hysterically, when you have been reduced to parody. Roth lands on the Jewish mother and the culture whose values she represents as the causes of human life being so reduced, so wasted. But they are only the agencies. The real causality is in the ethos that denies the viability of nature. The symbolic Jewish mother, with all her cooking and housecleaning, manages to make her son impotent and her husband constipated. She fouls up the mechanisms of nature. The culture and values she represents, then, are an antidote to nature, stopping it up, distorting it, killing life. Portnoy's complaint, a disorder in which the mind and body are at war, is a satiric statement of the theme of ethical disorder that runs through pornographic comedy. Comic pornography prescribes an enema, and if they can sell the script to the movies, just as the tube goes in, the camera eye will move in for a close-up of the anal apperature in good working order. It's messy, but a thing like that, believe it or not, is good for the soul.

8.

How to Make the World Safe for Pornography

AFTER being "five times fairly lost in supreme rapture" with the fair Louisa, James Boswell in his *London Journal* admits to being "somewhat proud of my performance." Louisa, having greater moral sensibility than temperance, "said it was what there was no just reason to be proud of. . . . She said it was what we had in common with the beasts. I said no. For we had it highly improved by the pleasures of sentiment." Even in the sack Bozy and Louisa are deep in the usual sex bag: they deny what both *need, want,* and *do.* This mechanism of denial is itself worth pursuing because it connects us with the psychic process of displacement whereby sexual energy is transformed or sublimated. Advertising has for a good while recognized this, and when it drapes juicy ladies or chiseled he-men about a Dodge Polara, Aerosal shave cream, or Maidenform bra it woos our eager displacement apparatus to gratify sexual pressures by transforming them to less "dangerous" analogues. So, rather than loosing our lust on the world, we acquire a new car—another kind of potency. But as this advertising technique has developed (largely since World War II and the popularizing of depth psychology) its profound materialism has been not only obvious but disturbing. For a Judeo-Christian society, no matter how materialistic its practices, cannot *morally* justify them. The options are clear enough therefore: change the morality or change the practise. Which means, realistically, that there are no options and we are confronted with the time-honored sophistic problem of moral revisionism.

If, as Boswell's anecdote suggests, we will not change our habits; and if, as poor Louisa's lamentation suggests, we feel morally obliged to refute our bestiality, then we must understand how our intractable beastly behavior gets sublimated to civilized virtue, and we get made at peace with our nastiness. History, here in the guise of Boswell, shows us—our naturalistic selves have been, over the past 300 years or so, "highly improved by the pleasures of sentiment." Since Boswell's time, sentiment figures so centrally in our cultural tradition that it may be said to be the primary phenomenon in what Leslie Fiedler calls "the Break-through" to modernity.

In its largest generic sense, sentiment refers to emotion, and the capacity for emotion, as Boswell says, signifies those higher functions of mind by which we distinguish ourselves from beasts. It was used as an analogue of *affection, feeling, belief,* and *sensation* by such eighteenth-century philosophers as Hume, who were exploring the philosophy of consciousness and interior reality. But the scientific exploration of such psychic machinery required a more sophisticated clinical context, and the more popular and culturally significant use of the term was Laurence Sterne's moral elevation of humane *feelings* over the pompous absurdities of *reason.* Toby Shandy, the moral hero of *Tristram Shandy,* transformed the western heroic concept irrevocably when he, rather than killing, liberated a fly out the window saying, "This world is surely wide enough to hold both thee and me."

This fictional incident is very likely the source of that epithet which signifies for us the highest refinement of human sensibility—and Toby Shandy is thereby the sentimental model for Albert Schweitzer; neither of them would hurt a fly. Before Toby, this richly foibled and often fuddled image of human sensibility, Sterne routs the pretentions of reason and dialectic, represented in such characters as Walter Shandy, who regulates his connubial "obligations" by machine—the first Sunday of each month, after he winds the clock. In articulating this dialectical opposition *Tristram Shandy* may be the most profound and optimistic statement of humanism possible. It celebrates imagistically what theologians, philosophers, and psychologists have sought mechanistically. It celebrates mind, that elusive touchstone, the thing that makes men men. Thus the ubiquitous human urge for univocal morality was provided with a univocal image of moral virtue—the man of feeling. Moral needs were better served by an idealistic synthesis than by the disconcerting diffusion of scientific analysis. Sentiment, therefore, came to signify the apex of human virtue.

In the hands of an existentialist like Sterne such a theory was good, but it did not everywhere have such integrity. Samuel Richardson, for example, extracted sentiment from its existential roots and made it the rhetorical servant of a middle-class ethos. For Sterne, sentiment—the capacity for feeling—was its own standard of human being. It assumed the status of moral paradigm. But, while Sterne's sentimentality argued the philosophical case for moral idealism and its resultant ethical charity, Richardson's was made a tactical weapon of liberation for the culturally emerging business class. Thus sentiment was accommodated to commerce. What after all, beside a nicely turned haunch, has Pamela to "sell" Squire B. other than those hundreds of pages of high sentiment which punctuate the narrative of her heroic preservation of virginity. And a well-turned virgin haunch, as Fanny Hill's or Moll Flander's narratives tell us, was easily obtainable for any squire of the realm. So, though fine feeling has sexy packaging, it is nevertheless sentiment that is for sale. And Richardson makes the Squire buy his dearly. It cost him, and all his kind, a way of life. The battle between Pamela and Squire B. signifies a historic moment of natural selection in the cultural evolution of the West. The business ethos, in England for example, having shut down the theaters and having harnessed kings, had finally worked its way into art. It was not, of course, a revolutionary moment. The business ethos had no particular interest in a better world and certainly had no strategy to achieve one.

209

It did not want an end to aristocracy; it wanted to *be* the aristocracy. The profit principle (not to be confused with the greed principle, which is an unequivocal vice even in the business ethos), therefore, needed elevation in the cosmic moral scheme. When Pamela marries "up" into aristocracy she carries the middle class and all its baggage (servants, peasants) with her. It was the best deal Business ever made: exchanging what all men had a lot of—sentiment—for what up to that time most men had very little of—value. With Richardson, sentiment is transformed into commodity, and commodity, by this association, is transformed into moral virtue. Ultimately, in our time, it becomes *the* moral virtue. What is good for business is good for man.

The way, therefore, to make the world safe for pornography is to show it that sex is good for business. It sounds simpler, however, than it is. It won't do, for example, to say that sex *is* good business, because one becomes, then, a greedy sex monger. Greed and profit, remember, are not the same. Profit is good; greed is bad. How much profit is equivalent to greed? "If you don't like it here go back to Russia where you came from." Besides, we are enlightened now and we know that sex is bad only when it is *dirty*. How does sex get dirty? "It gets dirty when there's too much of it." How much is. . . ? "Well, you don't have to have your nose rubbed in it to know about it." Couldn't those with sensitive noses decline the gambit? "It would be nice to think that people knew their own noses, but it's not realistic." What has to happen, in short, is that one clean sex up and show that, though it is perfectly businesslike, it is not tainted by filthy lucre. For however much we may think money is its own reward, we will not risk its spoliation.

Playboy magazine, perhaps more than any other single pop culture phenomenon, has managed to change sex from a dirty joke into "entertainment served up with humor, sophistication, and spice," to purloin a phrase from its original apology. *Playboy* has been a paradigmatic force in making the world safe for pornography because it has always been careful to use sex for "higher" ends—essentially for the establishment of its fundamental image, the well-heeled Playboy who can and should afford his monthly Playmate. From its beginnings *Playboy* projected the image of a latter day (executive *né* business) man of mode; again from the credo of its first issue, "We like our apartment. We enjoy mixing up cocktails and an hors d'oeuvre or two, putting a little mood music on the phonograph, and inviting in a female acquaintance for a quiet discussion on Picasso, Nietzsche, jazz, sex." The audience was intended to be, as it has proved to be, "young men-on-the-move" (another *Playboy* PR phrase). It was intended to be and has become a magazine for the young executive, and, more inclusively, for the hopeful fantasies of aspiring pre-executives. But, more than anything else, it is a monumental pop celebration of commodity.

Playboy has grown, in fifteen years, from the twice-hocked furniture of its founder Hugh Hefner's apartment to a $54 million "empire," as we are told in the 1968 financial report from *Playboy;* and we are reminded by Hefner—president of the enterprise—that, being a private corporation, *Playboy* is not required to make a public financial statement. He does it, presumably therefore, because he *wants* to. And if there is any question about *Playboy's* most important product, one need only check its own public relations brochures. The introductory paragraph of one, the cover of which shows the new Playboy Building backed up by Chicago's Gold Coast, goes thus:

Topped with the world's largest aviation beacon, the Playboy Building at 919 North Michigan Avenue in Chicago is today the headquarters of one of the brightest lights in the world of entertainment for men—*Playboy*. A landmark since its construction, the building, formerly called the Palmolive Building, is a fitting symbol for a magazine and subsidiary enterprises which have witnessed lightning success during the past decade.

One might note here that after *Playboy* moved out of its old Ohio Street buildings it took the United States Post Office and the Museum of Contemporary Art to fill its "shoes." Another blurb entitled "The Playboy Empire," begins so:

The $12,000,000 Playboy Club-Hotel at Lake Geneva, Wis., represents one of the most ambitious projects in the history of the Playboy empire. It is the 19th Club in the international chain which includes locations in Atlanta, Baltimore, Boston, Chicago, Cincinnati, Denver, Detroit, Kansas City, Los Angeles, Miami, New Orleans, New York, Phoenix, St. Louis and San Francisco, plus Montreal and London. It is the second Club-Hotel to be operated by Playboy International, Inc.—the first one debuted in Ocho Rios, Jamaica, in January 1965. Today the Playboy Clubs have some 650,000 keyholders and additional Clubs and Club-Hotels are now being planned for areas including New Jersey, Southern Spain, San Juan and Acapulco.

So Alpha, and so Omega:

As *Playboy* grew, so did its related enterprises. A Playboy Jazz Festival featuring practically every name jazz artist was held in Chicago in 1959. It was the largest in history, with 68,000 people attending. Hefner conceived and produced *Playboy's Penthouse,* a syndicated latenight television show. A second TV show, *Playboy After Dark,* is now being shown. Playboy Press, the book division, and *VIP,* the magazine for keyholders, were organized. The Playboy Theater, specializing in outstanding U.S. and foreign films, opened in Chicago; Playboy Models was set up; and Playboy Products, marketing apparel and gifts, was initiated.

With the continuous growth of the Playboy empire, plans are now under way for a major expansion into the motion picture and television industries.

Commodity is the beginning and the end.

But profit is really the simplest and even most predictable of *Playboy's* achievements. More complex and more culturally significant is the cause of that awful success—*Playboy's* adroit use of sex. So adroit has it been, in fact, that one has the uncomfortable feeling that Pamela, our old flame, has not done with us yet. One feels, in the image of the Playboy, that Pamela's Squire has been mightily domesticated (and calling domesticity "urbanity" or "sophistication" does not relieve the anxiety). Yet again from the original credo: "Most of today's 'magazines for men' spend all their time out-of-doors—thrash-

212

ing through thorny thickets or splashing about in fast flowing streams. We'll be out there too, occasionally, but we don't mind telling you in advance—we plan on spending most of our time inside. We like our apartment." Et cetera. The rest we have already seen. And not the Playboy's broadest, knowingest wink, not even a desperate psychedelic discussion of Picasso, Nietzsche, jazz, *and* sex all at the same time can dissuade us that Pamela has not stuffed that velvet smoking jacket and silk scarf with the carcass of her long tamed Squire, put a highball in his hand, a cigarette holder in his teeth, an impressionistic nude on his paneled den wall, and called him PLAYBOY. At last Pamela and the Squire are on equal terms (a fact which *Cosmopolitan* magazine has recently recognized much to its own advantage), and Pamela, our vital parts firmly in her grip, demands, "and now Monsieur your wallet." Hemingway warned us, but we would not listen.

The first thing, then, that *Playboy* has done by equating sex with profit is to sublimate it from its fearful psychic depths to the heights of that "fitting symbol formerly called the Palmolive Building." And, by being made into capital, sex has been psychologically neutralized. It has become a contemporary (and historical) community standard: it is proved profitable and therefore socially redeeming. Concomitant, of course, with *Playboy's* showing cause for sex has been its cleaning up of the image of sex. Attributing the observation to a Kinsey Institute authority, Nat Lehrman, a senior editor of the magazine, says that *Playboy* has raised sex to respectability, made it fit matter for coffee conversation (along, remember, with Picasso, Nietzsche, and jazz). This is probably true, but in the beginning *Playboy* had some difficulty getting launched into the antiseptic sex imagery which is its latter-day hallmark.

The early foldouts, called "Playboy's Eyeful" then, were standard low-grade skin pictures. Nor did they have the now-familiar personality sketch accompanying them. It took three years for the Playmate image to find the girl-next-door quality that now has currency. *Playboy* legend has it that one Janet Pilgrim, a circulation secretary whose name is still on the masthead, went to Hefner requesting a new typewriter. He told her she would have to pose nude for it, *à la* Lady Godiva. She did, and the Playmate image was born—bright-eyed, bushy (I beg your pardon?) tailed, and clean, clean, clean. Up to this time (about 1955), as one editor acknowledges, the magazine was obliged to use either "hookers" or professional models for its foldouts and the image was, excepting perhaps the celebrated Marilyn Monroe calendar nudes featured in the first issue, more sleazy than piquant. And, though Jack Kessie, *Playboy's* managing editor, claims that the sublimated *Playboy* Image we can now perceive was planned from the magazine's inception, sleaziness pretty much describes its character for at least the first four or five issues. Such photographic features, for example, as "Strip Quiz," a Paris *bistro* strip routine, or Beaux Arts Ball, a portfolio of prurient snapshots, or illustrations of criminal assault, indicate something of the imagistic tone of the first three issues. The fourth issue, though, presented two marvellously prophetic features. One is called "Sex Sells a Shirt," and simply shows a girl taking off her clothes, including of course her shirt. The text, in its banal way, discusses sex and merchandising for a few column inches. It intends to say nothing, and it does. But this nevertheless is the first public presentation of the profit formula on which *Playboy* was to ride to fiscal glory. The other feature is billed as a pictorial history of surgery, and it is essentially a vehicle for naked ladies pictured in the context of medical history. Sex, thus, is both a delight and an instruction, satisfying not only classical poetics but, more importantly, providing the proper scholarly elevation for so base a subject. This kind of augmentation was also to become an editorial staple of the magazine's success formula.

Today's Playmate, through which the *Playboy* Image is projected, is the scrupulously antiseptic incarnation of almost virginal contemporary community standards, an occasional lapse into prostitution notwithstanding. And she even has sufficient social redemption potential to be rented out to colleges over football weekends. At which, to show her healthy respect for the Working Man (or Labor or The People or the Dollar—as you prefer), she will charge overtime for conversation above and beyond an eight hour day. (This really happens!) Playmates, lest their title be misleading, do not indulge idle pleasure for its own sake; the meter on these puritanic taxi-dancers is always running. And well it might, for Nathanael West to the contrary, a clean young girl is always worth more than a clean old man—especially on a college football weekend at an all-male college.

Especially too when one notes that *Playboy's* notion of its editorial "responsibility" is to serve, according to managing editor Jack Kessie, as a guidebook to the good life for the young, university-educated man. The vocabulary *Playboy* editors use to describe their magazine and its goals reads like Dr. Johnson's own lexicon of aesthetic terms: Balance, Proportion, Taste, Elegance, Imagination, Wit. And it is easily acknowledged that *Playboy* is the most balanced, tasteful, elegant, imaginative, and witty skin book in the business. (By "skin book" I do not of course mean *skin* at all, but rather skin sublimated to *capital*. In which sense one understands that *Playboy* is the more honestly pornographic analogue of *Fortune* magazine, though it is less honest, and therefore more obscene, than the *Evergreen Review*. Of all the terms in the *Playboy* vocabulary, "taste" is perhaps the most significant. "We present sex," says Kessie, "in proportion to its over-all degree of importance in man's life." This is true, but it is not the whole truth. In modesty, Kessie ignores the fact that, in making sex a respectable thing and in demonstrating its commodity quotient, *Playboy* expanded the popular horizons for sex's over-all degree of importance in man's life. What he means by *Playboy's* tastefulness is that *visually* there is no more sex showing than there should be.

This is elaborated in Kessie's notion of *Playboy's* editorial contribution to the culture. *Playboy* was, he says, the first to assert not only nudity and sex, but also something else—a rounded view of the good life. He points out, for instance, that if *Playboy* "advocates materialism, so do we advocate other things—civil rights, for example." And what, after all, is the end of Taste (not to mention Balance, Proportion, Imagination, and Wit) if not to give a rounded view of the good life? The *Playboy* editors are tastefully aware that "too much" of anything—such as civil rights activism, or an eyeful of genitals —is bad for standards, of both business and taste. Thus the Playmate has breasts with glamorized nipples, a groin without pubic hair, vagina, or urinary tract, and a backside without anus. She has feminine shape without female, or for that matter even human, function. She is not made for coitus or procreation or motherhood. She has body without consequence. So when it comes to nakedness (absolute nudity) as distinguished from nudity ("tasteful" nudity, guess whose taste: yes, Pamela's), the "cleanliness" of sex is threatened, and so, therefore, is business: "Our standard has been taste," Kessie says, "and of course there is the risk of legal action. We like to think of ourselves as trend setters, but here we have, for business and other reasons, to wait for society to know its own mind." So, despite the PR assurance that "It was Hefner's unorthodox belief (a belief he still holds today) that editing a magazine should be a personal matter, that the primary criteria for choosing content should be the editor's own taste and judgment rather than the preferences of a preconceived audience," there *is* in fact a preconceived audience—the young, university-educated man—and the taste of the *Playboy* editors has long since been determined by the sublime cultural marriage of commodity and morality. And *Playboy,* one of the massive offspring of that union, has as much as any other cultural product reaffirmed that its parents are indeed one flesh.

The effect of sentimentalizing materialism, that is, of giving it the moral value of an ideal, is to transform the natural world into a pop art toy which exists for the Playboy's *well-earned* amusement. After all, he brings home the fatback. (Nor can we, in honesty, be condescending to the *Playboy* Image, for it metaphors all of us, the whole consumer culture on which our egos, economics, and politics depend.) Therefore, all things are seen in the context of *Playboy's* peculiar ethos of amusement. Women, particularly, are *objets d'art,* created for the

Playboy fantasy by the photographer's air brush art and in the Image of *Playboy* by the sketch writer's Playmate-as-home-town-girl fictions. The mere idea of his Playmate menstruating, not to mention the disgusting *fact* of it, is enough to make the Playboy impotent. The Playmate is the Playboy's Beatrice. She does not function, she *is*. Like Shakespeare's Cleopatra, age cannot wither nor custom stale her infinite variety. Like Keats' still unravished bride of quietness, she is forever warm and still to be enjoyed, forever panting and young, far above the stinking breath of human passion, and with *her* we avoid after-sex hangover, that "heart high-sorrowful and cloy'd/ burning forehead, and a parching tongue." The Playmate is not an object of sex. She is an object of art, low art to be sure, but art nonetheless. And who put her on that pedestal and on the mantlepiece of our den? Pamela, we smell a rat.

Playboy's pornography consists in its transformation of women—that is, female human beings—into Playmates and bunnies, into erotic art objects designed to titillate the sexual sense and then sublimate it into spending money (in the Play-boy Clubs hopefully), or into fantasizing about spending money (in *Playboy* magazine). The greenback dollar, in the *Playboy* ethos (and the *Playboy* ethos is fundamentally the capitalistic ethos), is the sublimated analogue of sperm. Money and the mak-ing of it is the masculine symbol in this cultural climate. Spending it therefore is the masculine privilege. It is no accident that the verb *spend* is a common pornographic metaphor for male or-gasm. And since, in a capitalistic democracy, money can buy everything, women are, as they have really always been, com-modity; and all commodity is available to him who has the power to take it. Thus the power to buy becomes, in the capital-istic ethos, the sign of sexual power. So the world is sexualized, and sex is commercialized, and we have a pornographic image of the world—an idealized, socially lionized, metaphor of pros-titution as a way of life. And that, traditionally, is what pornog-raphy is—the literature of and about whores and whoring.

But then this process is rather subtle, and one is seldom conscious of himself as the Playboy. Nor does one think of his

217

woman as a whore. And so long as he has Playmates, Bunnies, and their analogues the movie sex stars (who of late have been knocking one another's knockers for the chance to be nude on *Playboy's* pages) he need not think of her—if he thinks of her at all, his mind being filled with more enticing fantasies—as such, or as property. She may continue in her time-honored rhetorical role of the sometimes dull, sometimes bright but always slightly irrelevant companion. So it is a curiously lonely bed that Pamela after all has made and in which she must lie. But she is not through yet. Having established her ethos, she labors now to imprint her personality. She has before her, therefore, the task of creating a feminine pornography.

Feminine pornography requires a fantasy structure in which women are invited, as women, to be sexually excited. For the socially redemptive pornography we have been considering this means an alteration of the sex-profit nexus. Theoretically it needs a shift from money and expenditure as an exclusively masculine symbology. Imagistically it involves a transition from the *Playboy* cultural mode to that of the Career Girl. The basic model still, of course, is that of *Playboy*. The emphasis is merely reversed—from male cultural potency to female cultural potency. The woman's magazine most perspicacious in recognizing the *Playboy* mode and in exploiting it for its own audience and purposes is the new *Cosmopolitan*. *Cosmopolitan* has only recently tapped in to the pornographic tradition we have been considering. And coming from its own imperial stock, the Hearst syndicate, it is not a pornographic empire builder but is merely capitalizing on the female potential of the ethos *Playboy* has by this time stabilized. And though *Cosmopolitan* has its own cultural significance as a feminist pornographic voice, it is not consequently as historically instructive or important as *Playboy*.

It emerged from the maze of what William Iverson, in a marvelously witty series of *Playboy* articles—"The Pious Pornographers" (1957 and 1964)—called "the bizarre bulletins on glands, guilt, grief, gynecology, and intercourse which are the peculiar specialty of some of America's most widely read sex books—the women's magazines." His general thesis is that women's magazines offer sentimentalized sexual voyeurism which takes the form of a "sick, sad sex approach to the problem of getting a man to drop his pants [or a woman to lift her skirts], so that a million-odd women [can] get a few vicarious kicks from 'playing doctor.'" Here is part of what Iverson calls a "sampler" of prurient ladies' home preoccupations:

"That inverted nipple seems better than it was," the doctor told Evelyn Ayres after he had concluded his usual examination. "Have you been pulling it out gently several times, morning and night, the way Mary Ann showed you?"

"Yes, Doctor . . ."

"I believe I told you that there is a difference of medical opinion as to the best method of toughening the nipples . . ."

". . . Your uterus is small and firm. . . . Your breasts show no signs of pregnancy engorgement . . ."

. . . This was an atavistic dream of a man and woman alone in a Garden of Eden, perfumed, flecked with butterflies. A red petal fell from the African tulip tree . . .

"Oh, Bill," she whispered, half-choking. . . . Then he kissed her. Her lips were like orchids—crumpled, soft, cool, moist. They clung to his. Her arms were around his neck . . .

The range of frequency in intercourse for couples of 25 to 35 is great. A few have intercourse as often as 20 to 30 times a month; others only twice a month. For the majority, the average is 2 or 3 times a week . . .

"If he has his way, it would be every night. It isn't that I'm a frigid wife, for I am not. Once a week (which is my preference) I respond readily . . ."

Q. What about the forceful technique of making love? Do you think that women prefer it?

A. Sometimes. Many couples think that variation in sex simply means a different position. Variation can also mean a different psychological attitude. If a man surprises his wife, spontaneously, on a Sunday afternoon, or in a different room of the house, aggressively taking her, this type of approach can make their relationship enormously more erotic . . .

"He said I was cold, and I said he was oversexed. Once he even wanted to make love at lunchtime!"

219

"Of course it's awfully hard not to. You both want to so much. Sure, Jim used to get fresh with me now and then, but I'd always handle it by saying, 'Look at the television or something.' But once I thought, Oh, why not? . . ."

"The hymen is a thin little membrane, Phyllis, stretched across the lower end of the vagina . . ."

"Am I afraid to use mine?" I said.

"No," George said, "like I say, you're naturally lascivious. You use your pelvis. . . ."

I did a little bump.

"But I wouldn't go too far," George said. I could feel from his neck that he was beginning to color.

"Why do men want sex to be like a burlesque show? Why can't they realize that it is a solemn thing?"

". . . And . . . well, one night I drank a can of beer in the car with him, and it happened again . . . I just couldn't help it. After all, girls want it just as much as boys do, don't they?"

The summing up, where Iverson recalls,

the curious saga of Evelyn Ayres, troubled heroine of another stirring episode of "Tell Me, Doctor," the *Ladies' Home Journal's* long-playing feature on clinical sex and gynecological horrors. Years of familiarity with its format of fear, disaster and medical salvation had led me to think of this everexpanding anthology of female malfunctions as a kind of cryptoprurient *Memoirs of a Woman of Misery,* in which Evelyn Ayres now starred as the anxiety-fraught Fanny Hill of Breast Feeding.

There is here a latter-day version of that same morbid sentimentalizing of the faithful servant woman (not Moll Flanders but Pamela) as she resists the forces of aristocratic evil and guile that Richardson exploited for his social class in the eighteenth century. The heroine is essentially the same, but, with her social and even economic success in molding the Squire into the Playboy, the nature of the villain has transformed itself to neurosis, obstetrics and gynecology, things unheard of in Richardson's day. That, if you are not too particular, is progress. But, being an extension of the long-familiar soap opera, it is pretty much predictable. And so one suspects that Iverson's anxiety (*Playboy's* anxiety) crowds his condescending wit.

For his real complaint, *Playboy's* complaint, is not that the women's magazines are *pornographic* (he and *Playboy* know all about that, although such language makes them nervous, being bad for business), it is that they are *obscene*. Nor is his objection to their piety (that is sentimentality); he and *Playboy* know all about that too, as we have seen. The problem is that these magazines undermine the Playmate image. Think of the Playmate. Imagine her with inverted nipples! Or menstruating! Or, worse still, imagine her being sexually unsatisfied *after* a bout with the prodigiously phallic Playboy! Smearing her neuroses, obstetrics, and gynecology all over the hard-earned sanctuary of his den. Not only that, as if it weren't enough, they also undermine the *Playboy* image. Iverson's citation of the following rebuke of vestigial "19th Century Puritanism" is revealing in this regard:

All shapes and varieties of marital anguish were laid squarely at the door of the clumsy husband. It was the man, the marriage manuals unanimously declared, who was responsible for success in sex, and equally responsible for its failure. For the enlightened readers of the manuals, making love became a kind of challenge . . .

Frequently couples spent so much time worrying about whether their technique was right, whether their climaxes occurred simultaneously as the book said they should, whether the wife really had an orgasm, that they lost all the meaning of marital intercourse, not to mention the pleasure . . .

"Pleasure" was a word that the ladies' books had seldom mentioned in connection with sex, and T. F. James' reference to it came as a welcome surprise.

Iverson argues, though with more clever outrage than analytical energy, for a "recognition of the need for greater sexual responsibility in women . . . (to) reduce the impossible number of restrictions . . . imposed upon the sexual deportment of the American male." The *Playboy* spokesman is annoyed that women, too, want some fun but aren't getting it and are imposing their frustrations on his fantasies. Women, alas, want to *feel* something down there and, alack and alas, they want to feel it more often than men want to make them feel it. *Play-*

221

boy may or may not acknowledge the problem. That isn't clear either from Iverson's articles or from *Playboy* generally. What is clear, however, is that *if* there is a problem it is a problem for *women,* so *Playboy* lays it discreetly at their door and strides manfully off to a rendevous with mood music on the hi-fi and a quiet discussion of Picasso, Nietzsche, jazz, and (still undaunted) sex.

Perhaps *Cosmopolitan* got the message, for five months after Iverson's articles had been concluded it appointed Helen Gurley Brown (author of the best-selling *Sex and the Single Girl*) as its editor. *Time,* in March of 1965, (the same month Miss Brown was appointed *Cosmopolitan's* editor), noted the magazine's transition from a "rather bland" character into a female counterpart of *Playboy.* And in July of 1966 *Newsweek* observed that Helen Gurley Brown had sexed *Cosmopolitan* up, especially in terms of its advertising and the identification of its audience. So *Cosmopolitan's* press noted the terms of its new formula very quickly. *Cosmopolitan,* or more likely the Hearst hierarchy, had recognized how *Playboy* was making the world safe for pornography, and it very neatly cut itself in on the sex-profit nexus. It took women out of the home, away from children, housework and such like dowdiness, and put them into careers. It imagistically counterpointed the Playboy with the Cosmopolitan Girl. This advertisement copy defines her, accompanied by the usual photograph of a sleek and sexy career girl: "A girl can do almost anything she wants to, don't you agree. She can tan instead of burn, look sexy but also look like a lady, have a job that PAYS because she's smart and still stay fascinating to men. I've done all these things and thank goodness there's one magazine that seems to understand me—the girl who wants everything out of life. I guess you could say I'm That Cosmopolitan Girl." It also counterpointed its editorial image with that of *Playboy.* If Hugh Hefner, complete with smoking jacket, pipe, hi-fi mood music, girls, quiet conversation on, etc., is the *Playboy* incarnate, so is Helen Gurley Brown the complete woman and therefore the Cosmopolitan Girl's ideal tutor. Her New Year greeting for 1969 repudiated the "sick, sad sex approach" with a vengeance:

222

Happy New Year! I can't even *hope* 1969 is going to be any good for me personally because 1968 was so great! Are you as superstitious—or fatalistic or *something*—as *I* am? I feel no matter *where* you start from—rich, poor, smart, dumb, beautiful, plain, or *whatever*—people have their good years and bad years. Mine have been running so good lately . . . marrying David, writing *Sex and the Single Girl,* getting to edit *Cosmopolitan* . . . I'm afraid it may be time for a change! I do think if you put a lot in every day . . . like you're too tired to pick up your dumbbells to do your chest exercises at night because you *gave* already that day . . . life gets better! Oh, the scruffy years a young girl goes through! In *my* teens I was at the doctor's three times a week with the worst case of acne *you* ever saw. Then into the twenties with *different* doctors . . . to cure all the psychosomatic illnesses brought on by terrible love affairs! Things only *began* to get better in my thirties and *now* (forties) I think is the best time of all. Honest! I can't help but try to impose my philosophies on *you,* of course, through the pages of *Cosmopolitan,* to tell you that if you hang in there and give everything you've got—yes, that means self-discipline and having ambition— every day the rewards can be scintillating, notwithstanding a "bad year" that creeps in now and then.

During the tenth scintillating month of 1968, I flew to Paris for the weekend to go to a party (Darryl Zanuck's gala for Maxim's seventy-fifth birthday and the world première of *A Flea in Her Ear* plus a fascinating short film, *The World of Fashion*). I love the sound of Paris for the weekend, don't you?—although I must admit I spent most of my non-party time flaked out at the George V trying to grapple with the time change! They *help* you in European hotels. The maids close the draperies so you can't tell whether it's day or night; consequently, you don't have to get *up.* The next week . . . off to Shawnee, Oklahoma, to see my mother. Mother actually lives in Osage, Arkansas (population: ninety-eight), but, since they don't have a landing strip in Osage yet—they only got a paved *street* twelve years ago—it was easier to meet at my sister's in Shawnee. It's *good* for a girl to go home to her family; no matter who you think you are in your own world, they see you as the not-altogether-*bright* creature you were thirty years ago and manage not to let you get too uppity. I went shopping at Sears, Roebuck . . . *still* the best values anywhere on earth . . . and visited an AA meeting (no, I'm not a member!). God, but they're fabulous. I can't even give up chocolate-chip cookies for five days (much *less,* cocktails), but some of the members I chatted with had not been *off* the wagon for ten, twelve, fifteen years.

What's in *Cosmo* this month? Oh, you know . . . making it . . . making good . . . making love . . . loving men . . . loving yourself . . . a great mystery novel, short stories . . . the usual birthday package. I hope you like *all* of it.

The *Cosmopolitan* "moral" is just the other side of the *Playboy* coin—every girl/woman can be rich, alluring, sexually satisfying and satisfied, and, if she wishes, happily married.

Cosmopolitan is not through with neurosis, obstetrics, and gynecology, but they are no longer occasions for morbidity. It fosters the fantasy that every woman can be taught what she doesn't know or be artificially augmented with what nature hasn't awarded her. A sampler of titles alone gives a fair idea of *Cosmopolitan*'s vast pornographic curriculum: Why I Wear My False Eyelashes to Bed; How to Make Your Figure More Perfect; What Keeps Some Girls from Getting Married and What to Do About It; How to Turn a Man On; Spectacular Beauties Reveal Their Special Tricks; Get Him to Marry You with this Revolutionary New Method; How to Make $100,000 Before You're 35 (Without a Man), and so on into infinity. There is also of course a good deal of voyeuristic entertainment (and mayhap instruction) in such features as, The Men Surrounding Jacqueline Kennedy—and the One Who's Winning Her (they pick wrong); One Young Wife's Shocking Marriage, or When a Young, Pretty Girl Discovers She's Married a Homosexual (which subject, incidentally, *Playboy* won't touch); Jim Brown is Coming on *Strong* and *Big,* and with what pun twister, we may desist. *Time,* in February of 1968, accused *Cosmopolitan* of exploiting every sexual anxiety and every sexual fantasy of "the 18 to 34 year old single women who are not knock-outs, who are unsure of themselves, who are searching for a man." This is probably true, though there is no reason to put a lid on at the age of 34. Voyeurism is for all seasons, and sexes too, for that matter.

But, if one can provide instruction while celebrating commodity, as both *Playboy* and *Cosmopolitan* do, then one has not only an acceptable but even a socially redemptive license for pornographic fun. The trick, quite simply, is to make it slick. The Cosmopolitan Girl may not be so slick or affluent as the Playboy, but then she is fifteen or so years younger, and it really does seem more difficult to sublimate gynecological messiness into profitable status than it does to do so with crudely simple phallic power. Bathispheres will never capture our imagination so well as space rockets, and the idea of a concave skyscraper with a miner's beam at its bottom just won't do. Nor is the Cosmopolitan Girl so intellectually pretentious as her Playboy friend. Miss Brown disclaims intellectual ambitions for her magazine. "We don't want very many cosmic pieces —about space, the war on poverty, civil rights, etc., but will leave those to more serious general magazines." But *Playboy* too made similar disclaimers at the beginning: "Affairs of state will be out of our province. We don't expect to solve any world problems or prove any great moral truths." So if the Cosmopolitan Girl has not yet devised let alone published a philosophy, she does at least read the poetry of Dorothy Parker, which the Playboy has never done. And the future lies, after all, securely ahead. Standing on the troubled shores of our land, looking neither too far out nor too deep in, haunch by hip these twin colossi, guarding the divine grace of capital, are beacons to the world that, with "taste" and a little Yankee ingenuity, all is safe for pornography.

Safe enough, in fact, that pornography's future lies easy. In fact its future is happening so rapidly that it is difficult to identify its present. So far as the progress of pictorial pornography goes, for example, Ralph Ginzberg and the *Eros* trials (1962–66) are classical history. Even innocuous magazines such as *Coronet, Pageant, The Woman, Companion*—designed primarily for "housewives" (as *Cosmopolitan* is designed for "career girls")—sport semi-naked voluptuaries on their covers together with such teasers as "4 Experts Tell How Successful Lovers Achieve Good Sex Without Anxiety," or "The Married Woman: How she Can Reach Her Deepest Response," or "New Clues—How to Satisfy a Woman," or "Sin

225

and Pleasure Playgrounds for the Rich." And *Mademoiselle* recently put out a special sex issue, its demure, dewy-eyed, wet-lipped cover girl flanked by promises of "what, when, and where is sexy" and "How *You* Can Have a Sexy Face" and "a Supersensuous romantic novel by the great Colette." If *Mademoiselle* can give Supersex, *Playboy* and *Cosmopolitan* have done their work well. So has Pamela, for all of these magazines —whatever the sexuality of their merchandising—are proper. Which is to say that they want their sexuality sublimated, to suit the tastes of the well-housed, clothed, and fed.

Not so the raucous pornography of the "underground" sex tabloids, *Screw, The New York Review of Sex, Kiss, Pleasure,* and so on. Following the lead of William Burroughs and such early laborers as *Fuck You, a Magazine of the Arts* and *Horseshit Magazine,* they have made "obscenity" the vehicle for "total assault" on bourgeois culture. Thus sex has, ironically, become another popular front for moral revolution. With brilliant instinct, the smut papers have become a flanking coordinate of the new left. Their political implication is much greater than has been generally recognized. For aristocratic western political traditions maintain themselves by infecting the culture with "good taste"—good taste in the arts, in speech, in journalism, and above all in behavior. Good taste means moderation. Moderation means, "agonize if you must but don't do anything." The new left defies good taste, but the new smut attacks its *source* with the reminder that good taste usually conflicts with spontaneous humanity and acts as a kind of high-toned old Christian woman with emergency police power. *Screw, the Sex Review,* because of its high spirits, self-parody, and absolute irreverence, is perhaps the leader of the smut peddlers' assault on good taste and its concomitant suppression of ego and humane personality. *Screw's* chief rhetorical weapon is parody, the characteristic mode of the pop art context from which it derives. In one marvelous feature ("*Screw* goes to Market,") the editors investigate "Nature's Way of Frigging." After complaining that the DUOSTIMULAR they had intended to report on had never been sent, they report instead on the frigging effectiveness of various vegetables: their conclusion: "For the best orgasms and healthiest results, stick to Cucumbers, Carrots or for the best fuck possible—Summer Squash." In fact, they are perhaps more into parodying than inspiring masturbation. The joke's on everything—from the Academy Awards ("The Academy Awards Peter Metered": 73% flaccid) to J. Edgar Hoover ("Is J. Edgar Hoover a Fag?": Yes) to Danish "fuckfilms" ("8 mm. Raunch"). *Screw* features are good, not because of their intelligence, which they more or less have, but because of their (surprisingly) discriminating spontaneity and happy irreverence. "Arlecchino," a *Screw* rock critic, is an example. In one review, after the premise that "The best rock music is fuck music," he asks, "Where is their [Buddah Records'] responsibility? Everyone has the responsibility to teach the young to engage in joyful fucking. . . . When the record buying public is so large, Buddah could certainly turn out a sound that would inspire the genitals to stir, rather than a sound that reminds you of a mechanical fart." Of Dylan's *Nashville Skyline:* "You, dear listener, are being put on because you are so eager to go on anybody's trip rather than invent one of your own." (This is, implicitly at least, the basic *Screw* motif, and perhaps that of all the smut tabloids.) Of the Electric Circus: "a horde of silly people working very hard at being cool . . . mechanical . . . joyless . . . uninspired." Finally, in despair, the *Screw* ethic: "You know what: find yourself a piece of ass and make your own music. That's all." This—make your own music—is another basic motif. But there are brief times when *Screw* provides less whimsical commentary on pornography, as in Al Goldstein's review of *De Sade Illustrated:*

Which brings us to another boring yet important question. Why did I find *De Sade* so much superior to *Che!* which is graphic but dull in all contexts except for the legal breakthrough it represented?

Briefly, *Che!* was not erotic even though it was sexual. The cocks and cunts of the performers were mere propaganda tools of dissemination while *De Sade* is pleasure-oriented. The lack of emotion as manifest by the lack of hard-ons in *Che!* destroyed the illusion of reality.

Those responsible for *De Sade* arrived at a brilliant solution. Tak-

227

ing the nihilistically revolutionary words of the Marquis, they contrast it with the frills and ruffles of the 18th century costumes worn by the cast and then illuminate the concept of seemingly contradictory realities by showing magnificent hard core pornography on a stage screen via reverse projection.

Theme and counter theme blended in a mixed media format that drove my cock into a frenzy. Some of the stuff on the screen *Screw* would be afraid to run and we are not known for our good taste. And then its not really a question of good taste but appropriateness.

The movie segments shown after "dialogue seven" of a masked guy lapping a hairy pussy was filled with more redeeming social significance (whatever that is) than all the Father Hills and Billy Grahams combined *ad infinitum*.

This work, in addition to being a plea for the right of the body to seek and receive pleasure, and a polemic for buggery and the joys of getting it up the ass, (read the Randy Wicker article as a further footnote or anus note), is a brutal assault on religion. The superior reasoning and incisive analysis by the father of sadism makes it very clear why society was so afraid of his works and sought to censor and dilute his message.

In short, as this passage indicates, the smut journals are not only having a lot of fun, they are also saying and doing things that should be said and done. Even if they (or we) occasionally find them "boring," they do at least have exquisitely bad taste. Nor, though their approaches to sex are antithetical, could *Playboy* or *Cosmopolitan* be more pleased than *Screw* is with its financial success:

We were warned by our distributors, printers, friends and parents that going weekly would bring with it a drop of about 30% in circulation. Well after only two weeks we have already surpassed our largest printing. If we were considered an underground publication *Screw* would now be the NATION'S LARGEST UNDERGROUND. As it is, since we no longer are underground, we still place pretty high in the ratings and will be over the 100,000 mark, probably within one month.

Screw has several new projects planned that will further knock the publishing world on its ass. We will announce it soon and try to keep the copy cats at *Rat, EVO* and the *Free Press* from peeking and doing their imitation act. Now that *Screw* is here to stay as we told all you skeptics, we have plans that include world-wide representation of global sexuality and branch offices in Copenhagen and Japan to bring you the best in erotica with the greatest disptach possible. And this is only the beginning. SCREW IS THE FUTURE! The shock of our totally new concept in journalism is over and we are first and best without question. Now comes the jump to more quality, more humor, more pictorials and lots more cocks and cunts to please your aesthetic needs as you pump your old peter (dink?).

But a paper that promises to put its profits into "world-wide representation of global sexuality and branch offices in Copenhagen and Japan to bring you the best erotica with the greatest dispatch possible," as well as a "jump to more quality, more humor, more pictorials and lots more cocks and cunts to please your aesthetic needs" can't be all bad. Nor can a paper that concludes its "fuckfilm" reviews thus:

The film cost eight kroner and played at the Vester Bio. Neither cock nor cunt were shown nor contact between them. It might have been the Scandinavian version of *War and Peace* for all I knew. It was a waste of time and the *Screw* tourist should pass it by and see *Without A Stitch On* a second time.

The bathroom in the Vester Bio looked like an old Nazi gas chamber. It had a community pisser and you just peed on the walls which deflected the flow down. (Seriously, would any other paper in America contain such information?)

Screw's success indicates that it has tapped a vulgar and naturalistic sexual sensibility in the same way (though not with the same magnitude) that *Playboy* has tapped a "tastefully" fantastic one. So the most interesting question posed by the smut papers is how their vulgarity, since it seems to be here pretty much to stay, will affect the character of pornography.

Historically, except for bigger and better repetitions each December, *Playboy* has nowhere to go. It has done its work so well that it is already, so to speak, a rear (!) guard. Not that its market is exhausted. Quite the contrary, its market continues to grow, and insofar as its tasteful middle-class sexuality serves the needs of a tasteful middle class it will continue

229

to grow along with the middle class. In fact *Penthouse, Playboy's* British imitator, has begun to distribute in America on the premise that "an affluent nation of 200 million people constitutes a market big enough and lush enough to support *two* magazines of the same genre . . ." Meanwhile, vulgarity is loose in the streets. Always has been, always will be. Now that it is more legal than ever our pornographic imaginations are promised more "quality" and more "humor," not to mention the unmentionables.

Humor in pornography is crucial, and a long time absent. The chief function of comedy is to exorcise the sense of cosmic disaster. And we are much in need of exorcising the subtle domination of sexual preoccupation that *Playboy* and Madison Avenue cultivate and exploit. Partly by parody and partly by making sex commonplace (that is, natural rather than "sacred"), by insisting that vulgarity and obscenity are perfectly "normal" and that discovering the full range of human normality is itself a humane and useful enterprise, the smut tabloids can through comic exorcism help us control rather than be controlled by (for example, as "consumers") our sexuality.

So far as quality goes, we might expect to get pornography of technical quality (as in films) and of greater imaginative character than we have been getting. Dr. Anders Groth, a Danish psychiatrist for the largest mental hospital in Denmark, observed to *Look* magazine's Foreign Editor J. Robert Moskin (*Look,* July 29, 1969) that "Good pornography is erotic art where people are people with human feelings. Bad pornography is pornography where people act mechanically and where they have feeling only concerned with sex . . ." This is a good and useful distinction. And, Denmark having now the freest pornography laws and the most vigorous pornography production in the world, it comes from appropriate experience.

Dr. Preben Hertoft, also a psychiatrist, suggests further that "If it is not against the law, you will get better pornography. It may be possible for people with talent to make some films that are artistic." In apparent accord with this notion *Screw's* "Peter Meter" evaluation of pornographic novels, movies, and what-not

230

gives priority to "Interest" (50%), followed by "Sexuality" (40%), and "Technical" (10%). The point is that maximum sexuality by itself will not get a high rating (imagine Peter Meter Awards, Telstarred from Copenhagen to Tokyo!). At this point in America the sex journals head the popular front for vulgar sex, just as *Mademoiselle* leads the ingenue, *Playboy* the young exec, *Cosmopolitan* the career girl, *Pageant* and *Coronet* the housewife, and so on, each to their own tasteful titillations. And vulgar sex helps define a vulgar (pop, if you prefer) poetics and artistic tradition. At this point, as Danish Dr. Groth says, hard-core pornography is not useful to most people. But with the helpful polemics of the sex papers, pornography may not only become "dirtier" and more fun in itself, it may also realize its as yet largely unexplored artistic possibilities. Besides, if one must choose (as many of our young men must) between obscene fantasies—choose, that is, between a world that is all fighting or one that is all fornicating—we should not be much surprised if they choose the latter.

Those of us who find pornography's expanding popularity to be a progressive cultural sign must acknowledge a certain debt to *Playboy*. Though its commercial and materialistic emphases are not healthy, it has that disease in common with the rest of the capitalistic ethos. But, even with its distortions, *Playboy* has demonstrated that the pornographic imagination was not only compatible with but complementary to our better cultural values. That these values need to be more comprehensively understood not only by *Playboy* but by the rest of the culture as well is another problem. The point is that American materialism was incomplete without an open exploitation of sex. *Playboy,* following through on the cultural logic, put pornography on equal footing with haberdashery, automobiles, deodorant, jazz, Picasso, and Nietzsche. That once done, pornography assumed a life of its own in the popular mind. The smut tabloids are an example. Now, as society begins to discover its own mind on the representations of sexuality, the popular pornographic imagination will take *Playboy* and its imitators in tow. Already *Playboy* is publishing pornographic stills from films; having

231

helped open films up to pornography, *Playboy* now follows its new leader. Without being an innovator, then, *Playboy* has nevertheless contributed to the process of cultural innovation by being a populizer of sex, perhaps the last remaining frontier of American commerce.

The culture is in motion. As its aesthetic market expands so must its aesthetic base. Our aesthetic is being intruded upon by popular taste. Thus our notion of the beautiful increasingly absorbs what previously was thought to be vulgarity. Our notion of the beautiful, in other words, takes on more and more of the natural and, correspondingly, less and less of the ideal. The conservative agents of this evolution synthesize the two. *Playboy* idealizes nudity, giving the illusion of nakedness with the camera, but glamorizing it to a discrete and sentimentalized nudity with photographic sleight of hand. Or *Cosmopolitan* plainly but, again, discretely drapes its nudes with the erotic elegance of high peek-a-boo fashion. The radical agents of pornographic evolution, however, antipathetic to the elitist sociology of such imagistic idealism, use nakedness as a naturalistic weapon of assault. So the smut tabloids flaunt "lots more cocks and cunts" at the culture, turning traditional journalistic exposé and sensationalism into a mode of moral revelation. Sex, having so long been culturally hidden and sublimated, has become associated with the many other hidden and sublimated things that make our society run, things like violence, greed, and injustice. Making sex rear its ugly head is dialectically analogous to making those other uglinesses emerge from their comfortable depths as well. The radical pornographic imagination has rejected the sentimentalized sexuality that *Playboy* popularized and the culture accepted in favor of a more nearly naturalized sexuality. The ethical implication of this is that the society that can learn to accept its nakedness can also learn, by analogous vision, to conduct itself more sanely. And, to more effectively make that point, it has developed a new aesthetic.

232

9.

Censorship and Human Dignity

BECAUSE censorship means action, and by definition a repressive action, we do well to inquire what it is that censorship wants to accomplish. Its first principle, generously described, is protection—protection of moral and ethical values, of social and cultural order, and of psychological health. Its legitimate means are the passing of laws and reasoned public persuasion. Abstractly, then, the ends of censorship are good. They are good, that is, insofar as they are in the interests of human welfare. But censorship is an act and it does not therefore exist abstractly but rather very much in fact. The question becomes, thus, whether the fact of censorship realizes or violates its ideal—human well-being.

The abuses of humanity that have been administered in the name of human welfare—from the Inquisition to the Red Guard —force us to consider with care and suspicion any premise that proposes to help us by taking something from us. Censorship takes things away. But, because common sense tells us that taking a loaded pistol from a child is good, we know that being deprived of something can be good. So, we ask, exactly what things does censorship take away? Are they good or bad, important or unimportant? Primarily it takes choice, and choice is a form of freedom, and so censorship takes freedom from us. That, decidedly, is important. But is it bad? If it will keep what we may all agree to as *trash* off the bookstands, for instance, won't that in fact be good?

That censorship can more or less keep trash from the public

is true. That, however, we can agree to what trash is, is not true. Nor is it true that we can agree that trash, or even some trash, *should* be kept from the public.

I, for example, feel that Walt Disney's *Wonderful World of Color* is, by and large, pernicious, that it sentimentalizes life so severely and so persuasively as to endanger our understanding of nature and happiness. If we were living in Plato's republic I flatter myself that I would someday be, if not a philosopher king, at least an elder. And I would thus censor Walt Disney's view of the world for obscuring or distorting the true order of things, remembering that it was for the purpose of living with truth that we had established our state. But, even at the sacrifice of such fine powers, I do not want to live in Plato's republic. The responsibilities there are too grand, and the truth there is too categorical. For, although I feel that Walt Disney's view is untrue and that it impairs our knowledge of what is true, I find that I live in as much peace as I can reasonably expect with a great many people who like and regularly watch Disney's program.

I and my friends feel it is trash; they and their friends do not agree. I, on the other hand, like *Lolita* and *Lady Chatterly's Lover*. They think these books are trash. But, by virtue of their respect for my human dignity and my respect for theirs, they do not color my world rose and I do not seduce their wives or debauch their daughters. We recognize mutually that we will never agree on what constitutes trash. Our rational stalemate on that account causes us to see that an attempt by either of us to suppress the other's "trash" will necessarily violate that mutual sense of dignity by which we live in peace with one another. Thus, the social and human risk of censorship turns out to be far greater than the risk in allowing one another our moral eccentricities. And so, because denying our freedom to choose trash would violate our human dignity and thereby undermine the commonweal, I conclude that censorship is indeed bad.

But what of obscenity? Surely, we can agree on *that?* I suspect not.

I, for instance, find many life insurance salesmen as obscence as pornography. I cannot take very seriously a community

234

standard that not only sanctions but encourages a life insurance salesman, for instance, to exploit my sense of moral responsibility to intimidate me into buying his product. It I may rephrase John Donne, every man's lack of human dignity diminishes me. The insurance man does it with a vengeance. The pornographer, at least, does not pretend to be interested in my welfare.

I find it neither more nor less filthy and offensive that a man should exploit my sexuality to induce me to copulate or masturbate than that he should exploit my insecurity to induce me to buy insurance.

I must admit, of course, that my argument here is based largely on the social desirability of respect for human dignity. But this premise is, it seems to me, one of the self-evident truths of the Declaration of Independence—the right to life, liberty, and the pursuit of happiness. It is axiomatic that liberty is the source of human dignity. And if liberty is good, it is absolutely good. It cannot be sometimes good and sometimes bad. And we have to recognize, therefore, that whenever we curtail liberty we, to that extent, deny human dignity. But, of course, we do this regularly and cheerfully, with criminals and children. Rightfully, for criminals have demonstrated a lack of respect for human dignity in direct ratio to the magnitude of their crimes. And children have not yet, we assume, come to an adequate knowledge of human dignity or its expectations and obligations. But, all the same, our curtailing of liberties even in these and like justifiable circumstances necessarily denies individual human dignity; it denies the right to pursue happiness. We must be very careful, consequently, when we sanction any suppression of liberty that the suppression is necessary and therefore, if not good, at least justifiable.

We are, thus, obliged to ask, as Judge Jerome Frank and Justice Douglas and the monumentally important report of the Presidential Commission on Obscenity and Pornography have, whether pornography constitutes "a clear and present danger" to society. We may just as reasonably, in fact, wish to ask if *censorship* constitutes a "clear and present danger." For censorship without a clear and present danger is itself a clear

235

and present danger. Proponents of censorship argue that to ask for evidence of pornography's antisocial effects is to beg the question. We can see their manner of argument in this statement by J. Edgar Hoover: "I say that we can no longer afford to wait for an answer. What we do know is that in an overwhelmingly large number of cases sex crime is associated with pornography. We know sex criminals read it, are clearly influenced by it. I believe pornography is a major cause of sex violence. I believe that if we can eliminate the distribution of such items among impressionable school-age children, we shall greatly reduce our frightening crime rate."

The reliability of this viewpoint is categorically destroyed by its first premise, that in effect we cannot afford to know what we are doing. There is frustration and hysteria in this statement, the same kind of frustration and hysteria that gave Jack Ruby the license to murder Oswald and so obscure the real facts of the presidential assassination forever. Waiting for answers is frustrating, but it is also the first principle of justice, *the* principle without which a rational democracy cannot exist. Mr. Hoover's statement attempts to assign pornography the responsibility not only for sex crimes but for the whole of "our frightening crime rate." But, because no serious or sensitive analysis of the problem could support such reasoning, he must deny the rudimentary sort of evidence we ask before reaching any kind of decision, let alone a judicial one.

He asks us to suspend our reasoning powers and to "believe" what he believes simply because he believes it, and he, after all, is the nation's foremost policeman. This is the kind of abuse of authority that we do not normally allow. But, whereas we act openly and reasonably in politics, we act covertly and hysterically in regard to sex. Thus, Mr. Hoover's argument is in fact a majority argument. Luckily, the constitutional fathers were aware that a preoccupation with police power may corrode one's sense of justice, and they provided that the legislative and judicial powers were distinct from the enforcement agency.

In regard to the first amendment—guaranteeing the freedoms of religion, speech, and the press—it has been the principle of *due process of law* that has time and again preserved our human liberties from our own hysteria. Our constitution forces us to realize, even when we don't want to, that a democratic society cannot afford *not* to wait for answers; it cannot afford ignorance of what it is doing.

In fact, we have evidence to work from in order to define causes of sex crimes and crime in general. Mr. Hoover knows this as well as anyone. The evidence indicates that the causes tend to be psychological and cultural. Mr. Hoover knows that the police can do nothing about such causes. And it is understandably frustrating to have to continue dealing with effects, the criminals, year after year. But that is the job of the police. It is necessarily frustrating. Its contribution to society is to prevent these frustrations from becoming the hysteria of vigilante or mob rule.

But the police cannot stop slums and social injustice and the consequent antisocial behavior. They cannot cure pathological minds and their antisocial behavior. These are the awesome problems of society at large. They are frustrating because they are slow of resolution. Meanwhile, we want results, something to see. A pile of burning books is something to see (not just Berlin in 1939, but Philadelphia in 1963). But if we want social results we have to go to the source of the social problem. It will do us no good and a great deal of harm to invent irrelevant bogeys.

Pornography—quite obviously a bogey—in fact, the whole history of pornography at its vilest and heaped on our heads like manure, cannot do the cultural and social and human harm that one instance of hysterically miscarried justice can. One need go no farther than the McCarthy era or the impounding of persons and expropriation of property to which the Japanese-Americans were subjected in 1941 or the Ku Klux Klan at work today to see that.

I think it is true that we censor not to protect a virtue (innocence) but rather to conceal a vice (moral inadequacy). It is no doubt true that when an author represents actions in life (e.g., promiscuity) so as to indulge them or sanction them or at the least not to condemn them, he provides some kind of authority for his reader to behave in the same way.

237

The problem, then, becomes one of personal character and the environment available for its growth and inquiry. It is by now axiomatic that one cannot prevent reality or knowledge of reality by either ignoring or suppressing it. It may be—or its consequences may be—deferred, but it cannot be prevented. And there is substantial psychological evidence that suppressions have serious psychic and even social effects.

Thus, the question is, how can the child be made a "match" for the books and authors under whose sphere of influence he may come. The panic answer is to suppress. However, we know that not only is that measure more dangerous than desirable, but it won't work anyway, except perhaps for short spurts.

The reasonable response to this challenge is to undertake to *make* the child a match. But that, of course, requires our maximal commitment to the development of his humanity. Not only does it mean that schools have to be given a priority for both teaching and experimentation, but still more difficult, it means that we have to commit ourselves *personally* to making our own children human. And there's the rub. We don't have faith in our *ability* for that task and so we have no *willingness* to undertake it. We can't, therefore, make our children equal to their challenges because we are too anxious about failure to want even to try. The consequence is that we resort to suppression—censorship—to counteract our own inadequacy. We know that censorship is futile, that our children learn on the street (or in the barn) what we deny them in books, that their own passions and impulses demand some kind of realistic interpretation, but what we lack in moral energy and responsibility we compensate for with desperation and censorship.

Censorship, then, is employed not to preserve an innocence that we know very well is doomed, but rather it is employed to cover our own failures, our *will* to failure.

Sex and pornography must be brought rationally into the context of our total nature. Maurice Girodias, of the Olympia Press, pointed up the irony of our naïveté when he observed that we are sending astronauts to the moon, and yet we forbid them to read Henry Miller. We must exercise some common sense about

238

corruption. It is likely that a man who fights the kind of war we are fighting in Vietnam, where women and children are killed regularly, is so morally innocent as to be depraved by the Marquis de Sade? Isn't it absurd to suppose that *The Lascivious Hypocrite* can corrupt a cultural climate like that in Alabama, where man may with impunity gun down housewives or splatter an integrationist's head over the landscape with a shotgun? Pornography is the very weakest kind of social threat that we confront. Our humanity withstood the horrors of Buchenwald and the Philippines—many of them sexual. Do we really believe that that humanity can be threatened by *Fanny Hill?*

Criminal behavior is pathological. A society which honors *power* over *humanity,* as the Nazis did, will encourage pathological behavior as a norm. But in a humane society, as a democratic one must be, man's individuality and privacy will be honored. Pornography may stimulate a man to sexual activity, but unless he is already pathological that activity won't be criminal.

The normal man responds to the prevailing moral standards of his culture; ours, after all, honors human dignity over power. And it cannot, therefore, be a reasonable suggestion that we formulate our laws according to pathological values. We are better than that. Our laws must provide for the widest latitude of human potential. The police power, the protective power, the censoring power—they are all one—should protect that latitude as best they can from abuse. A policeman's work, like a woman's, is never done. No house is ever kept permanently in order. And we deny the purpose of the house altogether if, to preserve tidiness, we keep men from living in it.

The real question to which my argument is liable, I know, is whether I can actually contend that pictures of Tijuana Toots in lewd posturings with Pope Pederast IV or stories thereof are documents of human dignity. The answer to that, of course, is no. But on the other hand, as Steven Marcus's book *The Other Victorians* shows, pornography can give us significant historical, sociological, and anthropological data about sexual attitudes and anxieties, etc. And, as Eberhard and Phyllis Kronhausen's *Por-*

239

nography and the Law demonstrates, a study of pornographic structure can tell us a good deal about the psychology of sex. In fact, as Masters' and Johnson's now famous studies show, pornography is being used in scientific research on sex. In this sense, then, we may say that pornography has a scientific interest. But it also has a literary interest that is consistently emerging in the development of modern literature.

Psychologists and anthropologists tell us that pornography, in even its crudest form, answers certain psychic needs and has therefore always had some kind of cultural role. Man's sexual image is a fundamental concern—psychiatric case histories document the one, and the advertising industry exploits the other. Pornography, comprehensively considered, may be defined as the literature of sexuality. That it began as writings about prostitutes and their work merely tells of the imaginative direction from which it comes. However unpleasant a comment on human nature it may be, this imaginative concern with sexual impulse is a reality in our nature. So much so that our laws even skirt the issue. Many states, for example, do not have laws prohibiting prostitution; that matter is left to local option.

Our sexual character is being scientifically explored medically, psychologically, sociologically, and morally. There is every indication that it is being and will continue to be explored literarily. And much of that literature will be pornography. Much of it will be bad. Much of it will be crude. Much of it will exploit a market. But those are not sufficient reasons to suppress it. We don't suppress bad, crude, exploitive books or movies or television programs that deal with politics, or marriage, or religion, or war. But we suppress sex, which is every bit as fundamental to our lives and every bit as in need of investigation— both documentary and imaginative. We will simply have to allow for bad investigation there as we allow for it elsewhere.

Modern writers are preoccupied with the grotesqueness of modern experience because they have been saturated by it. My generation (people around 30) have never, for example, lived outside the context of war. "The old dispensations," as T. S. Eliot called them—conventional religion, morality, and philoso-

240

phy—have not been adequate to this challenge. Having gone through World War II, we cannot be persuaded that "God is in His heaven and all is right with the world."

Out of those old dispensations modern science developed, and it kept faith by promising nothing and delivering only so much as the integrity of any given investigation would permit. We have benefited greatly by observing this simple faith. And it is unreasonable to suppose that we will give it up to return to old dispensations that could not benefit us.

Pornographic literature at its best—in the tradition of Faulkner, Joyce, Lawrence—is a part of this modern attitude. That some pornography, very likely a great deal—even most—will abuse the tradition is granted. But that we should preclude the true exploration of our sexuality by censoring what we suppose to be abuses of our standards is not only preposterous, it is impossible. The rhythm is too strong now to reverse. We no longer subscribe to the bogey articulated in the Faust legend—that knowledge will destroy faith and thereby we will damn ourselves.

In an age and culture of universal education we are past the juvenility that knowledge breeds pride. Knowledge, including sexual knowledge, breeds humility and honesty—the essential terms of humanity.

Pornography exists, not because unscrupulous fiends print and sell it, but because it is a part of our nature. There is, therefore, no question of whether we will have pornography. We will have it, as we have it now, and as we have always had it. The question is quite simply whether we can stand our own humanity.

Index of Names and Titles